Towards a New Relationship

Kenneth Cracknell

Towards a New Relationship

Christians and People of Other Faith

EPWORTH PRESS

British Library Cataloguing in Publication Data

Cracknell, Kenneth
Towards a new relationship : Christians
and people of other faith.
1. Christianity and other religions
I. Title
261.2   BR127

ISBN 0–7162–0421–5

First published 1986
by Epworth Press
Room 190, 1 Central Buildings
Westminster, London SW1H 9HR
Second Impression 1990

Typeset by The Spartan Press Ltd
Lymington, Hants

Printed and bound in Great Britain
by Dotesios Printers Ltd, Trowbridge, Wiltshire.

CONTENTS

PREFACE

To work for an organization like the British Council of Churches is not helpful for the production of books. I calculate that in the past seven years I have travelled not less than 50,000 miles a year. The theology wrought out in the book has been produced for the most part not in the calm of the study but on my feet, in response to the endless challenges and anguished questionings that living with religious pluralism brings to Christians everywhere. Committees, conferences, seminars and synods are the staple of my life. I have to believe that all real life is in meetings as J. H. Oldham almost but not quite wrote. I am deeply grateful for all who have raised profound questions of faith and belief with me in Christian gatherings concerned with evangelism and mission, with pastoral care and social policy, religious education in schools and theological education at all levels of the churches' life. I am equally grateful for the manifold challenges to my Christian exclusivism that have come through participation in gatherings with men and women whose obedience to faith is expressed in wholly other ways than mine. I have learned so much from so many people, I do not know how or where to begin to express my gratitude.

Many of these debts of thanksgiving are honoured in the notes – I find that for the main part those whose writings I used most in the text I count my personal friends. They will recognize how much else I have learned from them which is beyond me correctly to attribute. The best things in this book are theirs alone. Errors and omissions, misunderstandings and misrepresentations are on the other hand my own entire responsibility and for them I ask pardon.

To my intimate circle of friends and family who have helped in the physical production of the text I offer my love and gratitude, too. It would be invidious to name more names than just two. These are those of my two secretaries, Miss Gwen Morris and Mrs Myra Macpherson who laboured over the often execrable original typescript and fought with the BCC's word processor to produce the final draft.

Now I can only hope that my words will be useful in building the new relationship for, in John Macmurray's words, 'all meaningful knowledge is in order to action, and all meaningful action is in order to friendship'.

ACKNOWLEDGMENTS

Some of the material of this book has already appeared elsewhere. I am grateful to the Rev. John Stacey, Editor of the Epworth Press for the stimulus to set it out here in a more ordered and permanent form. But I must also thank other publishers and editors for their permission to re-use the following material. To the British Council of Churches, the original publishers of *Considering Dialogue* (1981) and *Why Dialogue?* (1980) for sections of chapters 1, 2 and 4. Chapter 3 first appeared in *Dialogue in Community: Essays in Honour of S. J. Samartha*, ed., C. D. Jathanna, The Karnataka Theological Research Institute, Mangalore, S. India (1982). Chapter 6 was originally part of a lecture on 'The Ethics of Inter-faith Relationships' given to the Society for the Study of Theology at its Nottingham Conference, April 1983, and subsequently printed in *World Faiths Insight*, New Series 9, Summer 1984. Appendix A was originally a bibliographical article in *The Modern Churchman*, New Series, Vol. XXVI, No. 2, 1984.

◢ INTRODUCTION ◣

There can be no question now but that the issues we face in the following pages have become central for Christians all around the world in the 1980s. My own experiences in travelling in four of the six continents, and in both eastern and western Europe, as well as the results of encounters with church leaders and theologians from almost all countries in the world suggest that everywhere we are wrestling with the question of how we are to be faithful to Christ in a religiously plural world. A host of vital theological and practical concerns arise as part of that central questioning.

First, there are those which wrestle with what is called the theology of religion. These are the intellectual questions raised by religious diversity for Christians (as for other believers): i.e. Why does God allow so many different forms of religious belief to flourish and prosper, to renew ancient insights and produce new understanding, to bring forth people of holy life and scholars of great learning and integrity, to attract new followers of their traditions and to wield great influence in the affairs of individuals and nations? What do all these ways and paths signify for his purpose?

Then, because Christian theologians are called to reflect upon those uniquenesses of God achieved in Jesus of Nazareth – his teaching, his death, his resurrection, his raising to heavenly glory – they have to go on to ask how does the Christian tradition and community of faith stand in relation to the faith and community of other peoples? Is the relation one of rivalry and mutual exclusiveness? Is the Christian church in the displacement business whereby it eventually supplants the others, or does it expect to take the others over by absorption, with some kind of spiritual asset-stripping as part of the activity? Or perhaps the relationship is that of having no relationship. Are we adherents of mutually contradictory truth-systems called to co-exist but who find it impossible to communicate? Yet another relationship might be one of close co-operation, indeed even of co-witness against whatever is perceived to be the chief derelictions of our age – its secularism and materialism and so forth. Or again, the others might be seen as fellow-pilgrims to the truth which no one has yet grasped in its immensity. Or we might develop theologies about the anonymous work of the hidden Christ in the other religious systems, going on to speak of them as normal ways of salvation for their adherents, and of their communities as the 'latent church', over against the supranormal redemption in Christ and the 'manifest church' in which Jesus is acknowledged as Lord and Saviour?

The answers to such questions have immediate practical relevance. For they determine the response that the church makes to everyday problems of policy and planning. In Britain, for example, the Christian community has to deal with the hundred and one challenges facing it because it lives in what is now a multi-faith society. What, for example, is to be done about denominational schools where nearly every pupil has a Muslim background? What sort of religious education ought to be offered in a county school, the majority of whose pupils are either Hindu or Sikh? And what sort of religious education should be given in a county school where the pupils do not have the advantage of living in close proximity to members of other religious communities, and yet who are going to have to live in a religiously plural Britain and a religiously plural world? How does the Christian community then advise those who have to plan the future education of the new generations of British youngsters? How does the Christian community support (with an adequate theology, and through sustained prayer and interest) those of its number who work in the schools and colleges of this country?

Such immensely important issues raised in just one sector of the nation's life could be matched by equally momentous considerations elsewhere: in the health and social services, for example. Living in a multi-faith society touches almost every aspect of social planning, from pre-natal care to the provision of cemeteries and crematoria, literally from the cradle to the grave.

But the church is not only called upon to reflect on such issues of social policy. It has also to offer appropriate pastoral care in situation after situation. So a Methodist minister phones me to ask for help with a young couple just coming for an interview about their forthcoming marriage. But one of the partners is a Muslim! A local church council is approached by a Hindu group wanting to use the church rooms for a wedding ceremony. A committee organizing One World Week has thought it a good idea to hold an 'inter-faith service' but members of the local Council of Churches are deeply divided about supporting such an event. A twenty-three year old young woman has just been killed in a road accident but she has been deeply affected by

Buddhism. Her parents are devout Christians and the minister has to speak at her funeral when many of her Buddhist friends will be there. How does he console the parents? How does he speak of the young woman's conversion to Buddhism in the presence of her Buddhist friends? Such examples, all based on real events in the past few years, can be multiplied *ad infinitum*.

So this book joins many others in which Christians of different traditions are found to be wrestling with such issues. The reader is entitled to know in what respects this one may be different and how its author thinks he is in any way especially qualified to add to the colourful profusion of material dealing with the theology of religion and inter-faith dialogue.[1]

For the past seven years (since 1978) the Committee for Relations with People of Other Faiths has been at work within the British Council of Churches. I have had the privilege of being its first Secretary, and have been associated with the production of a whole series of booklets dealing with one or other of the concerns already raised. In the production of all of these documents I have worked with expert theologians and educationists, with experienced pastors and visionary church leaders, and with men and women profoundly versed in other cultures and other religious traditions. Through all this I have seen a particular kind of British contribution to inter-faith issues being put together. One component of this can be found in *Relations with People of Other Faiths: Guidelines on Dialogue in Britain* (1981, revised edition 1983) of which some ten thousand copies are in circulation. As I reflect upon this BCC contribution I see an emphasis upon the distinctive quality of the personal relationships between believing people.

That this word 'relationship' is a key term is reflected both in the title of the BCC Committee and in the title of its Guidelines. I take it up as the key word in my own title *Towards a New Relationship*. Much of what follows therefore is an extended exposition of the theme of relationships as we have sought to work at them within the BCC, and as I have learnt about new relationships from countless of my Christian colleagues as well as from people of other faiths with whom my work has brought me into contact. For 'relationships' as we shall see, is a word which may be used to embrace many other terms which have been used in this area, among them words like 'mission', 'witness', 'presence', 'encounter' and 'dialogue' itself... words which have become rather tired and dog-eared through over-use in the contemporary discussions. The sixth chapter of this book in particular is an exposition of the 'four principles' on which the BCC

Guidelines are built up and which, I believe, are central to the new pattern of relationships between all people of different traditions of faith.

But one is well aware, always, when moving in predominantly church circles, how great are the tensions for Christians as they are challenged to enter into these new relationships. How may they do that and remain faithful to their own traditions? When David Brown, late Bishop of Guildford and first Chairman of the BCC Committee for Relations with People of Other Faiths, produced his influential booklet in 1976 about Christian-Muslim relations entitled *A New Threshold*, there was a review published in Denmark called 'A threshold over which we must not cross'. Eight years later a church newspaper in England headed its review of the Anglican General Synod report *Towards a Theology for Inter-Faith Dialogue* . . . : 'So keen are they to have dialogue they are prepared to betray Christianity'. It is necessary therefore to spend time to show that the new relationships advocated in the following chapters are *properly* on the other side of a new threshold, and in no way a betrayal of Christianity.

So we begin with a look at the old relationships that many apparently suppose are constitutive of historical Christianity. But we shall go on immediately to ask if all this should be seen as the authentic Christian tradition. In 1979 the World Council of Churches published its *Guidelines on Dialogue with People of Living Faiths and Ideologies*. As one would expect in a document from a world confessional community embracing people of all the major theological traditions except the Roman Catholic, many statements in these Guidelines needed fleshing out according to particular traditions and in particular contexts. In paragraph 23 there was this question: 'How are Christians to find from the Bible criteria in their approach to people of other faiths and ideologies, recognizing as they must the authority accorded to the Bible by Christians of all centuries . . . ?' This has always struck us within the British Council of Churches' Committee to be of central importance for British Christians, and accordingly I was asked to write for the Committee a survey of the biblical material relevant to answering this question. In the event the Committee thought this material of sufficient importance for local congregations to ask that it should be published in full 'as a first statement inviting a debate'. This was in my *Why Dialogue?* (BCC 1979) which is now out of print. Much experience of using this material both in local churches and with theologians not only in Britain but on both sides of the Atlantic, in South and East Africa, and in South India and Sri Lanka, suggests that it is both a valid contribution and still of vital relevance. In a revised form it appears in these pages as evidence against exclusivist, non-dialogical Christianity!

At the same time the WCC Guidelines raised another issue concerning 'the universal creative redemptive activity of God towards all humankind and the particular creative/redemptive activity in the history of Israel and in the person and work of Jesus Christ'. It seemed to me that one contribution towards answering such a question was to look at the biblical material about God and the nations both in the Old and New Testaments. This essay was published in *Dialogue in Community: Essays in Honour of Stanley Samartha*, edited by C. D. Jathanna, and published by the Karnataka Theological Research Institute in India in 1982. Again in a revised form this material is to be found in chapter 3 as part of the biblical evidence against exclusivity. I am grateful to Bishop Jathanna for permission to reprint this essay.

In this way we will have examined the biblical material in order to show that the canonical scriptures taken as a whole are not exclusivist in their understanding of God's activity in this world. This in itself is a great step forward. But nevertheless the basic question for the Christian remains. For however telling the evidence is for biblical understanding of God's activity beyond the boundaries of historic Israel and the new Christian community, the question that confronts us has to do with the specific activity of God in Christ. For the Christian community lives from its faith that the Word has become flesh, and that in Jesus we have beheld his glory, 'glory as of the only Son from the Father' (John 1.14). In a world of religious pluralism our questions have primarily to do with the uniqueness and finality of the revelation of God in Jesus of Nazareth. We confess this man to be the Christ, the Anointed of God. Therefore the christological question is unavoidable. And why should we want to avoid it? It belongs to the heart of Christian faith. Without an assertion of once-and-for-allness and a declaration of its cosmic implications, the Christian faith must change both its name and its nature. So we must tackle the issues of faithfulness in a religiously plural world as they come to us in the words of such often-cited verses as John 14.6: 'no man comes to the Father but by me'; Acts 4.12: 'there is no salvation in anyone else, for there is no other name by which we may be saved'; John 3.18: 'he who does not believe in me is condemned already, because he has not believed in the name of the only Son of God'. We must take head on the issues that are raised by such texts. As believing Christians we have to work out our theologies of religion and inter-faith dialogue against this background.

And this I try to do in chapters 4 and 5. I who believe that in Jesus's teaching there is a message like no other man's, that in his death there are cosmic significances, and that because of his resurrection there is indeed a new creation, must search for a christology that is inclusive rather than exclusive. I need a way of seeing that what I believe about Jesus opens doors rather than shuts them, pulls down barriers between people rather than builds them higher, and sets us free to enter into marvellous new relationships with just that sense of expectation and yet with just as much vulnerability as Jesus himself demonstrated when he walked the paths of Galilee and Samaria, and the streets of Jerusalem. Christology must affirm both our conviction that the symbols of resurrection and ascension remain central to Christian faith and at the same time that goodness and grace, truth and sanctity are to be found in individuals and communities of other than Christian faith. If a case for such a christology is not made at this point it would seem to me that nearly everything else I want to say in this book must be called into question. Whatever else it is, it has no particular claim to be called Christian.

Thus it is that I offer the last two chapters, the one about the ethics of inter-faith relationships and the other about new dimensions of spirituality, as the reflections of a confessional Christian theologian. I write as a believing Christian first of all to my fellow believers. But I know full well that men and women of other convictions will be looking over our shoulders to see what is being said or implied about them. Scores and scores of them will be my personal friends: Jews, Muslims, Hindus, Buddhists, Sikhs, Baha'is, followers of new religious movements as well as some who would not call themselves religious at all. I hope two things will come to them as they read. First of all, that they may see one Christian wrestling with an issue that confronts all people everywhere in every tradition. As I wonder how I am to remain faithful to Christ and yet make sense of the faith of other people, so, for example, a devout Hindu or Muslim must also have a conceptual framework which makes sense of the faith of those who are not Muslims or Hindus, Jews or Buddhists. They, too, in the words of Wilfred Cantwell Smith, must 'aspire to a statement of God and his diverse involvements with humankind'. Secondly, I hope that they will see, particularly in the last two chapters, the universal implications of what I am saying, though this be couched in Christian terms. For though I write of ethical issues in inter-faith relations as they now confront Christians, what is said there about the pattern of relationships ('the four principles of dialogue') applies across the board. What is said about the possibilities as well as the perils of praying together applies to us all.

⅃1⅃

About the Old Relationships

It is extraordinarily difficult to start from scratch when we try to come to a proper judgment about inter-faith relations and the attendant theologies of religion and mission. For Christians in the West it is almost a question of starting all over again in these areas. Every word that we are likely to use to discuss these matters comes to us with a cluster of inherited meanings. Every concept is laden by centuries of use and abuse. Take the word 'missionary'. On the one hand humorous magazines like *Punch* and *The New Yorker* can hardly do without their stereotypes of sun-helmeted sahibs and cannibal cooking pots. Far less humorously and at the other extreme just to have the word 'missionary' in one's passport is to guarantee the non-granting of visas for entry into many countries. For some people the missionary is a harmless buffoon. For others he or she is a menace, an agent of Western imperialism and a destroyer of indigenous values.[1] Even for people who live within the Christian community the word 'missionary' can provoke adverse reactions, as well as uncritical adulation.

The words used to describe the people among whom the missionaries laboured are equally laden with the freight of the centuries. Charming words like 'heathen', which originally meant someone who dwelt on the heath, or 'pagan', originally just a word for a country-dweller (cf. the French word *paysan*) or even a civilian, over the centuries have become terms of abuse. Even by 1593 'heathen' had come to have overtones of beastliness and abomination. Shakespeare writes: 'Most heathenish and most gross'! 'Pagan' has a similar history, and has lost all sense of its rural origins. Flower services and harvest festivals may well be in a proper meaning of the word 'pagan' festivals, but the 'godless paganism' of the modern city dweller is something else!

But all this is mentioned only in order to lead us to recognize the emotive issues that cloud our understanding of the new relationships necessary between people of different historical and cultural traditions. Let us try to pick out three strands that have to be dealt with before we can start all over again. These are: (1) the entails of the historical developments within the Western Christian theological tradition; (2) the legacies of earlier missionary theologies, especially as embedded in the propaganda materials produced for the supporters of nineteenth-century missionary societies and in missionary hymnology; (3) the prejudices stemming from the assumption of cultural superiority by colonizers and imperialists. These three elements roll up into one single, sad tangle and make it truly difficult for Western Christians to think in new ways. So we must unravel some of these unblessed ties that bind us in knots.

1 The Theological Entails

Any way the contemporary church may find to speak affirmatively about God's activity in and through other communities of faith must in itself deny important themes in the history of Christian theology. There is unhappily no avoiding such a negation. Our forebears were simply mistaken. Let us briefly review the statements and propositions of some great representative figures. These concern the exclusiveness of Christian revelation, the exclusiveness of the church as the locus of salvation, and the finality and uniqueness of Christ, at least in some of their historical expressions.

The exclusiveness of the church may be represented by Augustine's disciple, Fulgentius of Ruspe (467–533) who, taking up the extreme negative elements in his master's teaching, insisted, for example, that not only all unbaptized children, but even those who die in their mother's womb are doomed to eternal fire. Naturally Jews, heathens, heretics and schismatics will perish in that same fiery damnation. These fearsome doctrines were used in the definition of 'extra ecclesiam nulla salus' at the Council of Florence (1438–45).[2]

> The Holy Roman Church firmly believes, professes and proclaims that none of those who are outside the Catholic church – not only pagans, but Jews also, heretics and schismatics – can have part in eternal life, but will go into eternal fire, 'which was prepared for the devil and his angels', unless they are gathered into that Church before the end of life.[3]

Here the church is the Latin church of Cyprian's conception into which Augustine was baptized, witnessing as it were to God who is apart from the world, regulating human affairs from outside by the agency of commissioned delegates. The episcopate has been appointed to teach and wield authority as the vicar of an absent Lord. All grace and every operation of the Spirit is within this legally defined community, and the rest of humanity is the *massa damnata*, an abandoned heap, excluded *ipso facto* from salvation.[4] That this was not just a theological abstraction can be seen in the practice of even so great a missionary as St Francis Xavier (1506–1552). The contemporary Roman Catholic missiologist Walbert Bühlmann tells that 'On his journeys he was accompanied by a loyal servant, a pagan Chinese who stuck by him even when the Portuguese deserted him. He regarded Francis as a brother. Unfortunately it never once crossed his mind to adopt his master's religion. Suddenly he died, and Francis Xavier wrote: "We could not reward him for his goodness of heart, for he died without knowing God. We could never help him or pray for him even after his death, for he is in hell"'.[5] It would not be difficult to find echoes of this sentiment in the early Protestant missionaries. Indeed there is that which lingers as the Augustinian entail upon all our thinking.[6]

Now let me remind you of the beginnings of Protestant tradition by citing this passage from John Calvin (*Institutes*, 2, 2, 18). Spiritual discernment, he is arguing, consists of three things – the knowledge of God, the knowledge of his personal favour towards us which constitutes our salvation and the method of regulating our conduct in accordance with the divine Law. He goes on,

> With regard to the former two, but more properly the second, men otherwise ingenious are blinder than moles. I deny not that in the writings of the philosophers we meet occasionally with shrewd and apposite remarks on the nature of God, though they inevitably savour somewhat of giddy imagination. As observed above, the Lord has bestowed on them some slight perception of his Godhead, that they might not plead ignorance as an excuse for their impiety and has at times instigated them to deliver some truths, the confession of which should be to their own condemnation.[7]

A few lines later there is the notorious parable:

> Their discernment was not such as to direct them to the truth, far less to enable them to attain it, but resembled that of the bewildered traveller who sees the flash of lightning glance far and

wide for the moment and then vanish into the darkness of night before he can advance one single step.

Calvin is speaking in particular of the philosophers of the ancient world but had he been called upon to speak of the significance of the other religious traditions, presumably his judgment would have been the same:

In short, not one of them even made the approach to the divine favour without which the mind of man must ever remain a mere chaos of confusion.

The Calvinist entail is a negative judgment upon all human works: Barth is never writing more in a Calvinist mode than when he says 'Religion is unbelief'.[8]

The uniqueness and finality of Christ is expressed for us by Martin Luther. So central for him is the doctrine of *sola fide* 'salvation by faith alone' that he writes, frequently and characteristically, sentences like these:

In this article (. . . of the Creed, namely that Jesus is truly God and truly man) the Christian faith is set apart from every other religion and faith of men. It makes all the others false and useless . . . [9]

All worship (*Cultus*) and religions outside Christ are the worship of idols.[10]

Apart from Christ therefore there is nothing except mere idolatry – an idol and a false figment of God.[11]

For whatever is outside faith (*extra fidem*) is idolatry. And this moreover is the chief point of idolatry, that God is thought to be placated by our own works.[12]

Therefore:

Those who remain outside Christianity, be they heathens, Turks, Jews or false Christians [he means Roman Catholics] although they believe on only one true God, yet remain in eternal wrath and perdition.[13]

The characteristic opinion about the other world religions among Lutherans is that they are *autosoteriological*, spiritual do-it-yourself kits.[14] It is not surprising that the chief attack on the Sub Unit on Dialogue with People of Living Faiths during the Nairobi Assembly of the WCC was led by a Lutheran theologian from Norway and that the theological impasse experienced at the Conference of European

Churches consultation in Salzburg on 'The Church and the Muslim in Europe', February 1978, was in part caused by the Lutheran bloc. So along with the Calvinist and the Augustinian we may speak also of the Lutheran entail upon adequate systematic or dogmatic theological reflection concerning the theology of religion.

But it may seem to some that all the blame is being shifted away from the British situation. After all most of us never read either Calvin or Luther, and have never adhered to the exclusive ecclesiocentric formulas of the medieval church.

So let us briefly look at John Wesley as he expounds the nature and consequences of Original Sin in his Sermon XLIV. He is of common mind with both Calvin and Luther. 'We had, by nature, no knowledge of God, no acquaintance with him.' It is true, he continues, that 'as soon as we came to the use of reason, we learned "the invisible things of God, even his eternal power and Godhead, from the things that are made"'. But this knowledge of his existence in no way implies any personal knowledge of him. 'As we know there is an Emperor of China, whom yet we do not know; so we knew there was a King of all the earth, yet we knew him not.' John Wesley cites Matthew 11.27 as his corroborating text.

In his own context, surrounded as he was by the exponents of natural religion, deists and others who wished to 'speak magnificently concerning the nature of man, as if it were all innocence and perfection', we can see him insisting that humankind had 'by nature, not only no love, but no fear of God', although he does allow that 'most men have sooner or later, a kind of senseless, irrational fear, properly called "superstition"; though the blundering Epicureans gave it the name of "religion"'.

But although we are properly without the fear of God and 'Atheists in the world' we are not screened from idolatry. 'Every man born into the world is a rank idolater'. In pointing to the inward meaning of idolatry as he sees it, John Wesley adds his own comment on the world of other people's religions: 'We do not, like the idolatrous heathens, worship molten or graven images. We do not bow down to the stock of a tree or the work of our own hands.' Ah yes, Reginald Heber had only to re-phrase that thought:

> The heathen in his blindness
> Bows down to wood and stones.

But Wesley also uses the expression 'the most refined heathenism' to include those Greek and Roman philosophers to whom Calvin also referred: 'Many of the ancient Heathens have largely described the vices of particular men. They have spoken much against their covetousness or cruelty; their luxury or prodigality.' But none of them was apprised of the fall of man, and none of them knew of his total corruption. Wesley sees this as the chief distinguishing mark between philosophical Heathenism and Christianity, considered as a set of doctrines. In this sermon Christianity stands or falls by the truth of its radical assessment of the desperate need of humanity for a Physician, a Healer of Souls. To teach anything else is to join the ranks of Heathenism itself.

But Wesley is, as we might well expect, rather more ambivalent in his attitude than this one sermon would suggest. For he occupied rather a different position from either Calvin or Luther. In the first place he had some experience of working as a missionary. In 1735 he responded to the need of the Society for the Propagation of the Gospel not just for chaplains for the colonists in Georgia, but for missionaries among the Indians. Dr Martin Schmidt has dealt perceptively with Wesley's motivation for this extraordinary venture,[15] examining at some length Wesley's letter to John Burton of Corpus Christi College, a close friend and one of the Georgia trustees. From this letter we learn the following: 'My chief motive, to which all the rest are subordinate, is the hope of saving my own soul' but he also hopes 'to learn the true sense of the Gospel by preaching it to the heathen'. He also reveals himself as an eighteenth-century man, with the early Romantic or Rousseauesque notion of the 'noble savage'. He believes that those to whom he will preach are 'as little children, humble, willing to learn, and eager to do the will of God'!

As Martin Schmidt says, much of this is touchingly naive, and yet, despite all the harsh realities which destroyed such simple-mindedness, something of this awareness of innocence and goodness in others remained in Wesley to the end. Martin Schmidt comments in general that 'it would not be difficult to build up, by one-sided selection from his statements, a *theologia naturalis* of the heathen as a section of humanity pleasing to God'. For there is also in Wesley a pervading awareness of natural theology, of a certain proper insight of the 'Enlightenment' and certainly of a much larger world-scale than either Calvin or Luther could ever have conceived.

So let me do what Schmidt forbore to attempt, to build up by selective quotation a *theologia religionum* out of Wesley's writings. I do this only to show that it may be done, and leave the reader to decide whether he or she concurs with Schmidt's further opinion that it is 'exactly this unquestioning juxtaposition of two sets of ideas, those of the Bible and those of natural theology, which is significant both for the structure of English thought as a whole, and for the English theological "Enlightenment".[16]

Wesley was well able to conceive that true insights were to be found in what he called 'natural religion'. In the *Notes on the New Testament* on Acts 17.26 he says of the Hymn of Cleanthes to the Supreme Being that it is 'one of the purest and finest pieces of natural religion in the whole world of pagan antiquity'. He recognizes that 'the doctrine of divine providence has been received by wise men in all ages' citing Cicero and Paustoobee, a Chicasaw Indian (Sermon LXVII 'On Divine Providence'). Thus, too, he begins Sermon LXXI, 'Of Good Angels': 'Many of the ancient Heathens had (probably from tradition) some notion of good and evil angels', and again he cites a pre-Christian teacher, this time Socrates. Even more significantly he begins another Sermon 'On Working Out Our Own Salvation' (LXXXV): 'Some great truths, as the being and attributes of God, and the difference between moral good and evil were known in some measure, to the heathen world. The traces of them are to be found in all nations: so that in some sense, it may be said to every child of man, "He showed thee, O Man, what is good: even to do justly, to love mercy and to walk humbly with thy God". With this truth he has in some measure "enlightened everyone that cometh into the world".' This remained 'a spark glimmering here and there' among the 'immense rubbish of heathen authors' but the tone of all this is quite different from Calvin's parable of the lightning flash.

For Wesley is thinking on a much grander scale. We find several references to the computation of 'our ingenious and laborious country man Mr Brerewood' who in the seventeenth century 'travelled over a great part of the world on purpose to inquire, so far as was possible, what proportion the Christians bear to the Heathens and Mohametans' (see Sermon CXVI, 'Causes of the Inefficacy of Christianity'). Given this situation for Wesley, as for others, the question arises about the final destiny of so many ('five parts of mankind out of six are totally ignorant of Christianity') who have never heard the gospel. Wesley adopts several stratagems to avoid saying that these were created for damnation. First of all he can leave any judgment to the mercy of God, because, he says, 'I have no authority from the Word of God "to judge those that are without"', nor can he 'conceive any man living has a right to sentence all the heathen and Mahometan world to damnation'. It is far better to leave them to Him that made them and who 'is the Father of the spirits of all flesh; who is the God of the Heathens as well as the Christians, and hateth nothing that he hath made' (Sermon CXXV 'On Living

Without God'). Secondly, affirming again that 'he is not the God of the Christians only, but the God of the Heathens also' he goes on to say that he is 'rich in mercy to all that call upon him' according to the light they have; and that 'in every nation, he that feareth God and worketh righteousness is accepted of him'. Later in this sermon he implies a ground for such final salvation: 'True religion, in the very essence of it, is nothing short of holy tempers. Consequently all other religion whatever name it bears, whether Pagan, Mahometan, Jewish or Christian; and whether Popish or Protestant, Lutheran or Reformed; without these is lighter than vanity itself.'

Such an authentic Wesleyan note must be matched by an equally authentic stress upon faith: In Sermon CVI, 'On Faith', we find this quite remarkable passage: 'But many of them (i.e., the ancient Heathens), especially in the civilized nations, we have great reason to hope, although they lived among heathens, yet were quite of another spirit; being taught of God, by his inward voice, all the essentials of true religion. Yea, so was that Mahometan, and Arabian, who, a century or two ago, wrote the Life of Hai Ebn Yokdan. The story seems to be feigned; but it contains all the principles of pure religion and undefiled.'[17] Here the whole sermon is worth consulting for Wesley's attempt at a typology of faith: from the Materialist and Deist forms of faith, through to 'Mahometan' and American Indian faith, ancient Heathenism and into that of the Jews and the Roman Catholics. It might be possible to trace a direct line from this to those of our contemporaries who insist that faith is the central issue that we deal with in our relations with people of other faiths.[18]

But these last paragraphs remain something of a *tour de force*, and an effort at special pleading. For Wesley himself believed he was at his most orthodox in asserting what he believed to be the biblical teachings on original sin and total depravity. Nor does it faithfully represent Wesley's normal opinion of the Muslim world: so we close this section with Wesley on Islam and find him at one with Martin Luther:

A little, and but a little, above the Heathens in religion, are the Mahometans. But how far and wide has this miserable delusion spread over the face of the earth! Insomuch as the Mahometans are considerably more in number (as six to five) than Christians. And by all the accounts which have any pretence to authenticity, these are also, in general, as utter strangers to all true religion as their four-footed brethren; as void of mercy as lions and tigers; as much given up to brutal lusts as bulls or goats. So that they are in truth a disgrace to human nature and a plague to all that are under the iron yoke (Sermon LXIII, 'The General Spread of the Gospel').

I have spent so much time on all this in order to make the following three points:

1. For us Western Christians it is exceedingly difficult to break away from attitudes which we have had imparted to us – consciously or unconsciously, it scarcely matters – throughout the processes of our theological formation. Our residual Augustinianism – or Calvinism – or Lutheranism – or Wesleyanism (if we may allow Wesley, as we have examined him, to stand for a much wider English tradition as Martin Schmidt implies) acts upon us most precisely as an entail. The *Oxford English Dictionary* defines an 'entail' as 'a transmission as an inalienable inheritance, or qualities, conditions, etc.', and concretely, as that which is so imposed in the terms of a legacy. We all in the West have these kinds of entails in our thought patterns.

2. But it is possible to demonstrate in terms of the long continuities of Christian thought, that these Western forms of theologizing, juridicial and scholastic in shape as they are, are in fact long detours or diversions away from a more authentic tradition of Christian understanding. There is, for example, a quite different and certainly older tradition which passes from within the New Testament itself, through such figures as Justin Martyr and Clement of Alexandria and other Greek fathers, which surfaces again at the time of the Reformation in Zwingli and the Renaissance humanists (who were not necessarily non-Christians!) and in the seventeenth century in the Cambridge Platonists. In the nineteenth century there are the towering figures of Schleiermacher in Germany and Maurice in Britain. All these in their various ways widened horizons to enable Christians to see what their faith has to say about the unity and goodness of creation, the purposes of God in history, and about the universality of the action of the Divine Word.

3. It is therefore necessary to demonstrate that the entail of the past can be broken, that the inheritance is not an intolerable burden. Much better, indeed, it would be if we were to treat the past as past, and the opinions of even an Augustine, or a Calvin, or a Luther, or Wesley as conditioned by their own historical circumstances and limitations in their knowledge and experience. However, we need to be sure that we should not be committed to their various forms of exclusiveness because that exclusiveness belongs inherently to Christian theology. In various ways we shall return to these issues in the next three chapters.

2. The Missionary Background

We have already referred to John Wesley's missionary sermon on 'The General Spread of the Gospel'. Just a few sentences from this Sermon show that Wesley felt that he was living in the decisive age of mission, the very last days of the world, and the dawn of the millennial age. He speaks of the revival of religion in his own time and continues: 'Let us observe what God has already done. Between fifty and sixty years ago, God raised up a few young men to testify those grand truths (he means of course the truths of sanctification and justification at the heart of the Methodist preaching). This message has gone from Oxford into every part of Britain, and a few years after into New York, Pennsylvania, even as far as Newfoundland and Nova Scotia.' So he asks 'Is it not highly probable that God will carry on his work as he has begun? . . . I cannot think that God has wrought so glorious a work, to let it sink away and die in a few years. No: I trust this is only the beginning of a far greater work; the dawn of "the latter day glory".'

The dawn of 'the latter day glory' – these words take us into the heart of the cluster of impulses that brought into being the modern missionary movement of the last one hundred and ninety years.[19] For Wesley is at one with his contemporaries and near-contemporaries in believing that God was about to bring in the new age of which the biblical prophets spoke: 'It shall come to pass in the latter days that the mountain of the house of the Lord shall be established as the highest of the mountains, and shall be raised above the hills; all the nations shall flow to it and many peoples shall come and say: Come let us go up to the mountain of the Lord, to the house of the God of Jacob' (Isa. 2.2–3; Micah 4.1–2); then 'the earth shall be full of the knowledge of the Lord, as the waters cover the sea' (Isa. 11.9). Isaac Watts (d. 1748) had already given the English language one of the finest paraphrases of this eschatological vision, still one of the great hymns of the contemporary church:

> Jesus shall reign where'er the sun
> Doth his successive journeys run.
> His kingdom stretch from shore to shore
> Till suns shall rise and set no more.

John Wesley added his own kind of commentary to this in one of his own hymns:

> Eternal son, eternal Love
> Take to thyself thy mighty power;
> Let all earth's sons thy mercy prove
> Let all thy saving grace adore.

But it is his brother Charles who puts into verse his brother's sentiments most sharply:

> Saw ye not the cloud arise,
> Little as a human hand?
> Now it spreads along the skies,
> Hangs o'er all the thirsty land.
>
> Lo! the promise of a shower
> Drops already from above;
> But the Lord will shortly pour
> All the spirit of His Love!

The times are shortened, and the 'millennial year rushes on to our view'. Isaac Watts and the Wesleys are, however, only putting into verse the prevailing sentiments of countless other eighteenth-century divines. Jonathan Edwards in New England,[20] John Erskine in Scotland,[21] John Newton,[22] and John Gill[23] in England can be cited as typical of the thinkers that gave rise eventually to the founding of the first British missionary society in 1792. This was the Baptist Missionary Society.[24] William Carey, its most famous servant, had already published his seminal *Enquiry into the Obligations of Christians to Use Means for the Conversion of the Heathen* in Leicester in 1792. Carey was quite certain that he lived in millennial times. In the *Enquiry* he actually pictures the ships of the East India Company as the fulfilment of the prophecies concerning the Ships of Tarshish, as in Isa. 60.9. So, too, in the *Form of Agreement* which the Serampore missionaries, Carey, Marshman and Ward agreed upon on 5 October 1805 as guidelines for their activities we read these words:

> But, while we mourn over their miserable condition (i.e. of the 'poor idolaters' among whom they were working), we should not be discouraged as though their recovery were impossible. He who raised the Scottish and brutalised Britons to sit in heavenly places in Christ Jesus, can raise these slaves of superstition, purify their hearts by faith, and make them worshippers of the one God in spirit and in truth. The promises are fully sufficient to remove our doubts, and to make us anticipate that not very distant period when He will famish all the gods of India, and to cause those very

idolaters to cast their idols to the moles and bats, and renounce for ever the work of their own hands.

There is some evidence that Carey himself came to change his opinion about such a general condemnation of Hinduism, and indeed in himself paved the way for what later writers like T. E. Slater were to call the 'Higher Hinduism'.[25] We can state, however, with some assurance that the two main themes of Carey here stated in the *Form of Agreement*, i.e. that the objects of Christian mission, are followers of false religions and that Christianity is destined very soon to triumph over all these false gods, remain dominant themes throughout the nineteenth century and well on into our own times.

Thus through the missionary hymns composed in the nineteenth century, and sung with hearty gusto in the twentieth, British and American Christians were assured that 'O'er heathen lands afar, Thick darkness broodeth yet' (Lewis Hensley 1827–1905); that the song must go round the earth, so that 'lands where Islam's sway, Darkly broods o'er home and hearth' may 'Cast their bonds away' (Sarah Geraldine Stock, 1838–98); that 'Word of life, most pure and strong' must spread 'till from its dreary night/All the world awakes to light' (J. F. Bahnmaier, 1774–1841, in the translation of Catherine Winkworth, 1829–78); that those whose 'souls are lighted/With wisdom from on high' cannot 'to men benighted/The lamp of life deny' (R. Heber, 1783–1826). In this way the firm impression has been implanted cumulatively in the Western Christian consciousness that God is absent from his world until the missionary comes with the message of Christ. Charles Edward Oakley (1832–65) said as much in his striking hymn 'Hills of the north rejoice'. He wrote, 'Though absent long, your Lord is nigh/He judgment brings and victory'. Incidentally it is instructive to notice what has happened to 'Hills of the North' in two recent hymn books, *English Praise* (1975) and *Hymns and Psalms* (1983). The first lines of each verse remain but the theology has been completely re-written!

Sung endlessly in missionary meeting after missionary meeting, there is no doubt but that such hymns inspired the amazing succession of heroes and heroines who made up what Kenneth Scott Latourette calls the 'Great Century' of missionary expansion.[26] It is no part of my purpose to detract from that achievement or to diminish the stature of those who suffered unnamed hardships and privations, terrible sicknesses and fearful deaths for the sake of the gospel, and for that matter still do. My point is quite another one. Because of this willingness of our forebears to assault frontally the powers of darkness we can discern in their writings, in their letters home, and their public speaking when they were on leave, a tendency to see everything overseas in terms of spiritual darkness. They were, so to speak, programmed to see the darkest and basest side of the religions and cultures among which they ministered. Nor were they immune from that profoundly human temptation to compare the best in one's own culture and beliefs with the worst in that of other people. Like us they confused the ideal for the reality in their praise of Christian modes of believing and took the degradation and moral failure of communities among whom they worked as evidence of the inadequacy of the other religions' inspiration. In the words of a speaker at the General Conference of the Protestant Missionaries in Japan, held in Osaka in 1883: 'It is unfair to hold any religion responsible for all that is done in its name, or infer evil tendencies in a religion because it has been believed in by some very bad men. *Still it is not unfair to judge a religion in the light of the general conduct of the great body of its recognized teachers* . . . What then is the moral condition of the Buddhist priesthood of Japan? Are they held in repute for a high sense of honour, for an exalted love of truth, for great purity of life? Does not such a question seem ludicrous? Have they not a reputation for exactly the opposite characteristics?' (italics his).

Now this particular missionary was sensitive to the issue we raise, but it may well be argued that he was mistaken. His comment really tells us nothing about Buddhism as such, and certainly it would not be hard to find examples in the history of the church which would suggest that Christianity was equally impotent, were we to judge it by the same criterion. But much missionary propaganda then operated and still continues to operate in this way.

By no means everything that should be said about the nine-teenth-century missionary is included in these last comments. It is increasingly recognized that the lands to which they went owe all kinds of debts to the best of these servants of Jesus Christ. These are after all the men and women who pioneered in the study of languages, developed the then rudimentary sciences of anthropology and ethnography, and established quite new patterns of education and health care. As the nineteenth century wore on they came to quite different judgments about the religious phenomena they encountered whether in the great religious traditions of Asia or among the so-called untutored peoples of Africa and the Pacific. But that is another story, and we take it up again at the beginning of Chapter 4.

But such new understandings of the faith of other men and women rarely percolated through to the man or woman in the average British or North American pew. They went on singing 'O'er heathen lands afar/Thick darkness broodeth yet'.

3 'Ineffable Superiority' – The Cultural Assumptions of Imperialism

'Remember that we are English, that we are Christians' – Catherine Morland, heroine of Jane Austen's *Northanger Abbey* (1814) is being rebuked by Mr Henry Tilney. In his collocation 'we are English – we are Christians' there is implied both the assumption of natural English superiority and also that confusion of nationality with religious faith that has marked much of the last two centuries as far as the English have been concerned.[27] Catherine Morland had been entertaining rather foolish suspicions as a result of her attachment to the 'Gothick' novels of her period. Some mysterious apartments in Northanger Abbey had stimulated lurid imaginings. But Henry Tilney's shock on learning of the 'dreadful nature of the suspicions' is counterpointed by his equal astonishment that irrational ideas could have been so easily entertained: 'Remember the country and the age in which we live. Remember that we are English, that we are Christians.'

Much of the encounter with people of different religions took place against such a background. Not only were there serious theological entails in the nineteenth-century and early twentieth-century judgments upon other forms of religion; not only were there missionary preconceptions about idolatry and heathen darkness, there were also the obvious but little reckoned-with cultural prejudices which belonged to being English in this period. Henry Tilney speaks with the voice of a man of rational sensibilities, derived in part from the classical Renaissance, in part from the Enlightenment, in part from Deism. His Christianity was akin to that of William Paley and his Englishness to that of Lord Macaulay, both of whom overlapped in time with Jane Austen (1775–1827). Paley died in 1805, Macaulay was born in 1800. When Paley published his *View of the Evidences of Christianity* in 1794 he wrote:

> I desire, moreover, in judging of Christianity, it may be remembered, that the questions lie between this religion and none: for if the Christian religion be not credible, no one, with whom we have to do, will support the pretensions of any other.

These words, which form the second sentence of that vastly influential book, required reading for schoolboys and undergraduates throughout the nineteenth century, are themselves both the consequence of prejudice (what did Paley know about any other religious system?) and the means of implanting prejudice in others. As an earlier eighteenth-century writer Henry Fielding put into the mouth of his appalling Squire Thwackum: 'When I mention religion, I mean the Christian religion, and not only the Christian religion, but the Protestant religion, and not only the Protestant religion, but the Church of England.'[28] It is not without significance that those who drafted the 1944 Education Act required 'religious education' to be taught in schools but did not find it necessary to specify that the religion in question was to be the Christian one! So, too, it appears to be taken for granted that the compulsory collective act of worship was to be a Christian act of worship.[29] 'Consider that you are English, that you are Christian.'

Thomas Babington Macaulay likewise had an amazing influence throughout the mid and later nineteenth century. With his ebullient optimism and Whiggish enthusiasms themselves based not a little on essentially romantic views of history engendered by his reading of Sir Walter Scott, he was convinced that 'progress' was inseparably connected with 'Englishness'. From all his writings let us choose a passage which bears directly on our own theme. In 1833, in the wake of the 1832 Reform Bill, a new Charter was made for the East India Company. The Governor General of India's Executive Council was enlarged by the addition of a Law Member.

This was Macaulay. He arrived in India in 1834. Among his first tasks was to decide whether the Government in India could legally apply to education in English the annual grant ordered in 1813 and up to then applied to oriental studies. I quote from the document known since as 'Macaulay's Minute'. He is discussing what language can best be used in the place of the Indian dialects which, he says, 'contain neither literary or scientific information':

What then shall that language be? . . . I have no knowledge of either Sanskrit or Arabic . . . I am quite ready to take the oriental learning at the valuation of the Orientalists themselves. I have never found one of them who could deny that a single shelf of a good European library was worth the whole native literature of India and Arabia.

. . . (the English language) stands pre-eminent even among the languages of the West. It abounds with works of imagination not inferior to the noblest which Greece has bequeathed to us – in the models of every species of eloquence – with historical compositions, which considered merely as narratives, have seldom been surpassed, and which, considered as vehicles of ethical and political instruction, have never been equalled – with just and lively representations of human nature – with the most profound speculations on metaphysics, moral, government, jurisprudence, trade – with full and correct information respecting every experimental science which tends to preserve the health, to increase the comfort, or to expand the intellect of man. Whoever knows that language has ready access to all the vast intellectual wealth which all the wisest nations of the earth have created and hoarded in the course of ninety generations.

Lord William Bentinck, the Governor General at that time, put the recommendations of this Minute into effect in 1835. Education in India was to be through the medium of the English language. In due course this was the case not only of India, but of nearly every other part of the British Empire. But we note here not so much the profound historical consequences of 'Macaulay's Minute' but its tone of effortless superiority. There was but nothing to learn from Indian cultures or religions or philosophies. The die was cast, too, for rationalizing the quite monstrous refusal of the average monoglot English-speaker to learn any other language except for the most pragmatic purposes.

Thus 'Empire' and 'Christianity', two quite separate concepts, come here together. We find, too, other collocations: 'In every quarter of the globe we have planted the seeds of freedom, civilization and Christianity' (William Huskisson before the House of Commons in 1828); the British crown '. . . assists in diffusing amongst millions of the human race, the blessings of Christianity and civilization' (Earl Grey speaking of his own colonial policies in 1853); and even David Livingstone himself urged the duty before the Universities of Oxford and Cambridge in 1857 of spreading among the Africans 'those two pioneers of civilization – Christianity and commerce'!

The converse of such an arrogant set of equations was the ignorant belittling of everything that was strange as alien and exotic, childish and laughable, belonging to the infancy of the human race. This needs very little illustration.[30] In part it still lives with us in the jingoism and racism which can still be unleashed, quite shamefully, in the British by any one who is willing to exploit these feelings.

To be sure a fuller account of the nineteenth century would have to make it clear that there is another side of this picture. There were colonial administrators who behaved with profound sympathy for the cultural aspirations and values of those among whom they worked. There were missionaries from William Carey onwards who saw beyond the misconceptions and prejudices with which they had arrived in India or China. Novelists like Dickens and Trollope were clear sighted enough to satirize such pretensions, and Kipling is maligned if he is taken to be pure imperialist.[31]

It is, however, Kipling's phrases that stuck in the minds of the English: 'the White Man's Burden' and 'Lesser Breeds without the Law'. Not to have dwelt, even if only cursorily, on this 'non-theological factor' in the equation would be to have missed a vital element in the discussion. We have in the West confused Englishness or Scottishness, or Frenchness, or Germanness, or North American-ness with Christianity and civilization. Into the confusion has been tossed imperialism and commerce. And all that has led to a trampling on other people's dreams and hopes.

So how do we break free from all this and start all over again? I suggest we begin with the New Testament, and in particular with the story of the Apostle Paul in Ephesus.

⌐2⌐

Dialogue in the New Testament

In the world of New Testament scholarship the standing of St Luke as a historian is seriously challenged. Paradoxically his status as a theologian rises all the time.[1] It is far from my purpose here to vindicate Luke as an historian, although I do find many statements made by New Testament scholars over-sceptical when they deal with the historical events in the Acts of the Apostles. Ernest Haenchen, for example, in his great *Commentary* on the Acts of the Apostles grants little credibility to the statement in Acts 17.34 that Dionysius and Damaris became Christians as a result of Paul's preaching on the Areopagus.[2] For, he says, these two names are not mentioned in I Cor. 16.15. Instead the first converts in Achaia are the household of Stephanas in Corinth. But it does seem at least allowable that Luke as a careful historian may have had access to records in Athens which embodied an accurate tradition naming two of its founders. For as far as Paul himself was concerned Athens was not one of the churches he founded, whereas Corinth most certainly was.[3] There is no *prima facie* reason why Luke should be wrong at this point and Paul right, and it may well be that in their different ways both are correct. But whether or not this is the case, Luke certainly had profound theological reasons for including the success story of Paul's preaching in Athens, as we shall see in the course of the present exposition.

For we shall concentrate on a particular aspect of the missionary programme of the apostle Paul as Luke the historian/theologian wishes to present them to us. To do this we begin with Acts 19, the story of Paul at Ephesus. Here I am at one with Ernst Haenchen when he says 'We can estimate Chapter 19 aright only when we understand it in the total design of Luke's work'.[4] But a cursory glance at Haenchen's *Commentary*, will show that while he allows that Luke must have taken the historical details over from tradition (he adds 'what creates life out of this chronological-topographical skeleton goes back to Luke himself, whose style here is unmistakable'), he pays quite insufficient attention to what Luke means in telling us the story recorded in Acts 19.8–10.[5] Let us set this passage out in the translation of the Revised Standard Version:

> And he entered the synagogue, and for three months spoke boldly, arguing and pleading about the kingdom of God; but when some were stubborn and disbelieved, speaking evil of the Way before the congregation, he withdrew from them, taking the disciples with him, and argued daily in the school of Tyrannus. This continued for two years, so that all the residents of Asia heard the word of the Lord, both Jews and Greeks.

Let us begin by noting the two expressions: 'arguing and pleading' and 'argued'. In English translations in common use a whole range of words are used as variants: 'disputing' (Authorized Version), 'reasoning' (Revised Version), 'using argument' and 'continued to hold discussions' (New English Bible), 'held discussions' (Good News Bible), 'argued persuasively' (Jerusalem Bible).

There is indeed a very considerable range of meaning from 'disputed' to 'held discussions'! All these expressions are attempts to translate the Greek word 'dialogue' (there are two Greek words frequently used in the New Testament, *dialegomai* and *dialogizomai* and both have the force of 'to argue', 'to reason', 'to contend'). For the moment all we need to observe is that 'dialogue' is a word with biblical roots.

The next point to notice is the period of time involved. We see Paul virtually stationary for considerably more than two years. This is not a man who must hasten from place to place 'lest souls pass into eternity and the torment of hell-fire without even hearing of Jesus Christ'. His missionary motive is clearly something other than that – there is a clue to it in this passage. We shall return to this in a moment. For the time being let us again contemplate the time-span: Paul is prepared to spend at least two years and three months in the activity described as 'reasoning and persuading', that is, in a programme of dialogue.

Where does all this activity take place? First, in the synagogue. Too much stress has in time past been laid upon words spoken in the heat of the controversy at Psidian Antioch. At that time Paul is recorded as having said to the Jews: 'Since you thrust (the Word of God) from you, and judge yourselves unworthy of eternal life, behold we turn to the Gentiles' (Acts 13.46). We gravely mistake Paul if we think that for him there was a sharp break between Jewish religion and Christianity. He was and remained a Pharisee (see Acts 23.6 and 24.14ff.). His undying concern for the House of Israel we shall see in some detail when we look at his letter to the Romans.

Paul on his own terms has no option but to spend time in the synagogue. He is there until he is forced by other people to leave. Only then does he move to his second location. This is the 'Hall of Tyrannus'. Actually the word translated 'hall' in the RSV is the Greek word *scholē*, our word 'school'.[6] Paul has moved into the physical environment of the Greek philosophers! In neither place does 'dialogue' take place on his own terms and in a neutral environment. The agenda and terms of reference of the conversations are set by the other parties to the dialogue. How different from our own habitual modes of operation – we very much tend to invite people to come into our structures (in both the physical and metaphysical senses of this word), where they will be able to listen to monologues of proclamation in an environment where we are totally at home. How much there is to learn about evangelism in general from even this cursory glance at St Paul's missionary methods.

1 The Subject Matter of Paul's Dialogue

At this point we may ask if Luke the historian gives us any clues as to the basic subject-matter of the dialoguing. In fact there are two such. In the synagogue the conversations turn apparently on the meaning of the kingdom of God. Clearly this is not in the first instance the offering of a set of proof-texts showing that Jesus is the Messiah, though presumably this would have been an element of the discussion. First and foremost it must have been about the shape of God's kingly rule in the earth: How are the human facts of suffering and impotence to be related to the rule of God in the light of the death on the cross of the Righteous Servant? Contemporary experience of dialogue with both Jews and Muslims makes me keenly aware that this still is the point of departure, the *crucial* issue – so to speak – when we Christians are trying to share our understanding of the ways of God with his creation, with followers of either of these two living faiths.

The second clue is embedded in that strange expression 'All the residents of Asia, both Jews and Greeks heard the word of God'. Either Luke is wildly exaggerating or he has something else in mind. 'All the residents of Asia' simply did not hear, in a literal or physical sense. Luke means that as a result of the intellectual wrestlings: with Greek philosophical concepts, with their underlying thought- patterns, with various gleams of true understanding in the systems and doctrines propounded in the lectures in the School – whether Stoic or Platonic or even Epicurean – Paul had put himself in the position to 'tell the story properly' to the mind of Asia. (It is incidentally fascinating to see that some manuscripts of the New Testament say that Paul taught in the School of Tyrannus 'from eleven o'clock to four', that is, when the school was not otherwise in use. It is a nice speculation as to what might still have been written on the ancient equivalents of the blackboard while Paul was talking!)

It is Luke's view that the Christian movement was being prepared here for the thrust into the Hellenistic world whereby Christianity out-thought all the pagan philosophies. We may see in Paul's own letters as well as in the other writings of the New Testament how early Christianity took over concepts from the old thought world in order to explain the mystery of Christ. Thus we have, e.g. Stoic concepts like *Logos* and *Plērōma*[7] used as 'tools' for christological statement, see John 1.1 (with caveats that we shall note in our detailed exposition of St John's Prologue later) in Colossians 2.9 and Ephesians 1.23. Incidentally it is worth just remarking that all these pieces of literature have associations with Ephesus, this city of 'dialogue'.[8] Luke no doubt believes that here is the part for the whole – a kind of 'first-fruitage' of all this – now all Asia could really hear the gospel in a language addressed to its mind as well as to its heart. Were we Christians more generally to take this model seriously, we would be far more concerned than we often appear to find ways of expressing our faith so that Muslims or Marxists, Hindus or Humanists could really be said to have 'heard the Word of God'. For many people of other faith the gospel story just has not yet been properly told.

2 Dialogue and Other Aspects of Paul's Work

There is still more to be said about Paul at Ephesus, for it would be highly misleading to suggest that 'dialogue' was the only form of mission in which he was engaged. Actually there were at least three other forms. One was a kind of ecumenical or intra-faith dialogue with some disciples or followers of Jesus who 'knew only the baptism of John' (see the well-known story of Acts 19.1–7). Another form of mission was the frontal attack on spurious and false religion – what we probably would call a 'new religious movement' with Jewish syncretistic elements, practising exorcism and magic arts (see Acts

19.13–19). The human world of religion is always ambiguous, indeed is often open to invasion by demonic forces. Dialogue is not the appropriate stance when confronted by the likes of the seven sons of Sceva, then or now. The third kind of mission is what we might call the 'unmasking' of an ideology. The one prevailing in Ephesus was connected with the cult of the goddess Artemis, 'Diana of the Ephesians'. In an almost Marxist sense, the worship of Artemis both buttresses and is buttressed by the economics of big business. This surely is how we must read the story of Demetrius and the silversmiths, Acts 19.23–41.

Dialogue with people of other faiths and ideologies is misunderstood if it is presented as the only way of mission or if it is represented as being complacent and tolerant in the face of evil nonsense. But with the example of Paul before us we may equally conclude, in the strongest possible way, that evangelism is distorted if it is presented as happening only by monologue, by one-way proclamation. Paul at Ephesus shows us that the way of dialogue is a way of patience, often very time consuming. It shows us that the way of dialogue means meeting the other person on his or her own terms and really attending to what they say, believe, feel. We also see that it is a way seeking to share persuasively the best of our own conviction, to share that which has most persuasively laid hold of our own minds and hearts. It was a way that plainly made many friends for Paul in Ephesus – what a significant little comment that is in Acts 19.31 'some of the Asiarchs also, who were friends of his . . . '![9] But perhaps Paul is the best one to sum it all up, for in a letter he wrote during this period in Corinth he bears his own testimony to the way of dialogue:

> To the Jews I became as a Jew, in order to win Jews . . . to those outside the law I became as one outside the law. To the weak, I became weak . . . I have become all things to all men, that I might by all means save some. I do it all for the sake of the gospel, that I may share in its blessings (I Cor. 9.19–23).

In this way Paul speaks of what we today would call empathy and identification and of a deep loving concern for the other. In the last words we have what has been called 'the purest missionary motive of all' – we share in dialogue because we want to share in the blessings of the gospel.[10]

Having thus established Paul's own commitment to and programme for dialogue from his activity in Ephesus, we are in a position to read three passages from earlier parts of Acts with fresh insight.

3 Paul on Mars Hill

The first of these is in Acts 17 (we are working backwards from
Ephesus!) where there is the account of Paul's meeting with the
Athenian philosophers on the Areopagus (Mars Hill). The com-
monest way of expounding this passage (derived it appears from Sir
William Ramsay)[11] goes something like this: Paul arrived in Athens
from Beroea, almost unintentionally, and while he was waiting for
Silas and Timothy to catch up with him, he went on a sight-seeing
tour of the city, 'his spirit was provoked within him when he saw the
city full of idols' (Acts 17.16). Therefore he 'argued' or 'disputed' in
the synagogue and the market place with the result that he caught the
attention of the Stoic and Epicurean philosophers who 'took hold of
him' and brought him to the Areopagus (Paul all unwillingly as it
were, in the midst of taunts and jeers). Despite all this Paul makes the
most of his opportunity by attacking their superstitions, 'for', he says,
'as I passed along and observed the objects of your worship, I found
an altar with this inscription "To an unknown God". What, therefore,
you worship as unknown this I proclaim to you'. Then according to
this style of exposition, he made a bad mistake. He tried to use
intellectual arguments to win these intellectuals to Christ. This
naturally was a total disaster and he left Athens a chastened and a
wiser man. It is no surprise therefore that when he got to his next port
of call and began his ministry in Corinth he had this thought
uppermost: 'I did not come to you proclaiming the testimony of God
in lofty words or wisdom, for I decided to know nothing among you
except Jesus Christ and him crucified' (I Cor. 2.1–2).

There is however, a quite different way of reading Acts 17.
Certainly one great German scholar writing just a little later than Sir
William Ramsay saw the Areopagus sermon in quite a different light.
He called it 'the greatest missionary document in the New Testament'![12] Even without our modern concern for dialogue this scholar
had perceived here an attempt to set out the beliefs of the new religion
in incisive and summary form yet seeking at the same time such points
of contact as were possible with the older world-view. In the light of
Paul's activity at Ephesus we can go even further than this.

Let us be clear first of all that there is no evidence that Luke thought
that he was portraying a failure in mission. Why ever should he use
his valuable space to do this? On the contrary the evidence is of a large
measure of success. St Paul's words gain at least two converts whose
names were significant enough to have been recorded, Dionysius and

Damaris, and there were others, (Acts 17.34).[13] Rather few contemporary sermons, we think, are as successful as this! In addition and very significantly for our purpose there is a group who say: 'we will hear you further about this'. Can it really be supposed that the great apostle did not rejoice in this? What nonsense to suppose that he moved off to Corinth with his tail between his legs. How much greater nonsense to suppose that he would not have welcomed with open arms an opportunity to continue the dialogue!

Secondly we note in Acts 17 the presence of the word 'dialoguing' itself – that is, the word translated 'arguing' or 'disputing' in verse 17. If we use the translation 'reasoning' or 'discussing' it might help us to see that perhaps Paul was not quite so hostile as he is made to sound. Further reading may disclose to us that the word in verse 22 translated by the AV as 'superstitious' is rendered by our word 'religious' in the RSV and 'scrupulous' in the NEB, that is, in quite a favourable sense.[14] Already then new light is being cast on the Aeropagus Sermon. When, therefore, we meet with the quotation(s) from the old poets and philosophers (Aratus of Soli, Cleanthes of Soli, Epimenides of Crete or whoever),[15] it is clearly by design and with total approval. Thus an old pagan philosopher contributes to Holy Scripture: 'in him we live and move and have our being' and 'indeed we are his offspring'! One aspect of our approach to people of other faith is in being aware that they will already have some insight into the truth of God and his ways. Here is Paul, in Luke's view, setting a pattern.[16]

We conclude, therefore, that the words of I Cor. 2.1–2 have nothing whatsoever to do with Paul's experience in Athens – from the internal evidence of the Corinthians correspondence it is much more likely that Paul was dealing specifically with the so-called gnosticizing tendencies of the Corinthians – but that's another story. It would make far more sense to draw a vastly different conclusion – namely that Paul was so intensely convinced of the need to come to grips with Greek Philosophy that he deliberately planned, as soon as there was an opportunity, to spend his valuable time in just such a centre as the School of Tyrannus.

4 Paul and Barnabas at Lystra

We can be much briefer about this. In Acts 14 we see the apostolic message meeting the paganism of the rural hinterland of Asia Minor.[17] But what Paul has to say to those who would have made him and Barnabas into gods is extremely impressive in the retrospective light of Acts 17 and 19. Even the most deluded and astray are not without some clue as to God and his grace. We need only instance Acts 14.16–17, 'In past generations he allowed all nations to walk in their own ways, yet He did not leave himself without witness, for he did good and gave you from heaven rains and fruitful seasons, satisfying your hearts with good and gladness' (RSV). The NEB is even more explicit in translating verse 17 'he has not left you without some clue to his nature in the kindness he shows . . .'. Also note in this verse the term *euphrosunē* 'gladness, good cheer'; in the same context in Hebrew the word would be *simchah*: (see Acts 2.28; Num. 10.10, and in many other places; it is a word which belongs to salvation, well-being, in the presence of the Lord). We shall see in due course how consonant this is with the understanding both of the Hebrew scriptures and the articulated teaching of St Paul in the Letter to the Romans. Meanwhile we content ourselves with noticing that here again as far as the Acts of the Apostles is concerned all is not total darkness in the heathen world.

5 Peter's Encounter with Cornelius

On the subject of the account in Acts 10 and 11 of the launching of the mission to the Gentiles Krister Stendahl writes: 'The slowness and resistance of the Church when it comes to such momentous new insights and new steps is described not primarily as a critique of the Church. It means to show the glories and the greatness in new applications of God's love and lack of partiality (Acts 10.34), this beyond the limits to which one was accustomed.' Later he adds, 'The Cornelius story shows that it is not easy for God to teach the Church that He does not practise partiality. To many of us the signs are strong that He has many ways of working in his world'.[18]

Let us add just one point to what Bishop Stendahl has written. It concerns the status of Cornelius in the sight of God prior to the time of his conversion to full Christian faith. Explicit and precise descriptions of Cornelius' manner of life at that time are given in Acts 10.2, 10.22 and 11.31. Let us pick out some of these expressions: he is a 'devout man', he 'feared God', he 'gave alms liberally to the people', he 'prayed constantly to God', he was 'an upright and god-fearing man' his prayers have been 'heard' and his alms have been 'remembered before God' (so the RSV translations, note that many of them are in the Greek New Testament exactly the words used in the Septuagint to describe saints of the Old Testament).[19] Peter expresses an authentic biblical judgment concerning the 'good man' who lives outside the

Covenant in these salutary words: 'I perceive . . . that in every nation any one who fears him and does what is right is acceptable to him' (Acts 10.34). Those who live according to the Torah, the Law, are God's people even though they live outside the boundaries of Israel.[20] That this echoes exactly one of the strands of the Old Testament teaching we may see from the material to which we now turn.

6 Paul's Theological Inheritances from the Old Testament

That the main theme of the Old Testament is the calling of a special people to whom the Lord God binds himself in a covenant relationship is not for a moment in dispute. 'I will be your God and you shall be my people' is at the very heart of things. It is no intention of the survey which now follows to belittle the biblical doctrines of election and all its implications for the freedom before God of the human spirit. Lesslie Newbigin has recently written eloquently about this in his *The Open Secret*. 'God's way of universal salvation,' he says, 'if it is addressed to man as he really is and not to the unreal abstraction of a detached "soul", must be accomplished by the way of election – of choosing, calling and sending one to be the bearer of blessing for all'.[21] Such a one is Abraham. Through his calling 'all the families of the earth shall bless themselves' (Gen. 12.3).

But we need also to be aware of the historical and contemporary misunderstandings which cluster around the concept of 'election'. There are great and desperate pitfalls surrounding 'election' when its exclusivism and particularity are stressed to distortion. The American theologian Donald Dawe has also recently pointed out the distortion that occurred when the Christian church took over the Jewish scriptures and applied the separatism of some of the ancient Israelites to its own manner of relating to the world. 'The Christians then gave this covenant theology a new twist to heighten its particularism. They expelled the Jews from the Covenant relationship to God and put themselves in their place. The argument was that a "new covenant" had been established through Jesus Christ that superseded the old one in Abraham and Moses. The church alone now was the holy people of God, the saved amid the damned . . . By the time of Cyprian (*d.* 258) this theology was established as the basis for interpreting all the covenant traditions of the Bible. It was summed up in the dictum "Outside the church, no salvation".'[22]

Of course, that must be seen as nonsense. Even in terms of the special covenant it distorts the purpose of God. Biblical election is never in order to privilege and security but to service and witness, so that all nations may share in blessing (see Ch. 3). But our point in what immediately follows is that there are yet two more grievous errors. These persist in our relations with people of other faith, first because of the failure to understand the special covenant in the context of the universal covenant of God, and secondly because of a failure to understand that God has never at any time abrogated any covenant – either universal or special – and that all God's covenants remain in force.

7 *The Universal Covenants*

The first eleven chapters of the Book of Genesis are the necessary prologue to the whole biblical story of redemption. Those who put together the stories and traditions contained in Genesis 1–11 knew exactly what they were doing. God's great saving acts: the calling of Abraham, the deliverance from Egypt, the giving of the command-ments, the entry in the promised land – all that which makes up the Torah, the Law as it is set forth in the Pentateuch could be made full sense of only in the context of God's dealing with all the nations of humankind. Hence the importance of the extended study of this theme that makes up the third chapter of this book.

At this point we simply want to speak of the universality of the Covenant. So we begin at the beginning. The God of Israel is the God of all the earth. He is creator of all human beings. They are all made in his image and likeness. All human society is under his watchful eye. Later Jewish teaching saw the act of creation itself as a covenant between God and all humankind in the primal couple, and spoke of the Covenant with Adam:

> The Lord created man out of the earth . . .
> He made them in his own image . . .
> He granted them dominion over beasts and birds . . .
> He filled them with knowledge and understanding
>   and showed them good and evil.
> He set his eye upon their hearts
>   to show them the majesty of his works.
> And they will praise his holy name,
>   to proclaim the grandeur of his works,
> He bestowed knowledge upon them
>   and allotted to them the law of life.
> He established with them an eternal covenant.
>   (Ecclus. (Ben Sira) 17. vv, 1, 3, 5, 7 and 8–12)

The teaching that follows makes clear that all the nations are continually watched over by the Lord (v. 15): both their iniquities and their good works are seen by him (vv. 20 and 22). Indeed the figure of Cornelius is immediately in our minds when we read:

A man's almsgiving is like a signet with the Lord, and he will keep a person's kindness like the apple of his eye (Ecclus. 17.22).

In Genesis chapter 9, there is specific mention of the 'covenant between men and you, and every living creature that is with you, for all future generations' (v. 12). The Rainbow sign is witness to all humankind of the all-transcending love and concern and graciousness of God the Creator towards the whole of his creation. The covenant with Noah is thus supremely important. It is totally unconditional upon any response from human beings themselves. It is established in the full recognition of the wickedness and weakness and foolishness of the human frame. It is made entirely upon the initiative of God and it will be sustained by his faithfulness alone.[23] Jean Daniélou has rightly called this 'the cosmic covenant' and careful reading of the Old Testament will show that this cosmic covenant was never forgotten.

It is perhaps our characteristic preoccupation with redemption, with 'saving acts' and 'Salvation-history' that makes us miss so often the biblical feeling for God as universal creator and sustainer (see Ps. 50.10; Jer. 8.7; Ps. 19.1 and many other places).

The Adamic and Noachic covenants makes it impossible to picture the church as the 'saved amid the damned'; the Old Testament scriptures cannot be taken over as support for the dictum 'outside the church, no salvation'.

8 Could St Paul have supposed that God 'spoke' outside the Covenant made with Abraham?

There will be many who would readily agree that God rules over the affairs of the nations with deep personal care and concern (on the basis of such words as those of Amos 9.7 where the Lord speaks of how he brought the Philistines from Caphtor and the Syrians from Kir, or Isa. 19.23–4, where the coming together of Egypt 'my people', and 'Assyria the work of my hands' with Israel 'my heritage' is foreseen). But there might be considerably more hesitation in admitting unequivocally that God has actually revealed himself, 'spoken' to men and women outside the special covenant people. Yet there is considerable evidence within the Hebrew scriptures that God has done precisely this, and that those who, under his guidance, shaped the biblical tradition were not in the least surprised that this should be the case. Let us now set out some of the biblical material that should be carefully reflected upon.

9 Dialogue in the Torah

Genesis 14.18 tells us of Melchizedek, King of Salem. He is described as 'priest of God Most High', and blesses Abram, as he then was, in the name of God Most High. The Hebrew Canon clearly understands this as an authentic 'word from the Lord'. But as E. A. Speyser makes clear in the *Anchor Bible Commentary* on Genesis, the situation is even more intriguing. Some firm historical traditions lie behind the record here. As a Canaanite priest Melchizedek naturally invokes his own deity by name: 'Blessed be Abram by *El-Elyon*, Creator of heaven and the earth'. Abram, two verses later, uses terminology known to him, i.e. he uses the word *Yahweh* to which he adds *El-Elyon*, creator of heaven and earth. In this latter formulation the phrase *El-Elyon* appears to be descriptive especially in apposition to 'creator of the heaven and earth'. But Melchizedek, the Canaanite priest, seems to be employing *El-Elyon* as a personal name. This terminology is independently attested.[24] But this is worth pondering. As Speyser goes on to comment: 'That later religious Hebrew literature should have identified *El-Elyon* with Yahweh, quite probably on the basis of this passage, is readily understandable. But this appears to be the only late reflex of Gen. xiv. The narrative itself has all the ingredients of historicity.' We see here then Abraham accepting a blessing from the non-Israelite priest, and offering him tithes in return. The missiological implications of this are spelt out for us by Caroll Stuhlmueller: 'Even while God was calling the patriarchs away from "your country and your kindred" (Gen. 12.1) to be the parents of a unique elect people, it was being done in such a way as to show the *positive* contribution from secular environment and pre-existing "pagan" religions. A message is being flashed to us that religion is never a new and pure creation by God but a synthesis of the best under a new inspiration from God' (italics his).[25]

Genesis 20 contains the poignant story of the encounter of Abraham and Abimelech. Few Commentaries focus their attention upon Abimelech, choosing rather to dwell upon the scriptural impartiality in relating the failings as well as the virtues of its heroes. But Abimelech is clearly portrayed as a man of high moral quality. He has acted, as he says, *betam lebabi*, 'in the integrity of my heart', and God in his reply to him agrees, 'Yes, I know that you have done this in the integrity of your heart *betam lebabka*'. God is speaking to him in a dream to ensure that he does not sin. When he eventually meets Abraham again, he asks him 'why have you done this thing to me?' Abraham replies, significantly, 'because I thought that there was no fear of God (*'eyn-yirath 'elohim*) in this place'. This is the same 'Fear of the Lord' (*yirath yahweh*) which 'is the beginning of wisdom' (Ps. 111.10). It is also the quality predicated of Job (Job 1.1; 2.3 etc.): Job is 'blameless' (*tam*) and upright and fears God. The Torah adds its testimony. In Abimelech's person is found the 'fear of God' beyond the boundaries of Israel, and certainly where Abraham did not expect to find it.

In *Exodus 18* there is the account of Jethro, Moses's father-in-law. He is described as 'the priest of Midian' (v. 1). This story is fascinating in terms of the history of Israel's religion, and has given rise to the so-called Kenite Hypothesis, i.e. that Yahweh was originally the God of the Kenites, and that Yahweh first revealed himself to Moses at the Burning Bush (Ex. 3.16). This hypothesis may be the explanation of verse 11: 'Now I know that Yahweh is greater than all the gods'. H. H. Rowley, the Baptist Old Testament scholar of a previous generation, was among those who accepted the Kenite hypothesis, and he says about Jethro's words: 'his joy at the manifestation of Yahweh's surpassing power would be more intelligible if Yahweh was the God he served'.[26] But whether or not Yahweh was a Kenite God, there are obvious implications in the inclusion within the *Torah* of this story of a priest of Midian offering a true sacrifice on behalf of the people of Israel. But we may note nevertheless that some later editor had discerned the oddity of this story. For clearly Exodus 18 has been displaced from its original context (see Ex. 17.1 and 19.1). It has been suggested that this later editor took offence at the notion of a Midianite priest sacrificing to God at Sinai after God had revealed himself to Israel and had anointed Aaron to the priesthood (see Ex. 28 and 29). To avoid the issues raised by this, the editor has moved this post-covenant happening to its present position as chapter 18. But what is to be emphasized is that the tradition is quite assured: Yahweh was known and spoke outside Israel.

In *Numbers 22–24* we have the early and intriguing narrative about Balaam, the son of Peor. In 22.8 the name of Yahweh is placed upon the lips of a non-Israelite soothsayer. It may be true, in the words of one commentator, 'that it is not necessary to hold that the pagan diviner was a worshipper of the true God'.[27] But it is clear that those

who were responsible for the Book of Numbers in its final form found
no difficulty in allowing that non-Israelites had fundamental insights
into the will of God. Dr J. H. Hertz, a former British Chief Rabbi,
quotes with approval this judgment: 'This recognition of God's
revelation of His purposes concerning Israel to a non-Israelite is
striking evidence of the universality of Judaism.'[28]

10 Dialogue in the Prophets and the Writings

In *Ezekiel 14.14 and 20* we have a reference to three righteous and
potentially redemptive figures: Noah, Daniel and Job. These are
three men from pre-Israelite times. Noah we have no need to speak
about at this point, for we deal extensively with the Covenant with
Noah in the next chapter,[29] but it is worth commenting on the other
two personages.

Daniel is first mentioned in a long epic text from Ras Shamra ('the
legend of Aqhat'[30]) where Daniel is said to be a King who dispenses
justice: 'He judges the cause of the widow, and vindicates the cause of
the fatherless.' His name means 'God has judged', and we may
presumably take it that in the contemporary prophetic tradition he
was held up as a paragon of wisdom and justice, even though he was a
Syrian and a non-Jew.

The Book of Job has as its setting the land of Uz. Most likely this was
Edom, though some have reckoned it to be elsewhere, maybe north of
Transjordan. But in any case Job is portrayed as a man of the desert, a
Bedouin sheikh. Whatever date we give to the Book of Job or however
strongly it may be insisted that in its final form it is the product of the
culture and theology of Israel, the epiphany of God (the tremendous
'answer to Job' out of the whirlwind in ch. 38) is presented in its pages
as taking place outside the borders of Israel and to one who does not
belong to Israel.

Alongside Job we may put the name of Ruth, on any reckoning one
of the 'holy pagans' of the Old Testament even before she speaks the
moving and beautiful words of Ruth 1.16.

But there are other figures inside the Old Testament which bear
just enumerating with no further comment at this point: Abel, Enoch,
Nimrod, Lot, the Canaanite women Shua and Tamar (Gen. 38.2–6),
Asenath (Gen. 41.50), Pharaoh's daughter (Ex. 2.5), Rahab (Josh.
2), Ithra the Ishmaelite (II Sam. 17.25) and, we could add, the sailors
in the story of Jonah who call upon the name of the Lord, in Jonah
1.14.

So the *Law (Torah)*, the *Prophets* and the *Writings*, those three elements that make up the Hebrew scriptures carry in their own ways evidence that God is at work and touches men and women outside Israel. In the next chapter we shall survey God at work with 'nations'. When we grapple with the christological issues in Chapters 4 and 5 we shall return to the theme of 'wisdom' – that incipient theology that tried to make sense of God's universal activity, and which is partly touched upon within the Old Testament. But we may conclude this particular section by affirming that the Hebrew canon could take a positive as well as a negative view of those outside the covenant people.

All this cumulative evidence surely must support the straightforward interpretation of Malachi 1.11 (that is, that it refers to the Gentiles, and not to the Jewish diaspora scattered among the nations):

> For from the rising of the sun to its setting my name is great among the nations, and in every place incense is offered to my name, and a pure offering; for my name is great among the nations, says the Lord of hosts.

11 A Note on Idolatry in the Old Testament

This is added here because a BCC Document on Inter-faith Services (April 1968) showed concern lest much biblical evidence was being deliberately ignored by advocates of the dialogue approach. It asked if we were taking seriously the Bible's 'vigorous attack on idolatry and unequivocal assertion of the Lordship of the God of Abraham, Isaac and Jacob, the God and Father of our Lord Jesus Christ'. Max Warren gave much attention to this at that time, and we here summarize his conclusions.[31]

The first point he made is this: the inimitably unambiguous witness of the Old Testament prophets to the evil of idolatry was in the breaking of the Covenant between God and Israel, as in Jeremiah 3. Jeremiah 18.15 gives us a cry from the heart of God: 'My people have forgotten'. Ezekiel hears God's verdict: 'these men have taken their idols into their hearts' (Ezek. 14.3). The marriage settlement of the covenant has been repudiated. Hence, we may add, idolatry is adultery.

His second point was that compared with all this, the Old Testament is remarkably reserved on the subject of idolatry outside the covenant people. There is indeed, he noted, prophetic scorn for the foolishness of idol-worship particularly in Isaiah (note particu-

larly Isa. 40.18ff.) and in Jeremiah (see for example, Jer. 10.3ff.) and
in certain passages of Hosea, Habakkuk and Jonah (see Hos. 8.6;
Hab. 2.18–19 and Jonah 2.8). But then he added 'what is more
striking and worthy of some study is the number of passages where the
idols of the nations are in fact conceived as symbols of the nations.
This is clearly the case in a series of passages in Jeremiah 46–51. The
same idea is present in Isaiah, Jeremiah, Ezekiel and Nahum (Isa.
10.10; 19.1; 21.9; Jer. 43.12; Ezek. 30.13; Nahum 1.14).'

We must, therefore, take his main point, that the Old Testament
testimony is not as 'unequivocal' or as 'unambiguous' as it might
appear at first sight. The prophetic concern for the relationship of the
people of the covenant with their covenant-making God is not
sufficient basis for us to start drawing inferences as to 'what should be
our understanding of the work of Christ, God the Reconciler, in the
world outside the covenant of Israel'. We are grateful to the memory
of Max Warren for this.

12 'For the Gifts and the Call of God are Irrevocable'

We return now to the theme of the special covenant with Abraham as
it was understood in the New Testament and, in particular, by St
Paul. We have already seen how, according to Donald Dawe, the
Christian church went astray in 'expelling the Jews from the covenant
relationship' and in putting itself in their place as the only covenanted
people of God, with the only source of salvation. We need now to ask
some searching questions of the Letter to the Romans, for perhaps
there are answers there which can help us to find some new ways
forward.

First of all let us concern ourselves with the 'universal covenant'.
What is Paul's teaching about this? As far as he is concerned all the
covenants remain in operation. Most certainly the covenant with
Adam does. 'Adam' is a basic category for him, see Romans 5.14ff.
and I Cor. 15.22 ('As in Adam all die so in Christ shall all be made
alive'). Like the writer of Ecclesiasticus (Ben Sirach) he knows that all
men and women live within range of the knowledge of God: 'ever since
the creation of the world his invisible nature, namely his eternal
power and deity has been visible in the things that have been made'
(Rom. 1.20; cf. Ecclus. 17.6–11). Paul knows that there will be 'glory
and honour and peace for everyone who does good, the Jew first and
also the Greek. For God shows no partiality' (Rom. 2.10–11; once
again compare this with Ecclus. 17.15–24, and with the Cornelius
story, Acts 10.34).

But also the special covenant of God with his people of Israel remains operative. All the yearning and longing for his own people demonstrated in Romans 9–11 testifies to this. We read these chapters properly only when we see that the mission to the Gentiles is only and essentially 'a colossal detour to the salvation of Israel, where the first become last. World history cannot end until those first called have found their way home as the last. In this detour Paul himself is nothing other than what John the Baptist claimed to be, namely the forerunner of the end of the world'.[32] This sheds floods of light on verses like Romans 9.4. 'They are Israelites, to them belong the sonship, the glory, the covenants, the giving of the Law, the worship and the promises . . . ' – (In this we note the present tense – nothing has been superseded here!); upon Romans 11.1, 'I ask then has God rejected his ancient people . . . why the very thought is unthinkable; on Rom. 11.13, 'their rejection means the reconciliation of the world, what will their acceptance mean but life from the dead'; on Rom. 11.28–29, for 'as regards election they are beloved for the sake of their fathers. The gifts and the call of God are irrevocable'.

Paul knows that through the 'inscrutable ways' of God (Rom. 11.33) they will receive mercy' so that 'God may have mercy on all' (Rom. 11.32). The immensity of this vision so overpowers him that it appears that he is almost lost for words: lost in wonder, love and praise he gives voice to the tremendous doxology of Rom. 11.33–36.

This all has massive implications for the dialogue today between Christians and Jews. I try to set some of them out in *Appendix A*. The literature there referred to shows how much has still to be done before we can get our Christian relationship to our Jewish fellow-believers right. There must be a repudiation of every form of anti-semitism wherever this appears in our inherited theologies.[33]

We conclude this section by reminding ourselves once again of the three months and two years of dialogue in Ephesus. We can see from the Letter to the Romans that Paul had been able to forge some powerful conceptual tools as he approached his partners in dialogue both in the Synagogue and in the School of Tyrannus. He had a positive way of understanding the presence of God in their midst. He could conceive that by sharing his faith with these others, 'for the sake of the gospel' there were future blessings which could become available to him (see I Cor. 9.23, again), some great new sense perhaps of the 'depth of the riches and wisdom and knowledge of God'.

⊥3⊥

God and the Nations

In the important theological statement in the *Guidelines on Dialogue with People of Living Faiths and Ideologies*, the question is put:

> What is the relation between the universal creative/redemptive activity of God towards all humankind and the particular creative/redemptive activity of God in the history of Israel and in the person and work of Jesus Christ?[1]

Alongside this question we may place a second from the same document:

> How are Christians to find from the Bible criteria in their approach to people of other faiths and ideologies, recognizing, as they must, the authority accorded to the Bible by Christians of all centuries, particular questions concerning the authority of the Old Testament for the Christian Church, and the fact that partners in dialogue have other starting points and resources, both in holy books and traditions of teaching?

I tried to set out some answers to these questions in an essay I wrote for a *Festschrift* in honour of Dr Stanley Samartha when this great servant of the church retired from the WCC in 1982.[2]

Accordingly I attempted to look at the way in which the story of the creative/redemptive activity of God in the history of Israel is set within a framework of universal creative/redemptive activity in the early chapters of Genesis. Then I tried to take notice of the way in which the literature of Israel itself expresses from time to time an awareness of God's creative/redeeming activity beyond the bounds of Israel. I did this by examining some of the eschatological perceptions in the Psalms and in the later Prophets. Lastly, I tried to indicate how some of these themes are taken up in the Book of Revelation. These, I argued, are clues to a new and juster estimate of 'pluralism' in the purposes of God, and that they may, therefore, enable us to affirm with some scriptural basis that 'partners in dialogue have other starting points and resources, both in holy books and traditions of teaching', that these are indeed 'treasures' which may be brought into the City of God.

1 The Concept of the 'Nations' in the Bible

Both Testaments have a great deal to say about 'nations' or 'peoples'. Unfortunately much of significance is masked from readers of the English versions by wide variations in the terminology employed to translate both the Hebrew and the Greek words. In the Old Testament the words most commonly employed are *'am* (pl. *'ammim*) *'le'om* (pl. *le'ummim*), and *goy* (pl. *goyim*), and in the New Testament, *laos* (pl. *laoi*), and *ethnos* (pl. *ethnē*). Without constant reference to the Hebrew or the Greek text it is usually impossible to know which of these words is being employed in the original. But, more seriously, there is a tendency to use in translating *goyim* and *ethnē* the coloured and tendential expressions 'heathens', 'pagans' or 'gentiles'.[3]

One further difficulty in translation lies in the fact that neither Testament knows anything of the modern concept of the 'nation-state' in which miscellaneous notions of territorial sovereignty, racial identity, 'blood and soil' and so forth are conjoined as a result of European political history and illegitimate romantic illusions.[4] The biblical *'ammim* and *goyim* refer to genealogical, linguistic, geographical and cultural groups. Thus the great empires, Assur, Babylonia, Persia and so on were conglomerates of peoples, with now one or now another group dominating. The *ecumene* of the New Testament was similarly the known inhabited world, made up chiefly of provincial units in which were cities with their surrounding populations. Local languages did continue to be spoken (see Acts 14.11) but there is hardly any emphasis in New Testament writings upon the ethnic components of the Roman Empire. Greek and Latin were the common languages of a world in which there were neither nationality laws nor national boundaries as we know them today.

2 The 'Nations' in the Old Testament

Helmer Ringgren has rightly observed that 'geographically Israel was part of the Ancient Near East, and history and archeology inform us that its political relations with its neighbours were manifold and various'.[5] We might add also that its religious reactions with its neighbours were also manifold and various, as witness the researches of the scholars into 'pan-Babylonianism' (Delitsch and his successors), myth and ritual patterns (S. H. Hooke and his school), or into Ugaritic influences (Engnell and his followers). Indeed the 'distinctive ideas' of the Old Testament really stand out only when seen against this background.[6] So we are all profoundly aware of the pluralistic matrix in which the Old Testament came to birth. Yet too little attention has so far been paid to the theological implications of this world of many faiths and religious traditions even for the shapers of the Old Testament themselves.[7] How did they perceive the relationship between God's action in Israel and the 'creative/redemptive activity towards humankind' by the 'Judge of all the earth' (Gen. 18.2).

Our first answer to that question must be in looking at 'the doctrine of the first things', the protology of Genesis, in chapters 1 to 11, together with the first three verses of chapter 12. But first let us take to heart some words of Gerhard von Rad about this material. He writes, 'they can hardly be over-interpreted theologically! Indeed the danger appears greater that the expositor will fall short of discovering the concentrated doctrinal content'.[8] We limit ourselves to just one of the great themes in the great biblical prologue, namely that sequence of teaching that is linked by the word 'generations', *toledoth* (Gen. 2.4, 5; 6.9; 10.1; 11.10; 11.27). The conclusion of the magnificent liturgical setting forth of the creation of the world, in Genesis 1.1–2.4a, reads: 'These are the generations of the heavens and earth when they were created.' At this point is inserted the Jahwist account of creation and fall and the story of Cain and his descendants, until we come to Gen. 5.1. 'This is the book of the generations of Man.' Genesis 5.3 tells us of the new line of Seth, the true descendants of Adam, in place of the aberrations of Gen. 4.17ff. The *toledoth* are listed: Enosh, Kenan, Mahalalel, Jared, Enoch, Methuselah, Lamech until we come to Noah in 5.29. Here we have a gloss on Noah's name: 'Out of the ground which the Lord has cursed, this one shall bring us relief from our work and the toil of our hands' (5.29).[9] Noah is a redemptive figure. After the interspersion of the story of the *nephilim* and the growth of wickedness in the earth in Gen. 6.1–8, the Priestly narrative resumes in 6.9: 'these are the generations of Noah (*'elleh toledoth noah*)'. Then follows the masterly interweaving of both J and P Material concerning the Deluge. This ends with the Jahwist affirmation: 'I will never again curse the ground because of man . . . ' (Gen. 8.21).

Genesis 9 then resumes the Priestly narrative proper with its formidable presentation of a universal or cosmic covenant. This is both a covenant of preservation and a covenant of redemption.[10] God's intention to make this covenant is first mentioned to the redemptive figure, Noah, before the flood, Gen. 6.18. Like other Old Testament covenants it is made from the greater to the lesser, i.e., established by the more powerful partner in the bargain.[11] Here we may particularly notice that it is made in full recognition of the weakness of the human frame (Gen. 8.21). At the same time it is made with those who bear the image and likeness of God, Gen. 9.6, of Gen. 1.26–7 and 5.1–3, all material from the priestly tradition: the Hebrew terms are *tselem* and *demuth*. The Noachic Covenant is *berith 'olam*, a covenant for ever, 9.16, and 9.11. Like other covenants it has its sign, *'oth*: the *qesheth* which we usually translate as a rainbow but which is in fact the bow of war to shoot arrows of destruction. In the heavens the warbow is now reversed and points as it were towards the heart of God.[12] This, says God, will be a memorial to enable him to remember the everlasting covenant, *lizekhor berith 'olam*, (Gen. 9.16).

In all this the great Prologue of the Book of Genesis makes clear that the divine redemptive purpose is already at work in God's activity among peoples and nations who are seen as having their common ancestor in Noah, of the true line of Seth, son of Adam.

Now the compilers of the Genesis material turn to the tables of the nations again in the form of genealogies of the sons of Noah (Gen. 10.1ff.). As with other chapters of the Bible entirely composed of genealogical lists, Genesis 10 rarely appears in church lectionaries or selections for daily Bible reading! Therefore its main points are largely unfamiliar in the churches. However, they are exceedingly important. Let us briefly review them. First, Genesis 10 teaches that the expansion over the then known world of the peoples is within the purposes of God, as their location in their territories and in their family groupings. Indeed they are to flourish with his blessing, 'before the Lord', *liphne jhwh* (Gen. 10.9). Their common ancestry is repeatedly asserted and their common destiny to live in harmony in spite of racial and linguistic differences is implied. Note that Genesis 10 teaches a different view of the origin of language, seeing it somehow as within the providence of God. As Westermann has written,[13] 'The basis for the universalism of Scripture is to be found in this chapter' for the peoples of the world are all 'the families of the sons of Noah, according to their genealogies in their nations and from this the nations spread abroad on the earth after the flood' (Gen. 10.23).

As a counterpoint to this P narrative, Genesis 11 sets out the earlier tradition of the origin of language in the story of Babel. This begins: 'Now the whole earth had one language and few words . . . '! But this deeply significant and indispensable addition to the Genesis Prologue does not need to be expounded at this point: it is part of the human situation with which God has to deal in his redemptive activity in history. It is, however, interposed between the P account of the generations of Noah and their continuation in the genealogy of Shem at Gen. 11.10. This listing ends with the settlement by Terah and his son Abram in Haran (Gen. 11.31–2). Now the stage is set for the beginning of God's special redemptive activity through the one in whom all the families of the world bless themselves (Gen. 12.3; cf. Rom. 4.1–25; Gal. 3.6–29).

Before we conclude this review of biblical protology, let us see how some Jewish (rather than Christian) interpreters bear their particular witness to the 'universalism' which we have been trying to expound.

For the vital importance of the '*toledoth*' theme, we turn to a Rabbi from the second century of the Christian era citing: '"Thou shalt love thy neighbour as thyself" (Lev. 19.18). "R. Akiba said this is the greatest principle in the Law." (R. Simeon) Ben Azzai said the sentence, "This is the book of the generations of Adam" (Gen. 5.1) is even greater than the other!' (*Sifra* 89). Rabbi Simeon's thought is matched by a Mishnaic sentence: 'Again but a single man was created for the sake of peace among mankind, that none should say to his fellow, "My father was greater than your father"' (*M.Sanhedrin 4.5*). Finally here is the Talmudic creation legend: 'In the beginning, two thousand years before the heaven and earth, seven things were created: the Torah written with black fire on white fire and lying in the lap of God; the divine throne erected in the heavens – paradise on the right side, hell on the left side; the celestial sanctuary in front of God – having a jewel on its alter graven with the name of the Messiah; and a voice which cries aloud, *return O ye children of men*' (italics mine, *Peshikta*, 54a).

These voices represent an authentic tradition of the Jewish people: it has always known that the world was created for the sake of the Covenant – not just the Covenant with Abraham but also the Covenant with Adam (see Ecclus. (Ben Sirach) 17.12 and the Covenant with Noah), as we have already seen.[14]

3 The 'Nations' in the Eschatology of the Psalmists and the Prophets

From stories of the beginning we now turn to visions of the end. Both are important ways of doing theology. In this complex matter of God's universal creative/redemptive activity it is important to point to those moments in the Psalms and in the later Prophets when there is a breaking out of the bonds of religious nationalism and Jewish particularism.

(a) The 'nations' in the psalms

In the Psalms the word *'am*, people, is used to refer to the People of Israel, but it is not used exclusively so – other groups may be called by this term as in Ps. 18.43. Similarly, the plural *'ammim* may be used synonymously with *goyim* and *le'ummim* as, for example, in Psalm 9 vv. 5, 8, 12. Thus a statement like this needs to be treated with caution: 'Gradually, however, the custom became established of reserving the noun "people" for Israel, the elect people of God, the People *par excellence*; and of designating other peoples by the word "nations" with a depreciative nuance'.[15] The failure to see that Israel often thought of itself as among the *goyim* (as in Gen. 10 and 11) and equally often thought of those outside Israel as among the *'am* or *'ammim* of God leads to serious mistranslations of certain material in the Psalms. So, for example, in Psalm 47. 'Clap your hands, all peoples, *kol-ha 'ammim*, shout to God with loud songs of joy' (v. 1). 'God has subdued peoples, *'ammim*, and nations, *le'ummim*, under Israel' (v. 3). 'God is the king of all the earth, and reigns over the nations' (v. 8). Then in v. 9 the Massoretic text reads: *nedibe 'ammim ne'esaphu 'am 'elohe 'abheraham*, literally, 'leaders of peoples gather themselves people of the God of Abraham'. Here is a sample of what the translators of modern English versions have done with this: 'the rulers of the nations assemble with the people of the God of Abraham' (TEV); 'the leaders of the nations rally to the people of the God of Abraham' (Jerusalem Bible); 'the princes of the nations assemble with the families of Abraham's line' (NEB). Compare with these the RSV: 'The princes of the peoples gather as the people of the God of Abraham', and the KJV: 'The princes of the people are gathered together, even the people of the God of Abraham'. Limits of space forbid me to go into the reasons which were used to justify the first three of these translations. Suffice it here to notice the remarkable difference of meaning, and to reflect on the theological presuppositions that have made it impossible for some to accept the literal meaning of the Massoretic text.

However, a consistent reading of the Psalms leads us to think that the RSV is the only correct rendering. The concept of all the nations being also part of the God of Abraham is in line with Ps. 82.8: 'To thee belong all the nations', and with Ps. 87, where we have the graphic picture of the Lord calling the register of the *'ammim*. Rahab and Babylon, Philistia, Tyre and Ethiopia have all been mentioned in v. 5. As their names are called so he declares: 'This one and that one were born in her (sc. in Zion)'!

Psalm 87, like Psalm 47, is speaking of the eschatological pilgrimage of the nations to the city of Zion, the centre and the navel of the earth. Many other psalms see the same vision of the gathering of the peoples on the holy mount of God, e.g. 96, 97, 98, 99 and 100, for 'He comes to judge the world with righteousness and the peoples with equity' (Ps. 98.9). 'For the Lord is great in Zion, he is exalted over all the peoples' (Ps. 99.2). While, to be sure, there are some Psalms which express vindictiveness towards the nations, e.g. Ps. 149.7 or Ps. 147.20, the general theme is the action of God in the future whereby 'the nations, *goyim*, will fear the name of the Lord and all the kings of the earth thy glory' (Ps. 102.15). At that time men will 'declare in Zion the names of the Lord, and in Jerusalem his praise, when peoples (*'ammim*) gather together, and kingdoms, (*mame lakhoth*), to worship the Lord' (Ps. 102.21–22).

There is, moreover, a particularly striking feature of this End-time expectation in Psalm 102, namely a reference to an eschatological people! Here again is a random sample of contemporary versions as they translate verse 18: 'a people yet unborn shall praise the Lord' (NEB), 'a race still to be born . . . ' (Jerusalem); 'a people not yet born' (TEV), 'a people yet unborn' (RSV). The unanimity here is remarkable, but one may wonder if full justice has been done to the profundity of the Psalmist's insight. The words '*am nibhera*' mean literally 'a people to be created'! Notice here the very special Hebrew root *br'* which is used normally for decisive acts of creation on the part of the Creator God, as, e.g. in Genesis 1.1, 21, 27 etc., in Isa. 65.17 'I create a new heaven and a new earth', and in Isa. 65.18 'I create Jerusalem a rejoicing and her people a joy'!

Like Isaiah the Psalmist is concerned about a new people, fresh created. So the KJV translators were wiser than our contemporaries in saying: 'the people which shall be created shall praise the Lord'. In the context of Ps. 102.22, 'When peoples gather together, and kingdoms, to worship the Lord', the vision is clear: All humanity will be gathered in the new heaven and the new earth. We shall return to this theme when we come to look at Revelation 21 and 22.

(b) The eschatology of the 'nations' in the later prophets

The possibility that there will be a new time when all God's peoples shall be 're-created' is conceived within the prophetic framework in three places: Isaiah 19.19–24, the Book of Jonah, and in Malachi 1.11.

In general, the theme of the activity of God among the nations in the prophetic literature needs no great spelling out. Amos knew that the Lord had brought the Philistines from Caphtor, and the Syrians from Kir, Amos 9.7. Isaiah in eighth-century Jerusalem knew that Assyria would become the rod of God's anger against a godless nation, and a people of his wrath (Isa. 10.6). Jeremiah 18.7–10 equally affirms the constant intervention of the sovereign God in the affairs of the nations.

Much of this material is naturally associated with messianic Zionism. As in the Psalms, the nations will go up as pilgrims to Zion (see Isa. 2.2–4; 11.1ff.; Jer. 16.19–20; Zeph. 3.8–9). As Zechariah says, 'many peoples, and strong nations, shall come to seek the Lord of hosts in Jerusalem . . . for in those days ten men from the nations of every tongue shall take hold of the robe of a Jew, saying, let us go with you, for we have heard that God is with you' (Zech. 8.22–23). Now this is no clue to pluralism; it simply portrays an eschatological vision where the views and attitudes of one people are vindicated, in what Bengt Sundkler and Johannes Blauw taught us to see as a kind of *centrepetal* mission.[16] Just by remaining in one place and standing still Israel would fulfil the role of sign, (*'oth*), and light, (*'or*) to the nations.

But this is not what Isaiah, 19.10–25 is saying. It is widely agreed that we have in these verses a series of prose fragments which have been appended to the original poetic words of the harsh oracles against Egypt in verses 1–15. It is impossible to date these fragments with any accuracy but clearly their viewpoint is not merely historical. When these words were first uttered, Assyria had presumably long ceased to exist. With Egypt, it becomes a figure for all the nations who are called to share in the covenant formerly made with Abraham. Note that for Egypt the 'sign and witness' of the Lord in vv. 19, 20 is the pillar of the Lord at its border. For the Lord will make himself known to them in their own land, heeding their supplications and healing them (v. 22). The words of verse 25 have a luminous clarity: 'Blessed be Egypt, my people, and Assyria the work of my hands, and Israel, my heritage.' G. Ernest Wright comments: 'Israel will now be part of a larger community in fellowship with the Lord. Indeed this union of all mankind in the service of God, also expressed in 2.2–4, is precisely that which is the centre of the Christian hope for all the earth.'[17]

To this great passage of Isaiah, called by one French scholar, a religious peak in the Old Testament,[18] we add a comment on the real significance of the Book of Jonah. The prophet Jonah (his name means literally, a 'dove') is given a message of judgment against

Nineveh, a city which is the very epitome and symbol of military might and aggression. To the very great displeasure of the Israelite prophet, Nineveh repents! The message of judgment then becomes, as always in the Bible, a message of mercy and compassion. Like the elder brother and the labourers who had worked all day in Jesus' parables, Jonah finds this very hard to take and so calls forth the Lord's response in Jonah 4.11.[19]

But the message of the Book of Jonah is even more far-reaching than just setting forth a message of free and universal grace: in Edmond Jacob's words, 'The nations will know in their turn that God is not only the master of universal history, but that he is merciful and compassionate, and that his kingship is fulfilled in his love. From that point onwards *there is no need to go to Jerusalem; it is possible to be at the same time a citizen of Nineveh and a worshipper of Yahweh*' (italics mine).[20]

So with these two passages in mind let us turn again to Malachi, 1.11, 'from the rising of the sun to its setting, my name is great among the nations, and in every place incense is offered to my name and a pure offering; for my name is great among the nations, says the Lord of Hosts'. Scholars have sought to interpret these words as referring to the worship of proselytes, or to worship offered by Jews in the *diaspora*, or even as some kind of syncretistic ideal.[21] In the context of Isa. 19 and Jonah surely it must be seen as expressing an eschatological hope: the days are coming when there will be a pure offering among all the nations. At the same time Robert Martin-Achard is surely correct in saying that Malachi is aware of the realities in the contemporary world of nations.[22] He is obviously asserting that in their religious activity, as for example in the Persian worship of Ahura Mazda, they are concerned with the one true God. As H. H. Rowley wrote: 'Malachi claims for Jehovah worship that is not offered to his name but is sincere and validated by a pure heart.'[23]

I believe therefore that there are real clues to understanding religious pluralism in these prophetic writings. All the nations and peoples experience God's activity; he created them and he will redeem them. In the End-time they will all be gathered to him, not simply as incorporated into the people of Zion but as themselves, smitten and yet healed, made with Israel part of God's total heritage; a new eschatological people of God – the God who so spoke to Abraham that all the nations should receive blessing.

4 The Eschatological Vision of the 'Nations' in the New Testament

Here we confine ourselves deliberately to the End-time as it is portrayed in the last chapters of the Bible.[24] Mathias Rissi has graphically described how and why biblical and theological scholarship has tended to neglect the eschatological concepts in the Book of Revelation. But, he writes, 'anyone who takes the trouble to listen will discover with what astounding, truly prophetic power John has shaped the images of the future in the light of the historical revelation of Christ'.[25] We turn straightaway to the vision of the new heaven and the new earth, Rev. 21.1–22.5, in order to make these all too brief comments.

First, we point to the variant readings in Rev. 21.3c. Codex Sinaiticus and Codex Alexandrinus read: 'he will dwell with them and they shall be his peoples, *kai autoi laoi autou esontai*'. This is therefore the reading used in both *Textus Receptus* and the Nestle-Kilpatrick text of the Bible Societies' Greek New Testament. However, most modern versions prefer to read a singular, *laos*, people, see, e.g., the RSV, NEB, Jerusalem Bible, and TEV. There is some manuscript evidence for this, but this is to make the text conform to Ezekiel 37.27, which is actually cited by RSV, NEB, and Jerusalem Bible margins. But the more difficult reading is surely the plural form, and we ought to follow that principle of textual criticism which suggests that much more weight should be given to the 'more difficult reading'. One can easily see the power of Ezek. 37.27 to influence a scribe to inadvertently write *laos* for *laoi*; it is less easy to imagine the same scribe altering *laos* to *laoi*. Yet we have given some reason for supposing that there is a strand in the total Old Testament witness which saw that there was indeed an eschatology of peoples.

But the most important reason for reading the plural, 'peoples' at Rev. 21.3 is that it conforms with and helps to make sense of the greater vision of the nations, *ethnē*, in Rev. 21.22–22.2. In these six verses the *ethnē* are mentioned three times: the first reference is actually to the Light of the City by which the nations shall walk. There is no Temple in the eschatological city, for the temple expressed a promise which is no longer needed: God and the Lamb are all in all. God's 'universalist' light will be upon all his peoples (21.24; 22.5). Note how the author of Revelation has gone far beyond 'zionism': he is no longer concerned about the eschatological pilgrimage of the nations to Zion and its temple as described for example in Zech. 14.[26] Secondly, we are told twice that the *ethnē* will bring their wealth into the city (21.24, 26). Now, to be sure, this is in the context of the earlier chapter of Revelation, where the kings and the nations have been shown as in rebellion and warfare against the authority of the Lord and his Christ, and we are reminded that abomination and falsehood have no place in the city (21.27). Yet it would surely be right here to emphasize the positive aspect: the glory, *doxa*, and honour, *timē*, of the nations will be gathered into the city of God's End-time. This is no negative judgment upon the cultural traditions and religious achievements among the peoples of God. Thirdly, let us take note of the tree, the leaves of which are for the healing of the nations, *eis therapeian tōn ethnōn* (Rev. 22.2). Now this tree has always been something of a problem to the exegetes concerned about taking the apocalyptic chronology of the Book of Revelation at its face value. The comment of Dr Nigel Turner makes the point for us: 'the best sense is undoubtedly made by understanding this, with Charles, as during the millennium. There would be no nations to be healed when the eternal and final City is established'.[27] But perhaps St John is not trying to make this kind of sense. We would suggest that, with the words of Ezekiel 47.12 in mind, 'their leaves for healing' (the Hebrew root *rph*' here, as at Isa. 19.22[28]), he has deliberately widened the vision to include *the nations*. In the End-time the nations will still be recognizable entities, smitten indeed but being healed!

We conclude, therefore, having surveyed all too superficially some of the themes concerning the nations and peoples in these protological and eschatological teachings of the scriptures. At the very least this biblical material must set question marks against theologies, explicit or implicit, which speak of a *single* people of God,[29] and which suggest thereby that God has but one single pattern of working in his creative/saving action towards humankind. We may add, also that if God has been so at work in various and diverse ways, we may expect that our partners in dialogue will have truth in their holy books and validity in other religious traditions. How this may be so in the light of the Christian understanding of the uniqueness and finality of their Lord Jesus Christ is the theological issue to which we now turn.

⌐4⌐

A Pluralist and Inclusivist Theology in the Making

The earliest Protestant missionaries, whether Elliott, Brainerd, Thorowgood and others in the American colonies, or Carey and the early Baptists in India and their colleagues in the London Missionary Society, the Church Missionary Society and later in the Wesleyan Missionary Society, were motivated by strong eschatological considerations. They believed that they were living in the millenniary age, that the time had come that the knowledge of God should cover the earth as the waters cover the sea.[1] Their successors were motivated by eschatological considerations of a different order – believing in the pre-millenniary coming of Christ they were terrified by hell-fire. *The Fundamentals*, a series of tracts summing up the doctrines of extreme Protestants which first appeared in 1909 and indeed gave the name 'fundamentalist' to certain types of biblical literalists, are clear that the doctrines relating to everlasting punishment are but the other side of the coin from doctrines of heavenly rapture at the time of the Parousia. We have seen the doctrine of the Roman Catholic Church formulated at the council of Florence and then endorsed by the first Vatican Council. Outside Christ, there was no salvation, and outside the church no salvation. The only conceivable eschatology was the triumphalist picture of all the nations gathered in to the one fold.

But now Christians in various ways are finding these biblical images of the end, as well as the more lurid developments of these images in the history of doctrine, no longer adequate to deal with the realities of the world in which the great faith communities are renewing themselves and growing larger in proportion to the

Christian population of the world. In 1985 it is estimated that the Christian population of the world, however secularized, is approximately 33%.[2] By the year 2000, if we are spared the nuclear winter, that will have declined to some 25% or 20%. In line with this we are beginning to discern a theological understanding emerging in which the great traditional faith-communities will *not* have disappeared.[3] In the *eschaton* the Jews will still be the Jews and those professing Muhammad to be the *rasul* of God will still be Muslims, and those of the great Eastern traditions will still be recognizable as Buddhists and Hindus and the rest. Africans will still bear the marks of and be witnesses to the insights of their traditions and religions, and the Chinese will still be rooted in their ancient soil. They shall indeed come from the east and the west and sit down in the kingdom of God, yet without first becoming 'Christians' like us.[4] The tendency towards thinking this way is widely apparent. It comes in a clear form in the work of John Hick. We quote here not his widely used *God and the Universe of Faiths*[5] in which he speaks of a 'Copernican revolution' in the relations between the world's religions, but from an essay he wrote for the valuable collection of papers he himself edited entitled *Truth and Dialogue: The Relationship between World Religions.*[6] 'We may expect' he wrote, 'the different world faiths to continue as religious-cultural phenomena, though phenomena that are increasingly penetrating one another. The relations between them will be somewhat like that now obtaining between the different denominations of Christianity in this country. That is to say, there will in most countries be a dominant religious tradition (as Anglicanism is dominant in England today), with other traditions present in varying strengths, but with considerable awareness on all hands of what they have in common, with osmosis of membership taking place through their institutional wall, with some degree of interchange of ministry and a large degree of practical co-operation.'[7]

Dr Hick goes even further in an essay first published in 1974 but now made more widely available in the most recent collection of his lectures and papers *God has Many Names*. In this essay, called 'Whatever Path Men choose is Mine', he writes, 'A single world religion is, I would think, never likely, and not a consummation to be desired. For so long as there is a variety of human types there will be a variety of kinds of worship and a variety of theological emphases and approaches. There will always be the more mystical and the more prophetic types of faith, with their corresponding awareness of the ultimate Reality as non-personal and as personal. There will always be the more spontaneous, warm and Spirit-filled forms of devotion, and the more liturgical, orderly and rationally controlled forms. There will always be the more vivid consciousness of the divine as gracious love or as infinite demand and judgment. And so on'.[8]

Wilfred Cantwell Smith approaches the vision of religious pluralism in his own inimitable way. Ordained as a minister of the United Church of Canada – and incidentally uniting in himself the strong Calvinism of his Presbyterian father with the warm Arminianism of his Methodist mother – he has worked all his life as a scholar in the field of the comparative study of religion. His name will appear again in these pages for I gladly acknowledge how much I have learnt from him over many years. At this point I want only to discuss briefly his contribution to understanding religious pluralism within the purposes of God.[9] He has made this on two levels. First, as historian he has taught us much about the sidetrack on to which we have been switched by our own Western intellectual tradition. In a series of rich and comprehensive studies he has shown that even the use of such terms as 'a religion' or 'religions', 'a faith' or 'faiths' is a comparatively recent development.[10] The use of the plural term 'religions' became standard only from the mid-seventeenth century, and common only from the eighteenth century.[11] He notes that it is impossible to use this plural form so long as one is thinking of something in the hearts of human beings, such as piety, obedience, reverence or worship. As I have already pointed out, the 'fear of God' is common to the outsider Abimelech and to the author of Psalm 111.[12] Speaking of 'religions' becomes possible only when 'one contemplates from the outside, and abstracts, depersonalizes and reifies, the various systems of other people of which one does not oneself see the meaning or appreciate the point, let alone accept the validity'. In the nineteenth century the plural form of the word 'faith' came into general usage, and has stuck with us, as in even the name of the BCC Committee 'on Relations with People of Other Faiths', and the WCC Sub Unit on 'Dialogue with People of Living Faiths'.

In Dr Smith's view this kind of usage is a disease of language, and forces us into repeated category mistakes. It allows particular external phenomena associated with religious traditions to be examined by an outside observer without participation (by sympathetic imagination, if nothing more) in the underlying commitments of personal faith. It allows us as observers to speak blandly of the religion to which another person belongs. 'Ought we not rather to concern ourselves with the religion that belongs to him? God is interested in persons and not in types.' So he affirms in his *Questions of Religious Truth*.[13]

We must take his central point here into our thinking. It is only since the Enlightenment that we in Europe began to speak of religions as intellectual systems and as patterns of doctrines that may be labelled Buddhism, Hinduism, Confucianism and so on.[14] He would much rather we thought of the 'cumulative religious traditions' of humankind in and through which individual human beings express that single indivisible quality known as 'faith'. Let me take now from Wilfred Smith a series of definitions of and affirmations about this quality of faith: 'Faith is a foundational category for all religious life, and, indeed for all human life . . . .'[15] For 'Faith is an orientation of the personality, to oneself, to one's neighbour, to the universe; a total response; a way of seeing the world and of handling it; a capacity to see at a more than mundane level; to see, to feel, to act in terms of a transcendent dimension'.[16] Yet 'Faith is neither rare nor automatic. Rather it is ubiquitously astonishing. It is the prodigious hallmark of being human'.[17] 'No man has faith who has not been in part educated to it by the legacy of others. Yet the religious history of mankind is ununderstandable if one does not allow that the faith of many men has fallen short of, diverged from, or transcended that expressed in the tradition available to them. Far from accepting, then, that the faith of men in all communities is really the same I would stress rather that the faith of men even within one community has not been the same.'[18] 'History is not a closed system; for in it stands man, open to the infinite. The study of religious history has been a study of the observable results of that fact, the data of the traditions. Yet it is an inadequate study of history if it omit or ignore the massive fact itself, the faith that the traditions have everywhere nurtured and expressed. The history of religion is the history of man's (Christian and other) continuing involvement, within history, in transcendence.'[19]

Wilfred Cantwell Smith will forgive me if I make one personal observation on a certain implication and correlation of his insights here. It is merely the briefest comment that a certain Wesleyan strain has surfaced in this kind of thinking. We have seen already that in John Wesley a willingness to discern faith in Jew and Muslim.[20] We remember, too, his emphasis on the Catholic Spirit which tried to look behind the outward name or rite. Preaching on the question of Jehu to Jehonadab in II Kings 10.15 'Is thy heart right with God?' Wesley asks. 'Dost thou believe his being and his perfections? his eternity, his immensity, wisdom, power, his justice, mercy and truth? Dost thou believe that he now "upholdeth all things by the word of his power?" and that he governs even the most minute, even the most noxious, to his own glory, and the good of them that love him? Hast thou a divine evidence, a supernatural conviction of the things of God? Dost thou "walk by faith, not by sight" looking not at temporal things?' (Sermon XXXIV 'On the Catholic Spirit'). In his *Journal* for 18 May 1788, Wesley committed himself to wide ranging tolerance in these matters: 'The Methodists alone do not insist on your holding this or that opinion, but they think and let think. Neither do they impose any particular mode of worship; but you may continue to worship in your former manner be it what it may.' There is no confusion of belief and faith for the founder of the Methodist tradition. Just as we may claim John Wesley in a certain sense for the Ecumenical movement of the latter half of the twentieth century, he may also be seen as a remote ancestor of a far wider ecumenism, the ecumenism of Wilfred Smith and many other direct or indirect recipients of the Methodist heritage who serve the new movement in inter-religious relationships. It is no surprise to me that so many of Mr Wesley's contemporary preachers are caught up in this, just as it is no surprise to see the massive contribution Methodists have made and still make to world Christian ecumenism.[21] I return to this matter when I consider the question of spirituality in Chapter 7.[22]

But let us return to Dr Smith's great theme. God is at work through forms of faith other than Christian. Indeed the fact that this is so is corroborative of our own Christian vision of God as active in history, redeeming and saving, reaching out to all people to love them and embrace them. As he says, 'If it had turned out that God does not care about other men and women, or was stumped and had thought up no way to save them, *then* that would have proven our Christian understanding of God to be wrong. For a century or so recently, much of the church seemed to take this line; and a good many members decided that Christian teaching must be wrong, and left'.[23] But like John Hick, Wilfred Smith has a vision wide enough to save the exclusivist church from its self-inflicted wounds.

So let him describe for us how he sees the missionary task of the contemporary church; 'One of the tasks that is open to us today, and beckoning to us, is to *participate* in God's creative process of bringing into actual reality what has been an ideal reality only, that of a worldwide human community'.[24] Wilfred Smith is writing here in the context of an essay which makes quite specific pragmatic proposals for the world missionary movement. It is a massive attempt to shift the discussion of mission forward from the unproductive and sterile models of crusading polemics and one-way proclamations. For Dr Smith such activity is not only ineffective but also unethical. It is a breach of the principle that we should do unto others as we would wish others to do unto us. If we are going to engage in mission to others we must allow others to engage in mission to us. He would argue even that we must *enable* these to engage in such mission. As the model of what he has in mind for this process Wilfred Smith suggests the case of Martin Buber. 'Here was a Jew, profoundly Jewish, who had something to say to Christendom, and said it. Christians agreed that he had something to say, and read him studiously and with profit. They learned from him, or should we, rather, say learned through him, about God, about themselves, about the Christian tradition in which they were participants. They welcomed him, applauded him, asked him to come back to give them more. I nominate Martin Buber as the model of a modern missionary *par excellence*.'[25]

Wilfred Smith goes on to instance examples from Hindu and Buddhist and Muslim backgrounds. But his underlying point, which he spells out in detail in his *Towards a World Theology* is that we have entered into a period in which we must speak of a common religious history of humankind. What is happening in his view is that we now have to think on a global scale of what men and women everywhere have to learn from all the religious traditions. The notion of Islamic or Hindu religious history is giving way to truer conceptions of the Islamic or Hindu strands in the total human religious history. The human religious configuration throughout the world is irretrievably and irrevocably altered.

But this is not a purely human phenomenon, however open it may lie to the scrutiny of the disinterested scholarly community. It is for Wilfred Smith a theological affirmation. All human history has been the history of salvation, not just the history of Israel in the Old Testament period, or of the community that proclaimed itself the new Israel in the New Testament. God has been at work in every religious community. 'This has always been true, but we are the first generation of Christians to see this seriously and corporately, and to be able to respond to the vision. We are the first generation to discern God's mission to mankind in the Buddhist movement, in the Hindu, in the Islamic, as well as in the Jewish and the Christian. Having discerned it, let us not fail to respond to it.'[26]

Though Dr Smith does not spell it out, clearly he expects that in the end God will still be surrounded by his different peoples in much the same way as we have already formulated it in the previous chapter. The treasures of the nations will be brought into the City of God. They shall come from east and west and sit down in the kingdom of God. The Son of Man at his coming will find faith on earth, even though it be not moulded and determined by the Christian cumulative religious tradition. But such a vision of religious pluralism raises an enormous christological problem, and to this we address ourselves in the next chapter.

Alongside the views of John Hick and Wilfred Smith I want to set out those of one of the Roman Catholic Church's leading missiologists. Professor Arnulf Camps is a Dutch Franciscan priest teaching at the Catholic University of Nijmegen. We may take him as representative of that vastly influential renewal movement in the Roman Catholic church associated with three great documents of the Second Vatican Council: *Lumen Gentium, Ad Gentes* and *Nostra Aetate*.[27] Since 1964 Professor Camps has been Consultant to the Vatican Secretariat for Non-Christians, the counterpart in Rome to the Sub Unit on Dialogue with People of Living Faiths of the WCC in Geneva. A series of books originally published in Dutch in the years 1976, 1977 and 1978, whose teaching I have sought to mediate elsewhere, have now happily been translated into English in a single volume entitled, significantly, *Partners in Dialogue: Christianity and Other World Religions*.[28] In fact this book is a mine of information about the last two decades and the mushrooming of Protestant and Catholic attempts to deal with religious pluralism. Camps works by summarizing the thinking of other people, then offering in each case his own incisive commentary upon their adequacies and deficiencies. It is not therefore an easy book to quote from, and deserves to be much more widely known and used than it is. But towards the end of the first section Camps writes: 'I agree with the authors treated extensively above who plead for a religious pluralism within Christianity. Christianity must be properly understood, however, as a group of human beings living the ideals of Jesus Christ. In a previous chapter we saw that these ideals of Jesus Christ are rooted in the general salvation history. Thus they are embedded in the interplay between God's invitation and humanity's response to his self-communication through the course of history. This pageant has gone through different phases and is still doing that. Every social response or religion has its own input into the dialogue.'[29] This means that there is now an enormous task set before the churches to make a new and positive response to other religions in the spirit of dialogue. It means, too, that other religions have their own specific contributions to make towards salvation. So inter-faith dialogue assumes that participants are open to each other, and that *together* they are working for 'the total salvation of the whole human race which is announced to us in the coming and already burgeoning kingdom of God'.[30]

To be sure we can see in these words, as throughout all Camps'
writing, a greater sense than in either Hick or Smith that the future
'pluriformity' will somehow be related to the Christian tradition. This
will happen as people work out in their own situations ways of
responding to their new perceptions of the kingdom. This will be as
the differing cultural and religious patterns absorb the ideals of Jesus.
Here Camps makes it clear that they will be recognizable forms of
Christianity in so far as they will be related to the reality that Jesus
represents: his vision of humankind, of the world, and of God. But
they will not look anything like the forms of Christian faith known to
us now. We see in this kind of thinking a distinct repudiation of the
Latin church's dream of unbroken unity and uniformity centred upon
the teaching authority of the Roman episcopate.[31] Camps is straightforward in his assertion that 'we are striving for a world Christianity ... But we fully realize that a long history lies before us
and that the real work has scarcely begun'.[32]

But a certain clarification of this position is necessary at this point.
In an article contributed to a *Festschrift* for the great Dutch
missiologist Johannes Verkuyl, *Zending op weg naar de toekomst*, Arnulf
Camps addresses himself to the question 'Is it necessary to preach the
Gospel to men of other faiths?'[33] He criticizes Verkuyl's position set
out in the latter's monumental *Inleiding in de Nieuwere Zendingswetenschap*,[34] wherein the human condition is seen as one of
brokenness, corruption and rebelliousness in relation to God. Consequently religious traditions are largely seen as autosoteriological, and
leading ultimately to disaster. Camps refuses to follow Verkuyl here.
He stresses rather the need for a broader concept of mission in which
there is a positive valuation of both other culture and other religion.
Within such a concept of mission, 'mission and dialogue join hands
harmoniously in such a way that dialogue teaches mission that God
has never left mankind alone (Acts 14.17)'.[35] 'Mission carried out in a
dialogical way' is 'mission because people are called to conversion
and to response to God's revelation in Christ, and dialogical because
this answer is not a contradiction of their former answer, but a
fulfilment of it, since the same Word of God is acting in creation and in
redemption. It is also a purification because no man and no religion is
perfect'.[36]

These last words of Arnulf Camps lead us straight into the
christological considerations necessary if we are to be at ease as
Christian men and women to hold at one and the same time
convictions about the decisiveness of the event of Jesus of Nazareth
and this kind of dialogical openness to the truths and commitments of

other men and women. For if we grant the proposition that God is creatively and redemptively at work in the faith and communities of other people, in the words of Kenneth Cragg, 'We shall have to think again about how we understand and state the finality of Christ and the meaning of the once-for-all Incarnation'.[37] Many theologians have done work of real significance recently on this christological frontier. The discussion here is limited to just a few representative figures. From the main streams of ecumenical and protestant Christianity I choose Bishop David Brown, the late Bishop of Guildford, and Donald Dawe, a Presbyterian systematic theologian teaching in the USA. Because it has special significance for Conservative Evangelicals we shall look at the work of Sir Norman Anderson. We shall take note of two Eastern Orthodox writers, the Metropolitan Georges Khodr and Bishop Gregorios (formerly Paul Verghese). Lastly we shall look briefly at the recent Church of England document *Towards a Theology of Inter-Faith Dialogue* . . . for that will take us straight into the exposition of the inclusivist christology which forms Chapter 5.

David Brown, Bishop of Guildford from 1973–1982, was the first Chairman of the 'Committee for Relations with People of Other Faiths' of the British Council of Churches. This Committee came into being partly as a result of the notable achievements of 'The Presence of Islam in Britain Advisory Group' which had previously been set up by the BCC. David Brown's *A New Threshold*[38] was written directly as a result of this Group's work and represented the pushing of the boundaries wider to enable British Christians to respond to their Muslim fellow citizens. It did this on the basis not only of the need for good community relations, but also and chiefly on the basis of an 'inclusive christology'. David Brown wrote 'Jesus of Nazareth revealed the eternal love of God in human acts of care and compassion; he revealed the creative power of God in human acts of healing and peacemaking; he revealed the holiness of God in human acts of rebuke and forgiveness'. Bishop Brown here spoke in the tradition of Justin Martyr and the Greek fathers generally. Then he continued 'Christ did not come to make God's love and power the exclusive possession of the Church, but to reveal the nature of him who holds all beings in his embrace'.[39] Here the points of reference are Christ the Second Adam, a concept which looks not towards the church but towards the world, and David Brown was always particularly insistent upon this: the telos (end) vision is the restoration of all things as in Revelation 21, Ephesians and Colossians, and as in I Corinthians 15 and Romans 11. Therefore the question arises, what does it mean that the modern church must cross a new threshold? It is to step over into a new awareness of what the divine love means, for 'God is to the universe as our Lord was to his contemporaries in Palestine'.[40] A clearer grasp of what is unique in the Christian faith will lead towards a genuine and universal catholicity. Then said David Brown, 'The Christian Churches will discover a joy and a glory which are not found in their present interim theologies'.[41]

Donald Dawe is Professor of Systematic Theology at Union Theological Seminary, Richmond, Virginia and one of the Editors of *Christian Faith in a Religiously Plural World*.[42] In a paper printed in this collection he gives an interweaving of themes derived from such people as Jean Daniélou, Karl Barth, Hans Küng, Richard Niebuhr and Paul Tillich. His teaching is in the context of the universal covenant with Noah and the special covenant with Abraham in the setting of radical monotheism 'not as the particularism of the saved against the damned' but as the 'particularism of a people that has been given a vision of God by which the world may be illumined (Isa. 49.6)'.[43] Concerning the meaning of the event of Jesus, Dawe says 'God is revealed not as the Protector God who saved his Elect One, his Son, from death nor his elect people from suffering. Rather, God is revealed as the God of resurrection who creates new possibilities beyond the power of death itself'.[44] He shows in compressed argument that God demonstrates in Jesus Christ how human relationships to him are fulfilled and how 'in knowing Jesus, Christian faith is provided with the *canon* – the measuring stick – by which the activity of God may be discerned and confessed because it is Christ through whom this salvation is ultimately given'.[45]

Therefore the presence of God may be actualized through many religious traditions. The form this takes is the renewal and fulfilment of human existence. It is a pattern of 'new being'. Christians know it and celebrate it because of what they know through Jesus Christ. 'Other traditions live out of the power of this being in accordance with the names by which they encounter and participate in ultimate reality. This does not make them crypto-Christians or members of a "hidden" or "latent church". They are and remain what they are – Hindus, Buddhists, Muslims or devotees of a myriad of other religions. This is possible because the "name of Jesus" is translatable. The "name of Jesus" is the encoding of the motif of death and resurrection as the key to new being. This motif is brought to expression in vastly different ways in various religions as they become vehicles for human renewal and fulfilment. But the crucial thing in identifying the "name of Jesus" is not in the verbalisms but in the "underlying pattern of new being at work"'.[46] Here he is trying to open up a way to deal with such 'sticking point' texts as Acts 4.12. We shall return to Dawes' thinking later.[47]

Sir Norman Anderson has been quoted as representing the exclusive stance.[48] 'The Christian must regard them (sc. the other religions) as Satanic Substitutes.'[49] We do need to register, however, that Sir Norman has thought a great deal more about the relation of the death of Christ in atoning love to those of other faiths who are godfearing and do what is right. Those of us who do not accept the kind of teaching about the propitiatory sacrifice in which Sir Norman believes may nevertheless be deeply moved by the way in which he seeks to set forth what Christ did at the cross to those who will live and die without ever becoming Christians. 'Our only hope is grace, and that on the basis of what God himself did in Christ at the Cross. And this is their only hope, too.'[50] Having established this Sir Norman is able to go even further. Surveying three possible views that Christians might take of other religions as systems, the positive as *preparationes evangelicae*, and therefore as related to the eternal Logos; the negative (as Satanic deceptions); or thirdly, as purely human aspirations after truth, Sir Norman Anderson is able to recognize that there is truth (though, not for him, the whole truth) in the positive teaching. What he had previously written about the saving knowledge of God held by the Old Testament Jews: 'Surely, here, we must think of the pre-incarnate Son as the Word, through whom alone all things that exist came into being, who was the life that was the light of men, and the true light that illumines every man' might equally well be said to apply to the other religious systems.[51] 'God' he concludes in 1970, 'has never left himself wholly without witness in his self-disclosures to mankind.'[52]

In 1980 we had Sir Norman Anderson's 'Henry Drummond Lectures', *God's Law and God's Love: An Essay in Comparative Religion*.[53] In these Professor Anderson is also wrestling with the problems of ultimate salvation for, and the source of goodness of, adherents of other faith-systems. He repeats the arguments of *Christianity and Comparative Religion* concerning the efficacy of the atoning death of Christ for those who will never call and confess themselves Christians.[54] We find him able to assert that ' . . . the Holy Spirit is not bound by conventional doctrines or traditional stances, and under his supernatural influence individual men and women may always be brought to an attitude of the heart that puts them within the passages of Scripture which affirm that he who seeks will find, and that to him who knocks "it shall be opened"'.[55] Having given the example of Rābi'a al-Addawiyya, the Muslim woman saint (Sir Norman's word) of the eighth century and having quoted her own saying 'our seeking of forgiveness itself needs a seeking of forgiveness', together with the further example of Ibrāhīm ibn Adham and his prayer 'Oh God, uplift me from the shame of disobedience to the glory of submission to Thee', Sir Norman Anderson goes on to suggest that such genuine search for God, such heartfelt pleas for forgiveness and such self-abandonment to God's mercy 'must, surely, be evidence of the Holy Spirit's inward working'.[56] He adds, movingly, that he 'cannot but believe that the seeking soul will either hear and receive the message of forgiveness and peace in this life, like Cornelius, or will wake up, as it were, on the other side of the grave to worship the Saviour in whom he found this mercy without understanding how'.[57] The far-reaching implications of these last dozen words take Professor Anderson very near to the theologians we now consider from Orthodox and Catholic traditions.

We suggested right at the beginning of this book that the problem of the theology of religion is chiefly as a result of Augustinian, Lutheran or Calvinist entails upon the Western church. Those who trace their place in the continuity of Christian thought by way of Justin and Clement of Alexandria are much more able to affirm the presence of the Universal Word in other faiths and communities. It is important therefore to listen to contemporary representative voices from Eastern Orthodoxy. We glance, merely, at two contributions whose implications would need to be teased out much more carefully by us Westerners.

'Christianity in a Pluralistic World – the Economy of the Holy Spirit'[58] is a christological contribution in the sense that its author, the Greek Orthodox Bishop Georges Khodr, refers to the teaching of the Greek fathers who distinguish between the 'economy' of the Son, and of the Holy Spirit. While the church lives in the realm of Son, the Spirit is at work far beyond the bounds of the Christian community, testifying to God among all the people and preparing them for the full knowledge of Jesus Christ. 'For Christ is everywhere hidden in the mystery of his self-effacement. Any exploration of the religions is an exploration into Christ. When grace visits a Brahmin, a Buddhist, or a Muslim reading his scriptures it is Christ alone who is received as light. Whoever dies as a martyr for truth or who dies for what he believes to be right is in communion with Christ. It was the single *agape* of St John that was lived out by the Islamic mystics, those great witnesses to the crucifying love.'[59] Father Paul Verghese (now Bishop

Paul Gregorios) wrote in the same collection of papers about 'Christ and All Men'. He interestingly begins with Augustine, or at least that strand of early Augustinian writing which was able to affirm that 'All who from the beginning of the world have been righteous have Christ for their head' (In Ps. XXXVI, Sermon iii, 4). But what Verghese essentially offers in these pages is not an argument based on patristic tradition, but the personal confession of a teacher of theology in the Indian Syrian church. We recognize the Athanasian dimension of such words as these:

> I believe that Jesus Christ has become Man, thus identifying himself with the whole of humanity. He is in fact the true being of all men, irrespective of whether they believe in him or not. This is an eschatological reality to be fully revealed on the 'last day' when Christ shall recapitulate 'all things' in himself. I believe therefore that the Incarnation of Jesus Christ gives a new status to all human beings, no matter when or where they were born or are to be born. He is the 'essence' or 'substance' of the new humanity that God has created anew in him. Because of this fact, I believe that the Incarnation has a saving effect for all men, whether they be Christian or not, though I am unable to define precisely the extent or nature of this.[60]

Because God's saving power is at work beyond the limits of the church, where, he affirms, the healing and redeeming powers of Christ and the Holy Spirit are actually available to the maximum, he goes on to say 'in the final dénouement, when the results of God's saving action in Christ are fully manifested, many people of other religions will be seen to benefit more from the redemption in Christ than even the vast majority of baptized members of the Christian churches.[61]

In 1981 the General Synod of the Church of England accepted virtually unanimously the British Council of Churches' document *Relations with Peoples of Other Faiths: Guidelines on Dialogue in Britain.*[62] In the course of the debate an amendment was carried which asked the Board of Mission and Unity of the General Synod to prepare a report on 'the theological aspects of dialogue'. Accordingly a group of specialists from various fields met over a period of three years to engage in a piece of corporate thinking, and produced for the General Synod's summer meeting in 1984, a document called rather tentatively *Towards a Theology for Inter-Faith Dialogue . . .*[63] In the course of this work, in which I as Secretary of the BCC's Committee for Relations with People of Other Faiths was intimately involved, much biblical and theological study was undertaken together with many consultations with leading Anglican theologians in the United Kingdom. In general the tendency of this report is towards an 'inclusivist christology', and it is worth summarizing some of its main conclusions here, specially as they concern the doctrine of Christ.

There is a strong sense throughout the document of God as Triune: 'The Triune God is a God who moved in creation into a relationship with all that is created; who as the Word, is incarnate in Jesus and yet encountered in other places; and who as Holy Spirit, present in the Church and in the lives of baptised Christians, is also active among those of other faiths and cultures. It is the same God whose saving grace is at work outside the Church as well as within it.'[64] What the authors of the report are affirming here is in the first place no less than what we have seen other individual theologians arguing for, namely the unqualified recognition that God has been and is at work savingly and redemptively in the lives of men and women in the other religious traditions of humankind. The report uses 'powerful biblical pointers' to explicate and inform our Christian understanding of our relationship with those of these other faiths. But it hastens then to add that 'What would be contrary to the biblical witness would be the abandonment of a defining loyalty to Jesus Christ as the one in whom God was reconciling the world to himself and any proposal that this message of reconciliation need no longer be offered to those of other faiths'.[65]

This 'defining loyalty' needs, however, to be able to specify how openness and commitment may go hand in hand. *Towards a Theology for Inter-Faith Dialogue* . . . accordingly addresses itself to the New Testament evidence where the story and the interpretation of the life and death of Jesus are inextricably bound together. Mark's Gospel begins with affirming that Jesus Christ is the Son of God, and leads its reader through to the point where one outside the community of Israel who witnesses the crucifixion declares: 'Truly this man was the Son of God.' Such language to describe Jesus arises out of the church's experience of the resurrection. 'The resurrection and ascension set the seal on this claim. Paul and other New Testament writers struggle to explain this mystery of God entering human history. They use their contemporary categories to express the divinity of Jesus and his pre-existence. They talk of Jesus as the divine Wisdom of God and the Word of God, echoing thoughts from both the Old Testament and Greek philosophy.'[66]

Not surprisingly, therefore, the section on 'The Incarnate God' fixes its attention on the Logos theology of the Fourth Gospel. 'The development of Logos theology has implications for understanding

God's activity in the world and is therefore important for any assessment of Christian relations with people of other faiths. While Logos theology understands the unique expression of God as being in Jesus Christ (there can be no surrendering of that belief), at the same time it takes seriously other manifestations of the Logos in other places and at other times'.[67] So Christians need to be open to the possibilities that they may have to recognize the working of the Word in other communities of faith, and if they so recognize the presence of the Word, they need then to learn how to respond to that Word. But how shall we recognize that operation or manifestation of the Logos in other traditions of faith? The report is quick to stress that this is the very reason which makes it necessary to safeguard the decisiveness of the revelation of God in Jesus, for this is the *canon* (here is an echo of the thought of Donald Dawe) 'by which we are enabled to recognise all other manifestations'. The use here of the term 'manifestations' has been criticized, but in the authors' original conception it was intended to be a synonym for the rather more technical term 'epiphany'. The implications here need perhaps rather more attention than is given in the Report, but it is clear to the authors that there are manifestations or epiphanies of the Word of God, the Logos, in other religious traditions. They then go on to use the expression 'other revelations': 'Furthermore in the encountering of those other revelations, new depths are encountered in that fullest revelation of God in Jesus Christ.'[68]

In part at least, this report is intended to function as a persuasive to the task of dialogue with those of other faiths. It certainly disclaims any intention to have spoken the last word on the subject and reminds its readers that theology is always provisional. But some kind of provisions for the traveller venturing into unexplored paths is essential. So its concluding paragraphs use this extended metaphor of a 'journey into unfamiliar territory' as the basis of its final reflections.[69] But however unfamiliar a field this may be to the great majority of Christians, it is not so to all. 'Those Christians who have already listened most carefully in interfaith dialogue acknowledge the richness of insight to be discovered in other faiths.'[70] Christian intellectual integrity demands an adequate rationale for the presence of such insight, and the authors state without reservation that in such dialogue we may expect to have our understanding of God 'illuminated by the insights, sensitivities and religious experiences of members of other faiths. This must be so from what we have understood from the Bible of the work of God the Creator, the Logos and the Spirit.'[71]

Because the authors of this Report were working within the strictest limitations of space, too many of the statements in it are in compressed and shorthand form. In the next chapter I want both to expand some of these statements and to add my own personal understanding of many of its themes. For as I have repeatedly suggested, it is an inclusivist christology that is most needed if we are to be faithful as Christians in an age of religious pluralism.

John 14. 6

⊿5⊾

A Christology for Religious Pluralism

'Christian students of comparative religion are well aware that if they expound the principles of another religion to a Western audience they are liable to be challenged with biblical texts such as, "there is no other name under heaven given among men by which we must be saved" (Acts 4.12) or "no one comes to the Father but by me" (John 14.6).' So wrote an outstanding Methodist scholar in this field, Geoffrey Parrinder in 1973.[1] As one who comes at the same issue from the rather different perspectives of the missiologist and the practitioner of inter-faith dialogue I can say the situation has not changed twelve years later. Indeed it often seems to me that these two texts are the only ones that the majority of Christians have in their repertoire when they are forced to think about the existence of other religions and, with them, the whole activity of God in his dealings with humankind. Geoffrey Parrinder goes on to comment that it is 'hardly agreeable to one's listeners to suggest that such verses are inauthentic, even if they are, and little more convincing to explain them away in the light of more universal texts'. He declares that what is needed much rather is a Christian theology of 'other religions, and of other saviours'.

I am completely in accord with Geoffrey Parrinder's main thrust here, and even more convinced that we must not 'explain away' or dismiss as inauthentic such texts as John 14.6 and Acts 4.12. They are both central to the Christian tradition, and express the profoundest commitment to the Jesus who is acknowledged as Lord and Master in that tradition. But I want to suggest in this chapter that rather than compelling us to the faith of Jesus Christ with a dogmatic exclusivity that leaves no place for other masters and other teachers, both John 14.6 and Acts 4.12 may be, and indeed ought to be, read in quite another way, and that they are of inestimable value to us in arriving at a Christian understanding of God's ways with his human children.

Both texts, and particularly the first, seem to me to offer indispensable guidance for a right understanding of other paths and ways in the light of what we corporately understand about the gospel of Jesus, and therefore as to how we enter into that 'new relationship' to which I believe we are called, wherein we are 'inclusivist' in our understanding of where God has touched the lives of other men and women but in which we maintain our exclusive loyalty to Jesus Christ.

So what follows now is an exposition of the implicit (and, I believe, in the Prologue to St John's Gospel and elsewhere, *explicit*) teaching of the New Testament concerning a christology which is inclusive, all-embracing, cosmic and universal in its scope, illuminating all the processes of creation and history and human creativity in culture, arts, music, science and literature. It is a christology of the Word, the *Logos* of God, to which the Fourth Gospel bears its astonishing witness.

We begin with a four-fold exposition of John 14.6. Some explanation of the procedure here is essential. My own reaction on the innumerable occasions where this text has been set before me as a challenge ('do you, or do you not believe that Jesus is the only way, and that no one comes to the Father but by him?') has always been to point out that it is quite impossible to give a yes or no answer to such questioning. Depending on the situation, the time available, and my perception of the theological preconceptions of my interrogators, I have found myself stating my position in any one of four differing ways: these four modes of response are now set out for the judgment of the wider Christian community. I am now quite satisfied in my own mind that none of these ways of interpreting St John's thought adequately conveys all that may be read out of (in the process of *exegesis*) the words of the Fourth Gospel. But I would be far less contented to think that they are adequate interpretations of the relevance of this Johannine text to the contemporary situation (in the process of *exposition*). Of the need for such a series of attempts at interpretation I have no doubt at all, and it is this that now emboldens me.

These interpretations are exposed on the one hand to criticism from New Testament scholars in terms of the exegesis, and from the systematic theologians in terms of the hermeneutic method. But I take comfort in the words of three greater risk-takers than myself. As I offer this four-fold exposition of John 14.6 I recall the words that

Gerhard von Rad used of the first verses of Genesis:[2] 'they can hardly be overinterpreted theologically. Indeed the danger appears greater that the expositor will fall short of discovering the concentrated doctrinal content'. These words may be even truer of the Fourth Gospel, for as Martin Luther once wrote, 'John speaks haltingly and simply as a child, and speaks his words out (as the worldly-wise might see it) in a quite child-like way. But there is such a majesty hidden behind this way of speaking that there is no one, however highly educated, that can either reach their depths or explain them to the fullest'.[3]

My third comforter is the Roman Catholic theologian, David Tracy, who asks, pertinently, 'Who is the Systematic Theologian, except the finite, historical, risk-taking interpreter of the religious classics of a classic tradition?'[4] It is safer to be a museum keeper, wrapping the past theological insights of our inherited traditions in our contemporary equivalents of the napkin in the parable of the pounds (see Luke 19.20). Let us then proceed and take some risks, and do our theology out in the exposed areas.[5]

1 The Answer to Thomas

No text is ever to be used as a pretext. Every scriptural sentence has an immediate context, and the first answer to those who want unequivocal answers to what they imagine to be the central proposition of John 14.6, is that John's words cannot be lifted out of their proper context and be made into a statement about the ultimate salvation or final destiny of any human being in relation to God. These words come to us in the immediate context of a conversation or dialogue between Jesus and Thomas. Thomas is for John both apostle and witness.[6] We must look first of all at the part he plays within the total narrative structure of the Fourth Gospel. This means that we must first rid our minds of the associations of ideas that spring into our minds when we hear the name of Thomas. Christian tradition has labelled him from the earliest times as 'doubting Thomas'. The preconceptions established by this sobriquet appear to continue to blind many to another possible reading of his function in the Fourth Gospel, namely that he is *believing* Thomas, the disciple who is the most committed to Jesus, and what he understands of Jesus's intentions. But even until today the foremost commentators on St John's Gospel tend to characterize Thomas as 'loyal but dull' (C. K. Barrett); 'a type of the unimaginative but loyal disciple' (F. C. Grant); 'loyal but literal minded' (William Temple); 'doggedly loyal but sceptically minded' (Lesslie Newbigin).[7] That great preacher of a previous generation, A. J. Gossip, wrote ' . . . Thomas, who always liked the feel of solid facts beneath his feet, and perhaps had not much poetry in his nature, blurts out, Lord, we do not know where you are going; how can we know the way?'[8]

So then we see that Thomas's loyalty is emphasized, but any possibility that he may be the vehicle for special insight is not ever taken into account. But I want to suggest that this is not a proper reading if we take into our thinking the other two incidents in which he figures in the Fourth Gospel. We first meet Thomas in the Lazarus story. Here he speaks words of amazing commitment and 'loyalty': 'Let us also go, that we may die with him' (John 11.6). Here we have a picture before us of Jesus and the disciples as they are faced with the urgent cry for help from the sisters of Lazarus. But they live in Judaea, which has become a dangerous place for Jesus. 'Rabbi, the Jews were but now seeking to stone you, and are you going there again?' (v. 8). Jesus responds with words about his own vocation and mission: 'Are there not twelve hours in the day? If any one walks in the day, he does not stumble because he sees the light of this world. But if anyone walks in the night, he stumbles because the light is not in him' (vv. 9–10). These strange, pregnant words, with their echoes of and cross-references to other Johannine imagery have to do with death and suffering. Note the associations called up by the words 'twelve hours': 'my hour is not yet come . . . ' 'my hour is come . . . ' (John 2.4; 7.8, 33; 13.1). Note also what 'to walk in the light' might mean for Jesus, as he reflects upon what it might be for him to walk in night. This is a forenote of the theme of Judas's leaving the supper table: 'and it was night' (John 13.30), and of the night scene in Gethsemane. Indeed, if there be truth in the suggestion that the Fourth Gospel is itself a commentary on the Synoptic tradition, which John is presuming that his readers already know, we could say that this incident in John 11 is the counterpart of the Gethsemane experience as recorded by St Mark: 'and going a little further, he fell on the ground, and prayed that if it were possible, the hour might pass from him' (Mark 14.13). This incident is missing from the Fourth Gospel and therefore it is here in chapter 11 that we have its counterpart in the momentous decision to cross over to Judaea. This might explain the strange detail of hesitation of 'two days' waiting in verse 6. Thus John gives his version of Jesus's setting his face to go to Jerusalem 'when the days drew near for him to be received up' (Luke's description, Luke 9.51). According to Mark, Jesus set out in the company of an amazed or shocked, certainly fearful group of followers (Mark 10.32). We know of course, but it is certainly possible that John knew too, and is therefore indirectly commenting on this tradition, that Peter is recorded as 'reproaching' Jesus for going towards Jerusalem. Matthew says Peter took hold of Jesus and 'began to rebuke him, saying "God forbid, Lord! This shall never happen to you"' when he was told of the sufferings that awaited the Christ (v. 21, cf. Mark 8.31–33). But whether or not John is making this deliberate contrast, it must strike us that there is so great a difference between the response recorded of Peter and the words John attributes here to Thomas: 'Let us also go, that we may die with him'. I suggest that this response is not to be interpreted as dull, unimaginative and literal-minded, but much rather as being spoken out of faith and commit-ment, a response to the poetry of Jesus's words in verse 9 and 10. In other words Thomas has discerned something of the mystery of redemptive suffering, and of the inner struggles of the one who must so suffer to redeem.

Thomas appears in the great culmination of the Fourth Gospel.[9] Indeed he is the one into whose mouth is put the supreme affirmation about the person and work of Jesus Christ in this gospel: 'My Lord and my God' (John 20.28). This should in itself warn us against any interpretation of Thomas in the Fourth Gospel which underplays his ability to discern mystery. Nevertheless there is a long expository tradition which says that Thomas required 'the grossest and most palpable proofs that the body he knew to have been killed in a specific manner had indeed been reanimated'.[10]

But, as so often, the expository tradition may mislead commentator and preacher alike. For there is another way of reading the Thomas story at the climax of the Gospel. It is this. John the story-teller who 'speaks out his words in a quite child-like fashion' but who is also the narrator of events of which it is impossible to reach their hidden depths, has really rather more to say to us than that Thomas was a crass materialist. The absence, therefore, of Thomas from the first occasion when the Risen Jesus appeared has its own narrative and theological necessity. This necessity is hardly for an extra (and hardly conclusive) piece of evidence concerning Jesus's resurrection. For the question of Thomas is not in fact about the physical fact of reanimation, i.e. with what has been called rather coarsely a 'conjuring trick with bones' but about the reality of suffering and death. 'Believing' Thomas, committed as he was to going to Judaea 'that we may die with him' stands here as the one who must be assured that the resurrection was not a docetic illusion[11] or a divine act of sleight of hand.[12] In David van Daalen's words: 'Thomas does not want proof that what the others have seen is not imaginary, but wants to identify the Lord. The real question therefore is not *what* has happened but *who* has appeared'.[13] John affirms this as a proper form of questioning by making Jesus use to him the exact words that Thomas himself had used (vv. 25 and 27). That Thomas is vindicated, so to speak, in his quest for the identity of the Risen One with the Crucified One is shown in his immediate response of faith. Note that after all Thomas does not, according to the narrative, actually physically touch the wounds: if in the mind of the evangelist he was actually seeking proofs of the grossest and most palpable kind he did not take the necessary step of ensuring himself that this was no waking vision or corporate hallucination.[14] John's point surely lies elsewhere, namely in the fact, as it would seem to him, that the words of the response 'My Lord and my God' are testimony that may be borne only by those who have discerned that the way of redemption is through suffering and death. Such a one is Thomas.

Now we return to John 14.6. Jesus has just said that he goes to prepare a place for them (v. 2), and that the disciples know the way where he is going (v. 5). Now the question here is whether Thomas does stand as a type of all who demand tangible proofs and precise definitions, or does he, rather, express a longing for a further glimpse into the nature of the redemption he believes Jesus to be about, and the manner by which such a redemption will be accomplished. Is he not then, the type of all who hunger and thirst after justice, the poor in spirit who long for peace, the pure in heart who yearn for truth? Let us therefore understand his question something after this manner: 'Lord, what is your ultimate intention, and how do we follow you in achieving so great a purpose?'

To such a two-fold question there is, can be, no easy answer. It is therefore a misunderstanding of the Fourth Gospel to suggest that Thomas is but a foil to provoke Jesus into declaring his purposes more plainly. For however necessary it might seem to later theologians or commentators that Jesus 'should clearly state the nature of the road by which His disciples can follow in His footsteps',[15] this is almost exactly what Jesus did not do. The great nineteenth-century Cambridge scholar, F. J. A. Hort is much nearer the truth of the matter in emphasizing the majestic obscurity of Jesus's answer:

> It was therefore impossible that Christ should mean 'I am the Guide' or 'I am the Example' when he said 'I am the Way'. These phrases may exact a slighter effort of thought; but only because they belong at best to a rudimentary and transitory form of truth. It

was doubtless hard for those who reclined around that table to understand in what sense one in fashion like themselves could say 'I am the Way'. Perhaps it is equally hard for us who have received Him through the Creeds in His Divine-majesty. Whether spoken from the human lips of Jesus or from the highest heaven, the words have a perplexing sound which no Jewish forms of speech suffice to make clear. They must always remain unintelligible as applied to the function of a simple Teacher or Ruler.[16]

How Hort goes on to offer his own interpretation of what Jesus does mean will concern us in the next section. Meanwhile let us remain with the issue he raises for us. New Testament scholarship since 1871 has developed in many ways, and it is doubtful now whether many contemporary scholars of the stature of Hort himself would write as though we have before us in John 14 a literal account of the Last Supper ('those who reclined around the table'). Hort nevertheless is deeply illuminating in speaking of the essential difficulty in a man like other men speaking such words, and secondly, in indicating that these words can be reduced to a set of propositions as though we all knew exactly what was meant. Just as poetry cannot be reduced to its prose content (otherwise it would have been written in the first place as prose), so John 14.6 cannot be reduced to a set of explicable theological propositions.

Hence the importance of the Thomas dimension in the answer: whatever else we do with the words of John 14.6 we must hold to the element within of mystery, redemptive suffering, life through death. In the broken and divided world we live in it is as well to remember that John 14.6 is not and cannot be a triumphalist slogan by which just a very few may minister to their own self-esteem and a concomitant sense of being rather especially favoured above all others. The shaping of the answer to Thomas points rather to the recognition of pain and perplexity, ambiguity and suffering. It also points to a 'beyondness', a transcendence and an ultimacy which has to do with the one whom John believes to be speaking these words: not indeed merely the Rabbi/Prophet of Galilee but the Word become flesh and dwelling amongst us, the incarnation of the *Logos*. We are at the heart of one of the profoundest christological affirmations in the New Testament.

2 'I am the Way'

Let us continue the quotation from F. J. A. Hort:

The claim which (these words) embody includes not merely a set of men moving in a world but the world itself which contains them. They convey a doctrine of Creation and Providence, not merely of historical mission; a claim on the part of the speaker to permanent supremacy in the whole manifold economy of circumstance. They are the practical and ethical expression of an all-embracing truth which we may perhaps apprehend best in the form of two separate doctrines: first that the whole seeming maze of history in nature and man, the tumultuous movement of the world in progress, has running through it one supreme dominating Way; and second, that He who on earth was called Jesus the Nazarene *is* that way.[17]

We shall need to take seriously both these splendid affirmations in what now follows. We have been taken into the heart of the christological questions that can never cease to occupy the church's thinking. Who is this Jesus? Is he man for us or is he God for us? Christian orthodoxy since the Council of Chalcedon has held that four propositions are integral within the worshipping, praying, witnessing community.

These are: Jesus Christ is truly human; Jesus Christ is truly divine; Jesus Christ is one Person; Jesus Christ is ultimately related to the more general action, presence and revelation of God in his world and supremely in human history. The history is long, and intricate, as to how this worshipping, praying and witnessing community has sought to hold all these four elements in their proper tension. There have been periods in that history when one or other emphasis has so dominated the others that serious distortion of Christian theology has arisen. Sometimes indeed this has led to heresy in its strictest sense, the deliberate breaking away on doctrinal grounds from the main community. But sometimes it has been the main body that has distorted the proper shape of christology, and taught e.g., the divinity of Jesus to the virtual exclusion of his manhood. We have lived, too, through a period of Christian theologizing in which it has seemed that the fourth element, i.e. that Jesus Christ is ultimately related to the more general action of God, action, presence and revelation in the world has been seriously under-played.[18] It is with this fourth aspect of the four-fold propositions of christology that I am chiefly concerned.

But we cannot consider that fourth element in isolation from the first three, even though it is not necessary to enter into a full discussion of how Jesus Christ may be at one and the same time 'perfect in Godhead and also perfect in manhood, truly God and truly man, of a reasonable soul and body; consubstantial (*homoousion*) with the Father according to the Godhead, and consubstantial (*homoousion*) with us according to the manhood; in all things like unto us without sin'.[19] How these two 'natures' may be united in one person, as the Creed of Chalcedon goes on to state, 'inconfusedly, unchangeably, indivisibly' and 'inseparably' cannot be discussed here, save for me to indicate that I stand broadly with the solutions advanced by D. M. Baillie in *God was in Christ*, but as supplemented by W. N. Pittenger in *The Word Incarnate* and *Christology Reconsidered*, and as recently adumbrated by A. T. Hanson in his two volumes *Grace and Truth* and *The Image of the Invisible God*.[20] That is to say, I find Donald Baillie's analysis of the 'paradox of grace' as applied to the mode of God's acting in Christ at once profoundly religious and deeply persuasive. The paradox of grace at this point expresses the Christian (and, as we shall observe shortly, not just the Christian) conviction that every good work and good intention found or accomplished by us is the result of the work of God in us, and not the result of inherent goodness in ourselves, for

> . . . every virtue we possess,
> And every conquest won,
> And every thought of holiness
> Are his alone.[21]

Harriet Auber was giving expression in this hymn to the great theme which runs from St Paul: ' . . . yet not I, but the grace of God which was with me' (I Cor. 15.10) through Augustine, Anselm, Thomas à Kempis, the Westminster Confession and the works of John and Charles Wesley. It is the common theme of Christian saints, and many who belong to other traditions.[22] Baillie goes on to say that if the saints 'experience the paradox of grace for themselves in fragmentary ways, and are constrained to say, "It was not I but God", may not this be a clue to the understanding of that perfect life in which the paradox is complete and absolute, that the life of Jesus which, being the perfection of humanity, is also and even in a deeper and prior sense, the very life of God Himself'.[23]

Donald Baillie has been criticized, perhaps justifiably, for never quite succeeding in indicating what was 'continuous' between the 'very life of God Himself' and the life of Jesus. Is it a continuity of grace such as may in principle, if not in fact, be experienced by all other human beings if they were to be able to make themselves as open to God as Jesus was, or is it an ontological continuity, and do we have to say clearly that it is the Eternal Word, the second 'hypostasis' in the Godhead who is incarnate in Jesus? This would be deliberately to espouse a *Logos* christology as Norman Pittenger does. 'My only important *addendum*' he writes, 'to Dr Baillie's discussion arises from my belief that it is necessary to see the relationship between God and man, both in our Lord and other men, as much more ontologically grounded than the Scots theologian appears to suggest.'[24] Thus Pittenger affirms, and in my view wholly appropriately, that it is 'the Eternal Word, consubstantial with the Father, who dwelt in Jesus'. I must now forbear to go into the detail of this and refer readers to the careful discussion of this 'indwelling' in Pittenger's and Hanson's own words.[25] I am, nevertheless, deeply indebted to both of them for perceptions of the importance of Trinitarian theology which have immediate bearing on the search for an 'inclusive christology' to enable us to affirm the reality of God's activity among people of other faiths with whom we are called to enter into qualitatively new relationships.[26]

So let us concern ourselves now with the fourth great affirmation of our christological tradition, namely that 'Jesus Christ is ultimately related to the general action, presence and revelation of God in his world and in human history'. And this, in the view of F. J. A. Hort is exactly that upon which John 14.6 bears: 'the whole tumultuous movement of the world in progress has running through it one supreme dominating Way' and then 'that He who on earth was called Jesus the Nazarene *is* that Way'.

It is fascinating at this point to turn our attention to the other religious traditions of humankind and to discover their nearly universal concern about the 'Way of God' and (and sometimes or) the way of men and women in the processes of salvation. Arnulf Camps, Professor of Missiology in the Roman Catholic University at Nijmegen, as we have already seen published in 1977 a book entitled in Dutch, *De Weg de Paden en de Wegen*, which may be translated literally as *The Way the Paths and the Ways*. In this he attempted to deal with some of the issues that arise in inter-faith dialogue between followers of 'The Way' and followers of the Paths and Ways. Happily this book now forms part of the English version of his seminal writings in this field now called *Partners in Dialogue* to which we have already referred.[27]

Camps is able to proceed as he does because he recognizes that 'Religions are not first and foremost institutionalized systems but Ways. Aren't the Old and New Testaments full of talk about the Way of the Lord? Weren't the first Christians called followers of the Way? (Acts 9.2). Doesn't the first Sura of the Koran talk about the straight Way? Doesn't Hinduism know three Ways to salvation? Doesn't

Buddhism talk about the Eightfold Path? Here it seems to me, we have a good starting point for dialogue'.[28]

I think we have in this insight not only a good starting point for dialogue as such, but also a good starting point for a Christian theology of religion which will enable us to enter into that dialogue relationship with profound expectations based upon our understanding of Christ as the 'supreme dominating Way' within the whole tumultuous world in progress. For Christians have always to realize that they have but the most rudimentary understanding of the cosmic significance of the Logos who was incarnate in Jesus of Nazareth. What we do, however, perceive is that the 'Way' in the cosmic immensities will not ultimately differ from the 'Way' we have seen lived in Jesus of Nazareth.

For what I am suggesting is not merely that it is of passing interest to see that the other religious traditions have used the term 'Way' or 'Path' as self descriptions. But rather, though unbeknown to them, they are immediately and directly in relationship to the One who is 'the Supreme dominating Way' in the whole tumultuous movement of the world in progress.

We are concerned therefore with the other religious traditions not because we are interested in religion as such. Were that to be so, we might go the way of attempting to distil the essence of religion,[29] of creating a new and universal form of religion,[30] or of comparing religious systems as we might compare educational or legal systems.[31] Because our concern is rather with God and his ways, and with human beings and their ways, our focus as Christian theologians lies quite elsewhere. What we affirm therefore in the first place is that other religious traditions are counterparts to Christianity. I mean by this that wherever people take their religious tradition seriously it determines their life-patterns, sets them ideals and gives them principles by which to live. In times of crisis and danger their religious tradition sustains them, comforts them, encourages them. But it can only do this because the religious believer can affirm within him or herself that the tradition's essential teaching bears some relationship to that 'beyond-ness' to which one can only respond by faith. The human phenomenon to which we give the name of religion has to do with transcendence. Because it has to do with transcendence, its teaching about the individual's 'path' has to have some correspondence with what is believed to be the 'way' of the universe, the cosmic order in which individuals are to find their own ways.

Thus, to begin with that community of faith which has accompanied the developing Christian church all its days, we find that Judaism is supremely concerned with *halakhah*, which means literally, 'walking'.

This is the technical term for Jewish teaching concerning all matters of the Law and all the everyday rules for conducting one's life. It is derived from Exodus 18.20: 'you shall show them the statutes and the decisions, and make them know the way in which they must walk and what they must do'. But we mistake this if we interpret this way simply as a form of legalism. One of Lionel Blue's delightful books, *To Heaven with Scribes and Pharisees* bears the sub-title 'The Jewish Path to God'.[32] Lionel Blue quotes at one point in this work from Moses Maimonides: 'on the dark path on which a man is to walk here on earth just as much light is provided as he wants to make the next step. More would only dazzle, and every side-light bewilders him'. Nevertheless Maimonides' *Guide for the Perplexed* was a work of theology.[33] The Jewish way of walking has to do with how God is perceived to be both in his ultimacy and in his relationship to the world.

The Christian tradition's other partner among the Abrahamic families of faith is Islam. Here is the first Sura of the Qur'an in A. J. Arberry's vivid translation:

> In the Name of God, the Merciful, the Compassionate
>
> Praise belongs to God, the Lord of all Being,
> the All-merciful, the All-compassionate
> the Master of the Day of Doom.
>
> Thee only we serve; to Thee alone we pray for succour
> Guide us in the straight path,
> the path of those whom Thou hast blessed,
> Not of those against whom Thou art wrathful,
> nor of those who are astray.[34]

No further comment is necessary. The following of the straight path is intimately linked with the perception of God as *Rabb*, the Master of the universe, and to the Muslim understanding of his purposes in cherishing and sustaining the world by his compassion.[35]

In Hindu tradition there are three ways to salvation, understood of course as *moksha*, release from futility, unreality, and the endless cycles of *karma* and rebirth. The answer to the prayer in the *Brihadāranyaka Upanishad* is strangely familiar to Western Christians:

> From the untruth, lead me to reality
> From darkness lead me to light
> From death lead me to life. (I, iii, 28)[36]

The Indian sages have taught that such aspirations are fulfilled in one or other *marga*, or path; *Jnāna marga*, or path of knowledge; *karma marga*, or the path or discipline of good works and *bhakti marga*, or the path of devotion.[37] No commentary of mine could even begin to touch upon the inexhaustible riches of the Indian religious traditions. But simply as illustrating the spiritual power that we are dealing with here let us set down first of all the verse from the *Upanishads* which Mahatma Gandhi thought summarized the Hindu tradition:

> Behold the universe in the glory of God (the Lord) and all that lives and moves on the earth. Leaving the transient, find joy in the eternal. Set not your heart upon another's possession. (The *Isā Upanishad*)[38]

Secondly, from India's most beloved scripture, the *Bhagavad Gita* which speaks of the vision given the charioteer Arjuna through the gift of a 'celestial eye'. Arjuna 'sees':

> Thou art Imperishable, the highest theme
> of wisdom, cosmic resting-place supreme,
> thou changeless Guardian of eternal Law
> the everlasting Spirit, thee I deem. (11.18)[39]

A few verses later Arjuna prays:

> And to my prostrate body bending low,
> O Lord adorable, thy grace bestow,
> as father bears with son, as friend with friend,
> as lover with beloved, God's mercy show. (11.44)

Krishna then imparts to Arjuna his divine teaching:

> However not as you behold
> can I be seen in such a guise,
> by austerity or Vedas,
> by gifts of alms or sacrifice.
>
> Only by undivided love (*bhakti*)
> can I in reality be seen
> in such a guise as you perceived
> and both be known and entered in.
>
> So work for me, intent on me,
> be free from ties, have love for me
> and lacking hate, whoever is so
> to every one to me shall go. (11.53–55)

The teaching of India's seers concerning the path to *moksha*, release, liberation, salvation, thus also depends upon theological notions concerning the Way (we use the upper case deliberately) the created order moves. To the concepts of love (*bhakti*) and grace (*prasād*) we shall return when considering the 'fatherhood' of God in the other religious traditions.

If *marga* is the Sanskrit word for path, its Pali derivative is *magga*, the word which Buddhists use for the Fourth Noble Truth, the Noble Truth of the Way. But other familiar terms to Westerners also contain the idea of the way: the best loved book of the Theravada Buddhist tradition is called the *Dhammapada*, literally 'the path of truth', and *Theravada* itself means 'the way of the elders'. The Buddhist self-descriptions of what we Westerners like to call 'Buddhism' are the Noble Eightfold Path, and the Middle Way. But we will all be aware that as touching the question of God the Buddha himself was inclined to be agnostic. Nevertheless the force of Ninian Smart's question must be taken seriously: 'What is the Christian . . . to say about the Buddha's teaching and experience given that in the Theravada at least it is hard to discern anything approaching a personal theism? Putting it crudely: Did the Buddha see God but not realize what he was apprehending?'[40] But few scholars of Buddhism would doubt that there is a sense of Way running through 'the way things are'. So the Professor of Buddhist Studies in Colombo University at once reiterates that the Buddha refused 'to be dragged into arguments and discussions which do not relate to this problem of the salvation of man' but then goes on to speak of a vision of salvation at the heart of the Buddhist world-view: ' . . . Buddhism starts with the culture of man and the elevation of his dignity. A first step in this direction is the insistence on the virtue of *maitri*, of the practice of loving kindness. It is basically the state of friendliness, of being a friend to *mitra* that links man to a society. It is no doubt extended to all grades of life, human and animal and further extends through time and space, leaving no room for caste, creed or ethnic differences. It is in fact interesting to observe that the future Buddha on whom the salvation of this present world is said to be hinged is named Maitreya. This insists as it were that the salvation of man rests on the mutual love of and respect for one another.'[41]

Lastly we must re-call however fleetingly the Chinese tradition. It is of particular interest to notice that the famous commentary on St John's Gospel by B. F. Westcott, Hort's contemporary and collaborator, actually refers to this Chinese tradition in the comments on John 14.6. Bishop Westcott, writing in 1880, belonged to that period when awareness of other religious traditions was just breaking in upon Western scholars, and he uses the opinions of one of the nineteenth-century pioneers in the study of other religions, the Dutch Professor C. P. Tiele. Westcott wrote: 'The use of the corresponding word (sc. 'the way') in the Chinese mystical system of Lao-tse is of interest. "In the mysticism of Lao the term (Tao, the way, the chief way) is applied to the supreme cause, the way or passage through which everything enters into life, and at the same time to the way of highest perfection".'[42]

So let us allow Lao-tzu (as he is better called) to speak for himself in words which the contemporary Chinese theologian Choan-Seng Song finds significant enough with which to begin his magisterial *Third-Eye Theology*:[43]

Impenetrable is the darkness where the heart of Being dwells
This being is Truth itself and Faith itself.
From eternity to eternity, they will never perish,
Who saw the beginning of All?
The beginning of All, one only knows through the perennial Spirit.

So

Man models himself after the Earth;
The Earth models itself after Heaven;
The Heaven models itself after Tao:
Tao models itself after Nature.

Our purpose in all this is not just to remind Christian theologians that to speak of the Christian path as but one way among many ways is no more than the empirically observable state of affairs. I am wanting also to affirm that the reason why these paths and ways have for so long inspired, consoled and encouraged the hearts of human beings is in their discernment that somehow their way is comparable to the Way of God in the things that can be felt and apprehended in the created order, as Romans 1.18ff. makes it clear. But, far from having deliberately distorted or suppressed the truth, becoming 'futile in their thinking' and darkened in 'their senseless minds' the greatest spiritual teachers of humankind responded to their discernment of the Way of God in the noble teachings and lives of faith and hope.[44] Nevertheless my purpose has not been to equate the unequatable: the ideas of 'grace', 'salvation', 'love', 'spirit' and of 'God' belong within the total conceptual frameworks of each tradition. We cannot create a syncretistic new religion by saying 'this is that'! Nor can we simplistically say that all religions teach the same things because some concepts appear to overlap. But we can affirm that what the Fourth Gospel is pointing to, when Jesus says 'I am the Way' is continuity with other religious traditions, as well as to a certain discontinuity.

For it is certainly not accidental that in chapter 14, as elsewhere, John uses specific notions and terminology derived from the religious traditions of his contemporary world. The Fourth Gospel has to be interpreted against the background of Gnostic dualism, Stoicism, Platonism, the Hermetic and Mandean literature, in short, what C. H. Dodd calls 'the general medley of religious beliefs characteristic of the Hellenistic world'.[45] In this there lurk the ideas of the mystical ascent or 'way' of the soul to God, or to those realms where there is truth and light.

But many scholars are sure that John never passes wholly out of the theological framework of his contemporary Judaism. Raymond Brown, for example, sees the primary reference of 'the Way' in John 14.6 to the 'Way of the Torah', and a secondary reference to 'the Way of the Qumran community, which appears to have designated itself absolutely as *ha-derek*, the Way. (Those who entered the community were those who had chosen the Way (1QS 1 x 17–18), and those who apostasized were those who 'turned aside from the Way'). There is likely also to be a third reference to the 'way' of John the Baptist. It is against this background of Jewish 'ways' that Jesus then speaks. John 14.6 then reflects a 'whole chain of usage of the imagery of "the way", originating in the Old Testament, modified by Jewish sectarian thought, and finally adopted by the Christian community as a self-designation'.[46] He goes on to note that it is not unusual for the 'Johannine Jesus to take terminology once applied to Israel (and subsequently adopted by the Christian community) and to apply it to himself'. He instances the imagery of the sheepfold and the vine, applied in the Old Testament to Israel and in the Synoptic Gospels to the kingdom of God. In the Fourth Gospel this imagery is found on the lips of Jesus: 'I am the good shepherd' (John 10.11). 'I am the true vine' (John 15.1). 'The same process', says Raymond Brown, 'seems to be at work in calling Jesus, rather than the Christian community, the "way".' He then suggests that this transformation of terminology could have been encouraged by the Johannine understanding of Jesus as personified divine Wisdom, and to this we shall return in the final section of this chapter.

So let us not lose sight of the manifold contexts to which Dodd and Brown point us. The multiplicity of religious ways and paths was an issue in the New Testament period. It is therefore clear that there is something to be said from John 14.6 about the theology of religions, and about the way in which we may 'attempt to communicate with a variety of dialogue partners'.

The longings and aspirations of humanity are to be recognized. They reflect the universal condition of all human beings, created in and through the eternal Word of God. Since they are created in and through this *Logos* it can be no surprise that they have so often sought to understand themselves as following a way which reflects the way of God in the created order. The discernment of the early Christian community in which the Fourth Gospel came to light is that such understandings of the human situation are in the profoundest sense 'true to reality' for 'the whole seeming maze of history in nature and in man, the tumultuous movement of the world in progress, as running through it one supreme dominating Way'. Here is the element of continuity.

But equally the Christian community believed then, as it must still do, that this Way of God has been most clearly discerned in the way that Jesus followed – the path of rejection and suffering, of abandonment and death. Thomas's question has still to be answered when we speak of Jesus as the Way. This way of Jesus is clearly discontinuous with all religious ways which offer false hopes or minister to human egocentricities whether on the individualist or on the communal level. Whatever path human beings choose is not necessarily a reflection of the way of God; ways which have not discerned somehow the mystery of suffering and the mystery of love are 'untrue to reality' whatever label they carry.[47]

For in the end of the day, 'He who on earth was called Jesus of Nazareth *is* that Way'. He is the exegesis of God (John 1.14). Whoever has seen him has seen the Father (John 14.10). But this 'seeing the Father' raises other enormous issues to which we now turn.

3 Coming to the Father

But what is it to 'see the Father', or 'to come to the Father'? One theme that runs on through the human attempts to speak of God is of the essentially impossible nature of that task: 'for my thoughts are not your thoughts, neither are your ways my ways'.[48] One of the greatest Greek philosophers, Plato, warned us that 'to find the maker and the father of the universe is a hard task, and when you have found him it is impossible to speak of him before all men'.[49] Many different strands within all the religious traditions speak of either the 'unknowability' of God in his essential being, or of his 'unutterability'. Within our own more recent tradition Blaise Pascal also warned us Christians, who can so glibly talk of the inner mysteries of God that 'every religion that does not affirm that God is hidden is not true'.

It is in the contexts of such perceptions among people whom we know to have been profoundly conscious of God that the Christian 'paradox' is to be set. For we do speak of the 'disclosed Father'. The New Testament tradition is ungainsayable: Jesus taught the Father-hood of God. He taught it moreover as having qualities of intensity and intimacy, and as being totally gracious and limitless in its scope. Indeed so far-reaching are Jesus's teachings about the Divine Fatherhood that it appears often that Christians themselves have not seen all the implications. But even as far as we have seen, it appears to us that such teachings have a quality of uniqueness and insurpassability. No one else to our knowledge has ever taught quite like this.

But here of course is the first challenge. Is it in fact true that other religious traditions have never found the Father, in the sense of meeting God as the gracious, the loving, the forgiving and yet the ultimate One, Maker and Sustainer of the Universe?

Franz Rosenzweig (1886–1929) is perhaps less well known than his near contemporary Martin Buber. But it could be argued that his significance for and contribution to Jewish-Christian dialogue is even greater than Buber's. He was the first, as it seems, among Jewish teachers in our own century to speak of Christianity as having a positive role to play in relation to Judaism. As Hans-Joachim Schoeps has written: 'Starting from this recognition of the other faith in its own depth of belief, Rosenzweig can admit what no Jew before him ever admitted of his own free will – and without this admission, in the future, no further discussion is possible – that not one of the nations of the world comes to the Father except through Jesus Christ.'[50]

Here, in Rosenzweig's own words is the reverse side of that proposition:

What Christ and his church mean within the world – on this point we are agreed. No one comes to the Father except through him. No one *comes* to the Father – but the situation is different when one need no longer come to the Father because he *is* already with him. That is the case with the nation of Israel (not the individual Jew) . . . The nation of Israel elected by its Father, keeps its gaze fixed beyond the world and history toward that last most distant point where he, Israel's Father, will himself be one and only – 'all in all'![51]

There is no doubt in my mind but that the wider context of these words gives not only a range of astounding insights for the Christian understanding of the continued existence of the People of Israel, but is also the agenda for the unfinished (indeed scarcely begun) task of dialogue between Christians and Jews. But here I have cited these sentences to focus our attention on to the Fatherhood of God as experienced in the tradition of Israel, i.e., in the Hebrew scriptures and in the religion and worship of the synagogue.

There have been far too many ill-considered comments in sermons and other contexts which have over-stressed the radical originality of Jesus's teaching about God as Father. It is not necessary to multiply examples of this implication that the relationship between the Jewish people and the God of Israel was less than adequate, and certainly not one which knew the intimacy of the Father's love. I may perhaps be permitted to cite the corporate delusion of the Christian community in one of the *Alternative Service Book*'s Collects for Good Friday:

> Merciful God, who made all men
> and hate nothing that you have made:
> you desire not the death of a sinner
> but rather that he should be converted and live.
> Have mercy upon your ancient people the Jews
> and upon all who have not known you
> or deny the faith of Christ crucified.
> Take from them all ignorance, hardness of heart
> and contempt for your word
> and so fetch them home to your fold
> that they may be one flock, one shepherd
> through Jesus Christ our Lord.[52]

While from the Christian point of view most of these petitions are justifiable, it is profoundly distasteful that the 'ancient people' should be spoken of in the same collocation with 'all who have not known you', and that in a contemporary liturgical expression, they should be charged with 'ignorance, hardness of heart, and contempt for your word'.

It is also thoroughly bad theologically, for the Jewish people have 'known God'. For the Christian God is none other than the God of Israel, and the church confesses him as Father because Jesus affirmed all that was already known about him in the scriptures by which he lived. As Karl Barth so strikingly expresses the matter:

> The Gentile Christian community of every age and every land is a guest in the house of Israel. It assumes the election and calling of Israel. It lives in fellowship with the King of Israel. How, then, can we try to hold missions to Israel? It is not the Swiss or the German or the Indian or the Japanese awakened to faith in Jesus Christ, but the Jew, even the unbelieving Jew, so miraculously preserved, as we must say, through the many calamities of his history, who as such is the natural historical monument to the love and faithfulness of God, who in concrete form is the epitome of the man freely chosen and blessed by God, who as a living commentary on the Old Testament is the only convincing proof of God outside the Bible. What have we to teach him that he does not already know, that we have not rather to learn from him?[53]

Now I would not readily assent to the idea that the existence of the Jewish people is the only convincing proof of God outside the Bible – indeed what I am implying in the suggestions that follow is that the argument for the existence of God *ex consensu gentium*, 'from the consensus of the peoples', is a very powerful one. But Karl Barth is certainly in order to move us towards accepting Franz Rosenzweig's central proposition. Both the historical evidence and the contemporary experience of Jewish worship in both home and synagogue suggests that Rosenzweig has truth on his side when he says that Israel (and not necessarily the individual Jew) knows the Father.

It would be otiose to offer a complete survey of the Old Testament evidence at this point. It must suffice to point to certain key moments in Israel's developing understanding of the nature of God. This begins with the earliest traditions of the Father-God in the Pentateuch in which the close relationship of God to the patriarchs is constantly stressed: God acts directly in human affairs and guides his people.[54] On one hand this understanding of God is tribalistic and clannish, and belongs to a nomadic type of society where all events that ever happen take place with the most limited of horizons. On the other hand it *is* a personal, non-mythological relationship, and is central to the understanding of the salvation-history of Israel. So in Exodus 4.22 (the J tradition) we read: 'Thus says the Lord, Israel is my first-born son' and in Deuteronomy 32.6: 'Is not he your father who created you, who made you and established you?' We may properly note at this point that the Pentateuch also implies a doctrine of the Motherhood of God in Numbers 11.12: here Moses is asking the

Lord reproachfully 'Did I conceive all this people? Did I bring them forth, that thou shouldst says to me, "carry them in your bosom, as a nurse carries the sucking child?"' The rhetoric of this is plain, and was not lost on Isaiah 46.3 with its feminine imagery: 'Hearken to me, O house of Jacob, all the remnant of the house of Israel, who have been borne by me from your birth, carried from the womb; even to your old age I am He, and to your grey hairs I will carry you. I have made and I will bear; I will carry and I will save.' This is feminine tender loving care.

It may be true to say that the further use of the title Father is rare in the Hebrew scriptures. But God is frequently compared to a father; or his activities compared to those of a father:

> Father of the fatherless and protector of widows
>   is God in his holy habitation.
> God gives the desolate a home to dwell in;
>   .he leads out his prisoners to prosperity.
> (Ps. 68.5–6)

> As a father pities his children
>   So the Lord pities those who fear him,
> For he knows our frame
>   He remembers that we are dust.
> (Ps. 103.13–14)

> My son, do not despise the Lord's discipline
>   or be weary of the Lord's reproof,
> For the Lord reproves him whom he loves
>   as a father the son in whom he delights.
> (Prov. 3.11–12)

But it is of course in the prophetic tradition that we find what appear to us the deepest insights into the nature of the love, care and compassion that is postulated of the best of earthly fathers. So Hosea uses fatherhood imagery (or perhaps better motherhood imagery!): 'I took them up in my arms, but they did not know that I healed them, I led them with cords of compassion, with the bands of love' (Hos. 11.4). Isaiah of Jerusalem allows God to say, 'Sons have I reared and brought up, but they have rebelled against me' (Isa. 1.2). The same thought, of God's disappointment that his children do not love him in return for his love, is found in Jeremiah: 'I thought you would call me, My Father, and would not turn from following me' (Jer. 3.19). The prophetic insight is that, despite all this anguish and disappointment, God never ceases to care:

> With weeping they shall come
>> and with consolation I shall bring them back.
> I will make them walk by brooks of water
>> in a straight path in which they will not stumble.
> For I am a father to Israel,
>> and Ephraim is my first-born. (Jer. 31.9)

Therefore God may be addressed as Father:

> Yet, O Lord, thou art our Father;
>> we are the clay, and thou art our potter;
> we are all the work of thy hand.

> Be not exceedingly angry, O Lord,
>> and remember not iniquity for ever
> Behold, consider, we are thy people. (Isa. 64.8–9)

Living Judaism continues to call upon this same God as 'Our Father' (*abinu*) and I have occasionally experienced the surprise of people visiting the synagogue for the first time to sense how intimately present or 'near' this 'Father' is to the worshippers. I take just one example from the Amidah:[55]

> Restore us, our Father, to thy Torah; draw us near, our King, to thy service. Cause us to return to thee in perfect repentance. Blessed art thou, O Lord, who art pleased with repentance.

> Forgive us, our Father, for we have sinned; pardon us, our King, for we have transgressed; for thou dost pardon and forgive. Blessed art thou, who art gracious and ever forgiving.

Abinu, malkenu, Our Father, our King, as forms of address mark other prayers of the synagogue, holding as they do the proper tension between majesty and intimacy. But here we must not be tempted into trying to say too much beyond this. Much here becomes the subject matter for common Christian and Jewish exploration of what it means to pray today (see Rabbi Jonathan Magonet's introduction to his remarkable anthology of Jewish writings entitled *Returning: Exercises in Repentance*,[56] and how we in both traditions speak of God as Father after Auschwitz).[57]

We turn our attention to teaching the fatherhood, and indeed the motherhood, of God in other religious traditions. For you will re-call that Franz Rosenzweig, in affirming Christianity's mission to the world insisted that 'not one of the nations comes to the Father except through Jesus Christ'. Before we express our gratitude to a scholar of another tradition for affirming for us what we already knew, we need to be sure that the 'nations' have in fact never discovered the Father, whether through calling upon him with that special title, or perceiving in some other ways the qualities of love, forgiveness, compassion and sustaining care that we attribute to 'fatherhood', especially as we have seen such qualities evidenced in the Old Testament texts.

Within three religious traditions which are quite independent of Judaism and Christianity[58] it is possible to find the Fatherhood (or Motherhood) of God explicitly affirmed both by the use of the word Father (or Mother) and also through the feeling and tone of manner in which prayer is made, where such evocation is to a gracious, loving, forgiving God.

Before we examine examples of such affirmations in these other religious traditions, I think it is important that we hold in our minds three considerations.

1. The use of the term Father (or Mother) is in fact extremely rare in other religious traditions. We cite these certain instances only in order to show that such expressions of the religious spirit have occurred.

2. All religious traditions are, as Hendrik Kraemer was once at such pains to teach us, 'all-inclusive systems and theories of life, rooted in a religious basis' which 'therefore embrace a system of culture and civilization, and definite structures of society and state'.[59] They are not merely speculative sets of ideas about the eternal destiny of human beings. The words in which the religious traditions are passed on carry freight from the total culture and world-view of the people who use those words. Isolated quotations tell us little or nothing of the far-ranging presuppositions which lie beyond the words of the quotations.

3. Nevertheless, the affirmations that follow are present within the traditions, and, most significantly, are increasingly emphasized by contemporary followers of these ways and paths in their own response to religious pluralism.[60] We may hazard our own guesses why this should be so, and indeed, in the light of our Christian understanding, we might find here a confirmation of the thesis that Jesus's teaching becomes the canon or benchmark or touchstone for measuring or assessing the good and the valuable in the old traditions.

(a) The 'Father' in Sikhism

We choose Sikhism for our first example of an Eastern path or way where we may have to admit the 'coming to the Father' otherwise than through Jesus's teaching. Let us consider this:

> O kind Father, loving Father, through thy mercy
> We have spent our day in peace and happiness;
> grant that we may, according to Thy will,
> do what is right. ·
> Give us light, give us understanding, so that we
> may know what pleases Thee.
> We offer this prayer in Thy presence, O wonderful Lord:
> Forgive us our sins. Help us in keeping ourselves pure.
> Bring us into the fellowship of those
> in whose company we may remember Thy name.
> (Through Nanak) may Thy name be forever on the increase,
> and may all men prosper by Thy grace.
>   Guru Gobind Singh (1666–1707)[61]

or this:

> O True King! O loved Father! In this ambrosial hour of the morn we have sung Thy sweet hymns, heard Thy life-giving Word, and have discursed on thy manifold blessings. May these things find a loving place in our hearts and serve to draw our souls towards Thee.
>
> Save us, O Father, from lust, wrath, greed, worldly attachment and pride; and keep us always attached to Thy feet.
>
> Grant to Thy Sikhs the gift of Sikhism, the gift of the Name, the gift of Faith, the gift of confidence in Thee, and the gift of reading and understanding Thy holy Word.
>
> O kind Father, loving Father, through thy mercy we have spent the night in peace and happiness; may Thy grace extend to our labours of the days too, so that we may, according to Thy will, do what is right. (*The Sikh Prayer*)[62]

We should set these thoughts from the devotional tradition within the context of Sikh theology. Happily, we have a fine, concise statement of Sikh belief from a Sikh theologian now living in Britain. This is to be found in a book with the appalling title, *Comparative Religions* (since there is no such entity as a single 'comparative religion' it is the grossest of solecisms to use a plural form!).[63] Let us set out some of the key expressions of the *Adi Granth*[64] as Piara Singh Sambhi selects them: 'My God is one, brethren, my God is one' (AG 350); 'This alone is his merit that there is none like him, there never was, nor will there be another' (AG 349); 'There is no place to go except God and he is but one' (AG 349). Piara Singh Sambhi points to a practice which runs through the writings of the Sikh Gurus when he comments on their use of many of the names of God current in their own times among Muslims, Hindus and followers of yogic ways. Guru Nanak favoured the term *Sat Nam* – 'Eternal Reality'; among contemporary Sikhs *Waheguru* – 'Wonderful Lord' is perhaps the most popular divine name. But the Sikh teaching is clear:

> Your names are countless, O Lord, I do not know their end, but of one thing I am sure, that there is not another like you. (AG 87)

God as 'Eternal Reality' is the gracious one, who hears prayer: 'Whoever cries out and begs at the Lord's door is blessed' (AG 349). Indeed as Piara Singh Sambhi stresses, this is a religion of grace. The message is 'evangelistic', a telling of good news. Thus Owen Cole interprets the calling of Guru Nanak as a 'deeply transforming experience, which resulted in the consciousness of being chosen to undertake the mission of revealing the message of God's name to the world'.[65] Owen Cole quotes both the *Janam Sakhi* narrative and one of Guru Nanak's hymns in support of this view. In the first of these, Guru Nanak explained that he had been taken to God's court and escorted into the divine presence. He was given a cup of nectar (*amrit*) and was told to drink it with the words 'This is the cup of adoration of God's name. Drink it. I am with you. I will bless you and I raise you up. Whoever remembers you will enjoy my favour. Go, rejoice in my name and teach others to do so. I have bestowed the gift of my calling upon you. Let this be your calling.'[66] So in the Adi Granth there is this hymn:

> I was a minstrel out of work,
> The Lord gave me employment.
> The Mighty One instructed me,
> 'Sing my praise, night and day'.
>
> The Lord summoned the minstrel
> To his high court.
> On me he bestowed the role
> of honouring him and singing his praise.
>
> On me he bestowed the nectar in a cup
> The nectar of his true and holy name.
> Those who at the bidding of the Guru
> Feast and take their fill of the Lord's holiness,
> Attain peace and joy.
> Your minstrel spreads your glory

> By singing your word.
> Nanak, through adoring the truth
> We attain to the all-highest. (AG 150)

A Christian theology of religion has surely to ask itself where the Word was when Guru Nanak had this experience. But even more precisely in this context, we have to ask, in the light of John 14.6 not only where the Word was in this experience, but what the Word has revealed of the grace and love of the 'Father'. Are we Christians to say that Nanak and the Sikh saints have not 'come to the Father'?

Before we leave the Sikh experience of God, it is worth perhaps pointing out that contemporary Sikhs do affirm that their faith is in the fatherhood of God. Thus N. S. Dhillon sets out in his *Practical Sikhism* ten central beliefs of Sikhism of which the first two are the Uniqueness and One-ness of God, and the Fatherhood of God for all alike.[67] '"The Fatherhood of God and the brotherhood of man" is one of the main themes of Guru Nanak's message' says Mrs Manjeet Kaur McCormack in her widely used *An Introduction to Sikh Belief*.[68]

(b) The Indian BHAKTI traditions

We have already noted the three Hindu paths *jnāna marga*, *karma marga* and *bhakti marga*. The last of these has been called 'India's religion of grace'.[69] In following this way, the emphasis is on loving devotion and self-surrender as the path to union with God. In Paul Clasper's words, it is 'the response of love to the Great Lover'.[70] As one aspect of the teaching of the *Bhagavad-Gita*, it is the reason why this work has become 'the most famous Hindu poem and scripture'. From Geoffrey Parrinder's verse translation we quote the following stanzas:

> Thou Father of the world, of motionless
> or moving things, dear teacher whom we bless
> in all the worlds no other equals thee
> none greater, unexcelled in mightiness.
>
> And to my prostrate body bending low,
> O Lord adorable, thy grace bestow
> As father bears with son, as friend with friend
> As lover with beloved, God's mercy show![71]

The worshipper or *bhakta* is to

> Go to him alone for refuge
> With all your being, by his grace
> You will attain the highest place
> And his eternal resting place.[72]

The promise to the worshipper is

> Show love to me, bear me in mind
> Offer me worship and revere.
> I promise you you will come to me
> Because to me you are so dear.
>
> Abandoning all things of law
> to me you must repair
> from every evil ever more
> I shall release you, have in care.[73]

How these words came to be understood across the centuries of India's spiritual searchings I have no need to detail. Again we may choose some poems from the *bhakti* tradition which seem to indicate not only a searching, but also a finding or a '*being found*'.[74] So some stanzas from representative poets, chosen for the most part from that remarkable collection of Indian devotional literature called *Temple Bells*, and edited by A. J. Appasamy.[75] First from Tukaram (1608–49)

> How merciful He is! In those who are helpless
>   He feels His chief delight
> He bears their burden on His head; He undertakes
>   the care of acquiring and keeping for them.
> He suffers them not to stray from the path, He takes
>   them by the hand and leads them.
> Tuka says, This is the reward if you follow him
>   with absolute devotion.[76]

From Tukaram again

> I proclaim these tidings, since I have power to do so; we are Thy children by loving service; we speak the language of close affection.
> By dwelling close to Thee we shall do away with doubt and fear.
> Tuka says, There is a genuine taste here: how can we go away.[77]

And Tukaram's 'casting his burdens on the Lord':

> No deeds I've done nor thoughts I've thought
> Save as Thy servant I am nought.
> Guard me O God, and O control
> The tumult of my restless soul
> Ah do not, do not cast on me
> The guilt of mine iniquity.
> My countless sins, I, Tuka, say
> Upon Thy loving heart I lay.[78]

Tukaram was from Maharashtra. Dadudayal (1601–1660) came from Gujarat and this verse bears the same marks of filiality and insight into unworthiness and the need of gracious love and mercy:

> Evils without number, countless vices are within me
> Many stains within me
> Not a single good deed have I done
> No virtue is there in me; no merit is mine:
> Yet forsake not thy sinful child, for without thee
> where is my refuge?
> Desire, pride and anger have misled me since my birth:
> O miserable man that I am!
> Thou only art my help: Father wash me with the nectar
> of Thy rich forgiveness and heal the mind that is sore.[79]

I will not go further at this point except to say that this poetic tradition continues to our own times. Many Westerners have discovered, for example, the work of Rabindranath Tagore, whose *Gitanjali*, or Song Offerings, have been through many editions since they were first published in 1912.[80] Since many of the Hindu people now living in the United Kingdom are nurtured in this *bhakti* tradition, it is, as I noted in the case of the first visits by Christians to the synagogue, something of a surprise for people when they make their first visit to a Hindu temple in this country to discover this form of worship and devotion. Instead of finding gross idolatry and superstition, as they supposed, they come face to face with people who in some true sense have 'come to the Father'.

(c) The 'Father' in African traditional religion

The religious patterns of India are diverse enough in all conscience, and we Westerners do ourselves no service in labelling them all 'Hinduism'. But as we turn to Africa we find an even more complex situation. Because there are very few written records Africa has happily been spared the systematizing process that took place in the study and library of the nineteenth-century Orientalist. We have no artificial intellectual construction called Africanism.[81] Nevertheless we are discovering in these days how much of the ancient tradition of Africa is still available to us, thanks to the devoted work mainly of Africans themselves.[82] We can trace the footsteps of God in that great continent where he has never left himself without witness (Acts 14.17). In these brief paragraphs I call attention to a widespread African awareness of the Fatherhood/Motherhood of God. In this I am indebted to the Kenyan scholar John S. Mbiti's *The Prayers of African Religion*.[83] Just four examples will suffice:

> Our Father, it is thy universe, it is thy will, let us be at peace, let the souls of the people be cool; thou art our Father, remove all evil from our path.[84]

> O my Father, great Elder, I have no words to thank you, but with your deep wisdom I am sure you can see how much I prize your glorious gifts. O my Father, when I look upon your greatness I am confounded with awe. O great Elder, ruler of all things both in heaven and upon earth I am your warrior, and I am ready to act in accordance to your will.[85]

> O Mawu Sodza (God) Mother of men, Mother of beasts. If thou givest to man, thou givest truly. If thou deniest to man thou deniest truly. In thy greatness I am great, and I agree to thy will.[86]

> God has turned his back on us
> The words of men have made him wrathful
> And yet he will turn about again
> God has turned his back on us.
>
> We are the children of our Maker
> And do not fear that he will kill us
> We are the children of God
> And do not fear that he will kill.
>
> How, in the time of deprivation,
> Will the people live?
> In the time of deprivation
> I will not fear
> Because I have prayed and prayed
> The word of the Lord will not be mocked
> His good word will ever keep thee.[87]

In these last words we overhear an act of faith akin to that great moment in the prophet Habakkuk where he says:

> Though the fig tree does not blossom
>   nor fruit be upon the vines,
> the produce of the olive fail
>   and the field yield no food

> the flock be cut off from the fold
> and there be no herd in the stalls
> yet will I rejoice in the Lord,
> I will rejoice in the God of my salvation.
>
> (Hab. 3.17–19)

Despite everything God, as John Mbiti says, 'remains true, loving, ever ready to forgive and help the people who are his children'.[88] As one who has worked as a Christian missionary in Africa, and, like many others, has learnt from the people amongst whom I was so much about the love of God and his ways with his children, I am still constrained to wonder how near they had already 'come to the Father' before they ever heard the message of Jesus. I asked then, and still ask (aware that there is a positive answer, though not an easy one): What have Western missionaries to learn rather than to teach in the presence of these 'manifestations' of the Word in Africa? It was this experience too that set me to thinking about how it could be God had spoken to the African peoples, and how indeed he had already received and accepted them within his fatherly/motherly heart. How could John 14.6 be still a guiding statement? I needed to turn again to the context of John 14.6 within the total framework of the Fourth Gospel.

4 The Logos by Whom We All Come to the Father

We come now to consider the Johannine teaching embedded in the Prologue to the Fourth Gospel. For just as the immediate context of John 14.6 is the questioning of Thomas, and we have seen that we cannot avoid the implications of that, so we now take note that John 14.6 cannot be taken out of the wider context of John's christology of the Word.

I see no need to add to the vast quantity of ink that has been used up in discussing John 1.1. These sentences of Raymond Brown are adequate to express the two major thrusts of the first words of the Prologue: 'The Prologue is a description of the history of salvation in hymnic form, much as Ps. LXXVIII is a poetic description of the history of Israel. Therefore the emphasis is primarily on God's relation to men, rather than on God in Himself.' Brown goes on: 'The Prologue says the Word was; it does not speculate how the Word was, for not the origins of the Word, but what the Word does is important.'[89]

In this hymn of salvation the Word plays a central role in both creation and redemption. All that is created is ultimately related to the Word, for it was created not only through him but in him (v. 3). The Word is not just instrumental in the creative process, but is also the principle in and through which everything coheres. This appears to be the teaching not only of the Johannine Prologue but also of Colossians 1.15–19. 'For in him all things were created . . . all things were created and for him. He is before all things, and in him all things hold together.'[90]

The Word's role in both creation and redemption is stressed again in v. 4. In the Word was life. Here the Greek word is *zoē* which is used elsewhere in the Fourth Gospel, exclusively for the concept of 'eternal life'. This life, says the Prologue, was the light of all men.[91] Here we come to the interpretative crux. On the one hand some scholars have noted that the gift of eternal life is associated only with the coming of Jesus (John 3.1; 5.40; 10.10). On the other hand to others it appears that the jump from speaking of the role of the *Logos* in the relation to the whole of creation to the specific mission of Jesus is far too abrupt. They also think that if vv. 4–5 refer to Jesus then the explicit references to the coming of Jesus would seem tautological. Thus Raymond Brown, for one, stands over against the Jesus-centred interpretation of these verses of scholars like Rudolph Bultmann and Ernst Käsemann. It is a matter of great importance how we read the text here, for on our reading depends our acceptance or rejection of the kind of inclusive christology for which I am arguing. In particular it seems the judgment we will make is itself dependent on what we understand to be John's purposes in writing the Gospel. I, for one, would read it as supremely a missionary document, one which sets out to open up a dialogue, and not to foreclose on the essential discussion of the role of Jesus in the universal salvation history. Let me make this clear by calling attention to the process of missionary communication as described by A. C. Bouquet:

> He [sc., the missionary] will begin by recognizing that if [his hearers] have enough serious purpose in them to want to talk about religion, or to listen to what he has to say about Christ, they have already within them encountered the Divine *Logos*, though perhaps unconsciously, have been found by Him, and have been moved by Him to take some step towards further knowledge and towards a deeper and more explicit relationship. This is perhaps what C. F. Andrews meant when he was asked how he approached earnest Hindus, and answered: 'I always take it for granted that

they are Christians, and as I talk to them, I often see the light of Christ come into their eyes'.[92]

Alan Bouquet comments in the same chapter that it is 'incredible how rarely commentators on the Fourth Gospel allow themselves to ask: "What did its author hope and expect that its readers would understand from it?" and goes on to add that it is inconceivable that he should have begun his work with a prologue which, dependent as it is upon the introduction of the technical term *Logos*, uses that term in a private sense completely misleading to his readers'.[93] One at least of the greatest commentators on the Fourth Gospel may be acquitted of such a charge, for he is clear that we have a missionary document rather than a work of dogmatic theology in our hands. C. H. Dodd writes that if we try to enter into the author's intention,

> it must surely appear that he is thinking in the first place, not so much of Christians who need a deeper theology, as of non-Christians who are concerned about eternal life and the way to it, and may be ready to follow the Christian way if this is presented to them in terms that are intelligibly related to their previous religious interests and experience.[94]

It is for that reason that those concerned with the theology of mission are most likely to see the first verse of the Prologue as speaking of the Universal Word at work everywhere.[95] The function of the *Logos* is to bring life and light to the world. All human creatures are within range of that light, however great the darkness, and in principle the light is stronger than the darkness. This *Logos* is the true light that lightens every man that comes into the world, v. 9. That light is the light of revelation.

It is therefore in my view not only perfectly proper but also quite essential to an adequate theological response to the discovery of 'truth', 'revelation', 'faith' and 'love' outside the Christian community to invoke the *Logos* doctrine, and in this way to speak of an inclusive christology.

That this is no new departure for Christian thinking may be established by a quick look at the writings of Justin Martyr and Clement of Alexandria. If we reflect upon the theological necessities that led them to write in this way, we will find light shed upon our own situation. For what they needed above all else was a 'salvation-history' which was concerned with the whole experience of human kind. Justin and Clement were seeking to affirm that God has always been at work. This was essential to their task of showing good reasons why people should give up the customs of their ancestors and adopt a new religion.

Formidable opponents of Christianity, like Porphyry and Celsus objected to the Christian position on the grounds that it was an upstart doctrine, a Johnny-come-lately religion with a vulgarly new theology. So we find the first argument employed by the second and third century writers was to insist that Moses and the Pentateuch are older than the Greek philosophers and that in fact Greek religion is indebted to them for much of its teaching. So we have the strenuous, if not strained, efforts in Clement of Alexandria (*Stromateis*, Book I, ch. 20) as with Tertullian (*Apology*, ch. 47) and Theophilus (*Ad Autolycum*) to prove the priority of Christian doctrine. With such a course of argument we are not concerned. But we have also their second line of interpretation, namely that the Word was in the world before Christ, though not in the same manner. It is this same *Logos* by whom the ancient sages were illuminated:

> Christ is the first-begotten of God . . . He is the Word in whom the whole human race shares. Those who live according to the light of their knowledge are Christians, even though they be considered godless.[96]

> . . . for whatever law-givers or philosophers uttered well, they elaborated by finding and contemplating some part of the Word.[97]

> I confess that I boast and with all my strength strive to be found a Christian, not because the doctrines of Plato are different from those of Christ, but because they are not in all respects similar, as are neither those of the other Stoics, poets and historians. For each man spoke well in proportion to the share he had of the seminal Word.[98]

> For not only among the Greeks did reason (*Logos*) prevail to condemn these things through Socrates, but also among the barbarians they were condemned by the Logos who took shape and became man and was called Jesus Christ.[99]

These four quotations are from Justin Martyr, the earliest of the Apologists to use these *Logos* doctrines for his missionary purposes. A more refined and sophisticated use of the *Logos* teaching is to be found in Clement of Alexandria, whose work it was to vindicate the alliance between the world of Greek philosophy and the new religion:

God was the giver of Greek philosophy to the Greeks by which the Almighty is glorified among the Greeks.[100]

Should any one say that it was through human understanding that philosophy was discovered by the Greeks, I find the Scripture saying that understanding is sent by God.[101]

By reflection and direct vision those among the Greeks who have philosophized accurately see God.[102]

In the whole universe all the parts, though differing one from another, preserve their relation to the whole. So then the barbarian (Jewish) and Hellenic philosophy has torn off a fragment of eternal truth from the theology of the ever-living Word. And he who brings together again the separate fragments and makes them one will, without peril, contemplate the perfect Word, the truth.[103]

Justin and Clement were both seeking a way of affirming the continuity of the Christian revelation with the rest of human experience. That is indeed one way of describing what we need, too. But note that this cannot be done in some broad and undefined way by which we abandon the particularities of the Christian tradition; the sense that in Jesus's teaching we have something that Plato did not teach, a 'revelation of the Father' with all the implications of that revelation declared once and for all in the cross and resurrection.

Similar motivations as impelled Justin and Clement lie behind one near classic contemporary exposition of christological doctrine that we have already noticed, Norman Pittenger's *The Word Incarnate*. We have seen how Pittenger wrestles in this work with the nearly two thousand year old question as to how we may speak of God's being in Christ, even though ultimately we can never solve this problem of how Jesus may be both 'perfectly man' and 'perfectly God'.

I find Pittenger's work is even more valuable in its constant attempts to explain how we can affirm that Jesus is not merely an outstanding religious teacher who saw further into the mind and purposes of God than, say, the Buddha or Confucius or Muhammad, but that, to use the words of another writer, 'He is the chosen means of the self-communication of God the Word, and hence his cross (climax of his life and passion) is the form under which we apprehend the suffering of God'.[104]

Pittenger argues the case for an explicit Logos-christology. On the one side there is his (and the Christian tradition's) central conviction that Jesus is man alongside us, a truly human being. Therefore he is constrained to say that 'the difference between us and all other instances of divine operation is of immeasurable degree, not of absolute kind'.[105] The *Logos* doctrine is of enormous value here, for he believes that all other forms of christological expression 'never really make our Lord other than a catastrophic and irrational intrusion into a world from which in any genuinely significant sense God is taken to be absent'.[106]

Here we are taken into Pittenger's other great concern: that we shall in our communication of the meaning of our faith in the contemporary world be able to speak of a 'salvation-history' which includes the whole cosmos – not only this world, but also all possible worlds.[107] How may we speak of the relationship of God to all this if we are limited to the 'inevitable but somewhat excessive Christocentrism' of practical Christian faith. By invoking the *Logos* doctrine Pittenger hopes to obviate 'the tendency to move over into a "Jesus-centrism" in which the human life lived in Palestine is thought to exhaust the possibility of knowledge of God and relationship to him'. It is for this reason that he states so clearly: 'But Christian theology does not see Jesus's significance in this fashion. He is the incarnation of the Eternal Word, God the Son "made flesh". Hence he who is incarnate in the man Jesus Christ is the second "Person" of the Holy Trinity; and it is this "Person" who is ultimately the Lord and Saviour, incarnate in Palestine in the first century of our era, but neither exhausted by or confined to that action'.[108]

'Neither exhausted by or confined to that action' is Pittenger's vivid but careful way of indicating that we may expect to be able to find 'disclosures' or 'manifestations' of the Word outside the Christian community of faith; as well as in other religious traditions as in the natural world, in human history, in music, literature, the fine arts and in philosophy; as well in scientific discovery as in the depths of the human imagination.

The Eternal Word is everywhere at work, creatively and redeemingly. He subsists eternally in God. He is that *hypostasis* in the Godhead who goes forth in creation, in revelation and redemption. As God in his self-communication, or in Pittenger's phrase 'the self-expressive agency of Godhead' it is *he*, not Jesus, who pre-exists.[109]

That this is the essential Christian orthodoxy should in fact need no belabouring, however much piety has led Christians into what variously has been called Jesuolatry, Christomonism or Unitarianism of the Second Person of the Trinity. It must be clear to everyone upon a moment's thought that there could never be pre-existence of the human mind, ego, self or personality of anyone who truly shares our human nature. This would fly in the face of everything we know about the development of the human psyche. Careful Christian theologians have never suggested anything else. Here, however widely they may diverge in other respects, William Temple and John Hick are at one. First of all, from William Temple, in his widely used *Readings in St John's Gospel*:

> From the beginning the divine light has shone. Always it was coming into the world; always it enlightened every man alive in his reason and conscience. Every check on animal lust felt by the primitive savage, every stimulation to a nobler life, is God self-revealed within his soul. But God in self-revelation is the Divine Word, for precisely this is what that term means. What is constituted within that divine self-communication, as one element composing it, is the energy of Life; this is what urges all kinds of living things forward in their evolution; and this is what is fully and perfectly expressed in Christ. So it may truly be said that the conscience of the heathen man is the voice of Christ within him – though muffled by his ignorance. All that is noble in the non-christian systems of thought, or conduct, or worship is the work of Christ upon them and within them. By the Word of God – that is to say, by Jesus Christ – Isaiah, and Plato, and Zoroaster, and Buddha, and Confucius conceived and uttered such truths as they declared. There is only one divine light; and every man in his measure is enlightened by it.[110]

Even here William Temple's language, the language which comes naturally to the believing Christian, might slightly mislead us. Can it really be by '*Jesus Christ*' that Isaiah and the rest spoke. Does Temple secretly think of the pre-existence of Jesus? Elsewhere he makes it plain that he cannot mean this. In his *Christus Veritas* he wrote of the purpose of the divine act of incarnation:

> That purpose would seem to be twofold – Revelation and Atonement. For the former, what is necessary is that Jesus Christ should be truly God and truly Man; for the latter what seems to be necessary is that human experience as conditioned by the sin of men should become the personal experience of God the Son – not as an object of external observation but of inward feeling (to use the language of human consciousness). Neither of these requires that God the Son should be active only in Jesus of Nazareth during the days of the Incarnation. 'The light that lighteneth every man' did not cease to do so when He shone in full brilliance in one human life. Jesus did not control affairs in Mars, or in China. But God the

Son, who is the Word of God by whom, as agent, all things came to be and apart from whom no single thing has come to be, without ceasing His creative and sustaining work, added this to it, that he became flesh and dwelt as in a tabernacle among us. . . . [111]

From quite another tradition, we have John Hick's carefully worded statement, which takes into account what may be said in the light both of recent theological and philosophical thought and the new awarenesses of religious pluralism:

All salvation – that is, all creating of human animals into the children of God – is the work of God. The different religions have their different names for God acting savingly towards mankind. Christianity has several overlapping names for this – the eternal Logos, the cosmic Christ, the Second Person of the Trinity, God the Son, the Spirit. If selecting from our Christian language, we call God-acting-towards-mankind the Logos, then we must say that *all* salvation, within all religions, is the work of the Logos, and that under their various images and symbols men in different cultures and faiths may encounter the Logos and find salvation. But what we cannot say is that all who are saved are saved solely and exclusively by Jesus of Nazareth. The life of Jesus was one point at which the Logos – that is God-in-relation-to-man – has acted; and it is the only point that savingly concerns the Christian; but we are not called upon nor are we entitled to make the negative assertion that the Logos has not acted and is not acting anywhere else in human life. On the contrary, we should gladly acknowledge that Ultimate Reality has affected human consciousness for its libera-tion or 'salvation' in various ways within the Indian, the semitic, the Chinese, the African . . . forms of life. [112]

The clarity of these statements from Temple and Hick is splendid, which does not mean that we are bound to agree with either of them in every point of detail, nor perhaps even with their underlying philosophical presuppositions (note the expression 'evolution' in Temple, and 'Ultimate Reality' in Hick). What both of them do for our argument is to indicate how *Logos* christology make sense as a means of describing God's working in all human lives: 'every stimulation to a nobler life', 'all creating of human animals into the children of God' is the working of the *Logos*.

But two important matters still remain to be discussed. The first is the human resistance to the *Logos*, what the Fourth Gospel points to when it says that the 'Light shines in the darkness'. For we are not to be either simplistic or naive about the world of religions. Religion as a human phenomenon is deeply ambiguous. Darkness can masquerade as light. Much in all the world's cumulative religious traditions has enslaved men and women's minds, distorted their perceptions of reality, corrupted their wills and hardened their hearts against their neighbours. People have put their trust in things that cannot save. Even mystical experience has often been a snare and a delusion. Fanaticism and bigotry stain and mar all religious traditions, and there is a profound sense in which we must admit that even Christianity as we have known it up to now can be called no more than the 'greatest of the non-Christian religions'. The 'measure of Christ' is applied to us all through the focussing of all that God means in the human life of Jesus of Nazareth.[113] He, to use the Fourth Gospel's language, is 'the only begotten of the Father' and as such the *exegesis* of God. In the face of all our human distortions of religion, we have the words of the Johannine Christ: 'No one has ascended into heaven, but the Son of Man who came down from heaven' (John 3.13). C. K. Barrett stresses that the Johannine understanding is that Christ 'alone is the link between God and man (cf. 1.15) and there is no access to God independent of him'.[114] We take this with deep seriousness: the way of Jesus's life and ministry led to conflict and criticism, crisis and judgment. Of course it did. The way to God is not as men and women often, in their foolishness and private 'darknesses', vainly imagine. Their images and conceptions of God are not infrequently far from the reality that Jesus declares. I would not want any of us to be unclear about that.

But the burden of the whole of this chapter has not been the problem of human wickedness and superstition, but rather – its corollary – the problem of human goodness and faith; how do we say yes to all that and affirm that 'the light shines in the darkness and the darkness has not overcome it' (John 1.5)?[115] To the insistent and inevitable questions that press in upon us as we contemplate the good and generous faith of other men and women who follow other 'ways' and 'paths' I believe we can respond only with joyful affirmation. We may speak ourselves with good and generous faith as we recognize the 'coming to the Father' of those who stand outside the Christian tradition. We must respond with grace and gratitude to the presence of truth and wisdom in the other religious traditions of humankind. For this kind of joyful affirmation, it seems to me a Logos christology like the one outlined here is vitally necessary.

We conclude then with one last reflection. If it truly is the case that all human beings are created in and through the eternal Word, the *Logos*, we can hardly suppose that it can be the view of the author of the Fourth

Gospel that because the Word has become flesh and lived among us, that primary relationship has come to an end. On the contrary, the argument must surely be 'how much the more' are all human beings likely to be related to God through that One who is now risen and ascended. Here we should use scripture to interpret scripture and notice the force of Ephesians 4.10: 'In saying, he ascended, what does this mean but that he had also descended into the lower parts of the earth? He who descended is He who also ascended far above all the heavens that He might fill all things'. We may understand John 3.13 and 1.51 (the verses cited by C. K. Barrett) in the light of these words. The risen and ascended Christ stands in direct relationship to all things.[116] Therefore we affirm that 'he alone is the link between God and man' remains true. Therefore, also we may go still further in expressing the conviction that there have been, that there are, and that there will be men and women whose prayers and actions are moulded by other religious traditions who are not only touched by, illuminated by the *Logos*, but who in their response actually 'come to the Father' through the One who is risen and ascended and fills all things, who is the link between God and humankind.

Thus I have tried to set out four ways of responding to the challenge that questioners imply when they set before me the words of John 14.6. In none of these four responses have I sought to explain these words away. Rather I have suggested that they have massive importance for our relationships with people of other religious faith, and that indeed they open up to us the possibilities of owning a rich and profound christology for religious pluralism. Which of these four emphases is the most valuable and the most worthwhile to pursue I leave to the reader to decide.

5 *There is No Other Name*

A similar process of exegesis and interpretation might be engaged upon with regard to the other much-quoted 'exclusivist' text, that of Acts 4.12 with its affirmation that there is no other name given by which we may be saved. In fact though the Lucan context is not so rich in connotation as that of the Fourth Gospel, and yields less profound material for reflection. But I think it important not to ignore it now lest I be charged with avoiding its 'plain' import as a conversation-stopper or deterrent to dialogue, and, more important, fail to point out its potentialities as we go further into establishing an adequate basis for the theology of religion in our time.

Lifted out of its context Acts 4.12 is a very formidable statement indeed. Salvation is uniquely through Christ. There is no other possibility. But our very first question must be about the context of this pronouncement by St Peter. Does it allow us to build up the universal dogma that no non-Christian has any hope for salvation?

Reading the whole narrative in chapters 3 and 4, we notice first of all that these words are the climax to a series of events arising out of a healing miracle. Peter has said to a man lame from his birth, 'in the name of Jesus Christ of Nazareth, walk' (Acts 3.6). In 4.9 he is still discussing with the Jewish authorities 'this good deed done to a cripple', and 'by what means this man has been healed'. Here we must take some notice of the Greek words used. In verse 9 it is *sesōstai*, healed. In 4.12 two other forms of the same root are employed: the noun *sōtēria*, healing, as well as salvation, and the passive infinite form *sōthenai* of the verb *sōzō*, to heal, make whole, save. All English translations have problems with these words – see for a striking example the various renderings of Luke 8.48: 'your faith has made you well' (RSV) 'your faith has cured you' (NEB), 'your faith has healed you' (J. B. Phillips) 'thy faith hath made thee whole' (AV and RV). It could also be 'your faith has saved you'! In the light of all this and given the healing context perhaps there is a case for translating 4.12 as 'there is no healing in any one else at all . . . there is no other name . . . by which we must be healed'. Of course the usual translation is the most likely, and healing is in any case an aspect of salvation, but clearly there must be some doubt whether there are enough grounds here to deduce an exclusive doctrine about who is ultimately acceptable to God.

Further close inspection of the textual evidence confirms that in any case St Peter is not making a general statement of universal validity but is appealing to the Jewish leaders that such a healing is reason for them to accept their Messiah. As Geoffrey Lampe wrote 'these words should be read in the proper context of Luke's reconstruction of the anti-Jewish polemic of the early church and not generalized beyond that context'.[117]

But as with John 14.6 there could remain something positively helpful for us for the dialogue with people of other faiths, were we to reflect further on Acts 4.12. Even if it is not available to answer questions we may put to it about the exclusiveness of Jesus as the bearer of salvation, there is clearly in it a centring upon Jesus and no Christian faith can avoid that, and still remain Christian. 'For Christian faith "Jesus" is the name by which the nature and activity of God is fully revealed. His name is the saving name because it affords the means by which human beings share in the grace and love that is the nature of God himself'.[118] This is truly said, and it is this that we would most want to share with our partners in dialogue. But our knowing this does not preclude the possibility that the grace and love which Jesus represents for us might be found under the names of the other religious traditions. Indeed, rather than pointing to an exclusiveness, Acts 4.12 might help us to think of ways in which the grace and love of God operate in the world without being named at all. The humility and 'un-knownness' of Jesus in his early life may point to a 'humility' and 'un-knownness' in the activity of God now in our own world. Only in this pattern, which for us bears the name of Jesus, is there healing, wholeness, salvation for the world: only in this way can any of us be saved. There is no other name given under heaven . . .

⌐6⌐

The New Relationship: The Way We Behave in Inter-Religious Dialogue

If Christians are able to look forward to a future in which they will be able to contemplate a plurality of religious traditions as within the gracious purposes of God, and more than that, to affirm God's gracious presence within people of other faith they will need some kind of theology like that outlined in the last chapters. But with such an understanding, they will be able to approach men and women of other religious paths without undue anxieties lest, not having been converted to belief in Jesus Christ in this life, the latter should be lost eternally. Our whole intention then in setting out the visions of a pluralist religious eschatology and especially an inclusivist christology is to make it possible for Christians to behave with a new freedom in the light of their understanding of Jesus Christ. We have argued that such an openness towards others is part of the obedience of faith in one whom we confess to be the Way, the Truth and the Life in the ways we have tried to outline in the last chapter. Our participation as Christians in inter-faith encounter will depend upon an understanding of God's purposes which allows us to be both open and honest, vulnerable and yet committed, and, in the words of the Fourth Gospel, 'to do the truth' in our time.

We turn now to the practical implications of this doing of the truth in the light of these understandings, first of all in the ethics of our inter-faith relationships, and then in the new forms of spirituality towards which we are called to move. Insights into both the ethical and spiritual issues that are raised will come from both within and from outside the Christian tradition, and from the rapidly increasing stores of experience that we and people of other traditions are gaining as we meet one another in new and profounder ways. In this chapter we begin to reflect on the ethical questions – the practical ground rules for our behaviour towards one another – and then we shall try to set, however tentatively and precariously, these ethical matters within a framework of prayer and spirituality, of faith and love.

'Begin to reflect' are words chosen advisedly, for though an enormous literature already exists on the theory of interfaith dialogue, and on the theology of religions, surprisingly little attention has been given to ethical questions in this encounter. The material we do have falls under one of four heads. There is a vast amount of writing on the rightness or wrongness of entering into the 'dialogue relationship' (whatever that is conceived to be) from confessional standpoints.[1] Such injunctions, either to embrace or to refrain from embracing the way of dialogue, are based, for Christians as for others (although they would not use the terminology), on considerations of systematic theology, the theology of mission and the theology of religion. That is why we have spent so much time on these in this book.

Under the second head, we may put such writing and reflection that deals with ethical questions which themselves form part of the content and subject matter of interfaith dialogue. To be sure, such literature very often contains both implicitly and explicitly profound insight into the ethical considerations which must govern right relationships between the religious communities, and we shall refer to such insight in this kind of writing several times in the course of this chapter. But in general ethicists and moral theologians have not themselves turned their full attention to inter-religious ethics as such.[2]

In the third category is the kind of writing which portrays actual inter-faith encounter.[3] This descriptive writing may so to speak come from 'within' and be personal stories of deepening relationships and enrichments. It may be story-telling about the situations and experiences of other people and groups. There is much sensitive material of both these kinds. Of its nature the ethical content is very considerable but as yet remains the raw material of the ethicists' reflection.

The fourth category is that of the burgeoning *genre* called 'Guide-lines'.[4] These are attempts by responsible groups within the faith-communities to set the rules of the game for those who wish to take part in this new activity. Very often such documents are in the nature of efforts to set down the parameters within which the new dialogue is permissible, with the strong suggestion that there are boundaries over which participants in such relationships may not go, thresholds which may not be crossed.[5] So they shade over into the first category, and should then be considered by those concerned with confessional theologies. Nevertheless, for our purposes this last category will provide us with basic material which may be discussed from the points of view of both descriptive and prescriptive ethics. At the same time we will be constantly reflecting upon how this 'Guideline' material is consonant with the ethical considerations in the other types of writing.

1 'Guidelines on Dialogue'

Guidelines on Dialogue between people of different faiths now come from all around the world and often reflect quite different situations. Very often they are what is called 'bilateral' in their scope, referring to what should happen between Christians and Jews or Christians and Muslims, or Muslims and Jews. We must hope that somewhere some scholar is monitoring all this material.[6] Other sets of Guidelines are 'multi-lateral' and refer rather more to the general principles involved in inter-religious encounter. For our purposes there are three sets of guidelines of the multi-lateral type: the *Guidelines on Dialogue with People of Living Faiths and Ideologies*, of the World Council of Churches (1979); the British Council of Churches' *Relations with People of Other Faiths: Guidelines on Dialogue in Britain* (1981); and, from the hands of one individual, 'The Rules of the Game' in Raimundo Panikkar's *The Intrareligious Dialogue* (1978).

I choose Panikkar's 'The Rules of the Game' for two reasons. Panikkar himself is a figure of extraordinary stature in contemporary inter-religious encounter. For him much of this encounter is within his own being, for he was born into two of the major traditions, the Roman Catholic and the Hindu. He described himself once, when someone said he was half Spanish, half Indian as 'fully Spanish, fully Indian'. He is reputed to be a difficult writer and indeed he does think in a most condensed way. But the major cause of the difficulty often seems his ability to think in no less than (and probably more than) four languages, and therefore through language to live at home in the religious traditions and cultures of which these languages are the vehicles. Out of this range of experience he has written some thirty books on inter-faith relations, or as he would prefer 'intrareligious dialogue', most of which are not translated into English.[7] The first reason is therefore his personal authority. Alongside this we set his being Roman Catholic. We have not yet so far a document from the Vatican which is exactly equivalent to the WCC *Guidelines*, but it would be grossly misleading to treat the ethics of inter-religious relationships as though the Roman Catholic church had not made some decisive contributions in inter-faith activity. The great Vatican II statements *Nostra Aetate* and *Lumen Gentium* are not in themselves formal guidelines for inter-faith relationships, but Panikkar's 'Rules' serve to make explicit what is often implicit. Panikkar's statement (despite his alleged 'difficulty') offers powerful descriptive and proscriptive ethical rules which deserve close attention.

The WCC *Guidelines* on the other hand bear all the marks of corporate thinking, the 'camel a horse designed by a committee' syndrome. A word about their provenance is therefore necessary. The WCC has had a Sub Unit on Dialogue with People of Living Faiths and Ideologies since 1971. In its earliest years this Sub Unit, (now known as the Dialogue Sub Unit but previously called the DFI) was much extended in the organization of high-level international encounters between leaders of world faith communities. No doubt these early ventures were open to the charge of élitism, and in fact they aroused a good deal of suspicion about the purposes of such dialogue. Was it to shape a new world religion? To eliminate religious differences? To engage in conscious or unconscious syncretism? To offer a substitute for mission and evangelism? The Nairobi 1975 Assembly of the WCC had an unsatisfactory and inconclusive debate on these matters and at this point the DFI programme nearly foundered altogether. It was therefore with a renewed sense of purpose that member churches sent their representatives to the DFI Consultation at Chiang Mai, Thailand, in 1977. This gathering produced a new statement entitled *Dialogue in Community*, and much of this material is incorporated into the WCC *Guidelines*. While one can take *Dialogue in Community* as representing an advance in ecumenical understanding of inter-faith dialogue across several fronts, for our purpose it is sufficient to note the new emphasis in the title: dialogue is 'in community', that is, where there are existing inter-religious or pluralist communities, and that these specific encounters take place in a world which is made up of communities, 'a community of communities'. This focus is ethical rather than theological, or, to be more precise, the concerns expressed are those of theological ethics rather than of systematic theology. It is this strand in the WCC *Guidelines* that we concentrate on, rather than such matters as 'syncretism' which also gets treated in Section E.[8]

The BCC Guidelines, *Relations with People of Other Faiths*, are dependent upon the WCC *Guidelines* in the sense that they are a deliberate working out for a national context of the WCC themes,[9] and in fact the BCC Committee for Relations with People of Other Faiths distilled from the disparate WCC material what are now called the Four Principles of dialogue:

Dialogue begins when people meet each other
Dialogue depends upon mutual understanding and mutual trust
Dialogue makes it possible to share in service to the community
Dialogue becomes the medium of authentic witness

In the pages which followed the BCC Committee showed itself concerned with prescriptive ethics for the Christian churches in Britain, treating such areas as community relations, pastoral care, religious education, denominational schools, and such issues as inter-faith worship and the sale of and the use of Christian premises to and by people of other faiths.

Since these Four Principles of Dialogue were first published in June 1981, they have been widely studied and in many cases wholeheartedly accepted by church decision-making bodies.[10] At the same time they have been expounded to people of other faiths in Britain who have affirmed that they too can accept them in the light of their own convictions or theologies. This unexpected development is felt to be extraordinarily encouraging, indicating that the 'Four Principles' have a general validity.

It is not therefore a matter of mere convenience if we use the Four Principles to give structure to the following exposition of the ethics of inter-religious dialogue.

2 Dialogue Begins when People Meet Each Other

This principle was derived from the statement in the WCC *Guidelines*: 'Dialogue should proceed in terms of people of other faiths rather than of theoretical impersonal systems' (Para. 20). Such a formulation reflects the concensus of people everywhere involved in constructive inter-religious relationships. This widespread agreement has, however, come to be expressed with varying emphases and we consider these now.

First, there is often a strongly proscriptive element: 'Dialogue', i.e., creative inter-religious encounter is not to be conducted in terms of religious or ideological systems, and this for two reasons.

On the one hand the practice of dialogue has led again and again to the discovery that no one person anywhere is the embodiment or personification of ideas and beliefs that are set out systematically in text books for the convenience of students and other interested

'outsiders'. We are learning not to say to one another: 'as a Marxist
you must believe in x', or 'you Hindus believe in the doctrine of y,
Zaehner says so'. Or even 'The Holy Qur'an says you Muslims
believe in z'. As we meet any given Marxist, or Muslim, or Hindu, we
discover that he or she may or may not, for whatever reason, believe x
or y or z. Deep learning in the history and comparative study of
religions is as much a hindrance as a help in meeting and listening to
actual men and women. The label of the faith or ideology in which
they have been brought up or which they profess is only a first clue to
discerning their rich individuality. It is sound ethical practice to
approach another person with as few presuppositions as possible, and
not to label or stereotype him or her.[11]

Alongside this we must put the experience of practitioners of inter-
religious understanding that to proceed in terms of systems rather
than of individuals is inevitably to enter a *cul-de-sac*. The propositions
of, say, Christian faith and the Islamic revelation are mutually
exclusive. Jesus Christ may not be confessed as Risen Lord if he was
taken up from the cross before he died.[12] Ultimate Reality cannot be
at one and the same time the impersonal Brahman and the God and
Father of our Lord Jesus Christ. Dialectical Materialism is incompat-
ible with theistic belief and so on. World views and religious systems
exclude each other but human beings with their common, everyday
concerns do not. In the words of the BCC *Guidelines*: 'What makes
dialogue between us possible is our common humanity, created in the
image of God. We all experience the joys and sorrows of human life,
we are citizens of one country, we face the same problems, we all live
in God's presence.' The right order of going, therefore, is to enable
ordinary people (including ordinary theologians) to meet each other.
It is almost instantaneously disastrous for future inter-religious
activity to invite the local bishop, the rabbi, the imam and the Hindu
pundit to share the same platform and to discuss religious questions.
This will almost certainly be a debate, not a dialogue. It will close
doors rather than open them.

These two practical considerations are given positive theological
and philosophical grounding in the positions advanced by writers
such as Raimundo Panikkar and Wilfred Cantwell Smith.

Panikkar's 'Rules of the Game' make clear general theoretical
positions discussed in his longer works, notably *Myth, Faith and
Hermeneutics*.[13] Summarizing himself, Panikkar insists: '*The Religious
encounter must be a truly religious one. Anything short of this simply will
not do*' (the italics are his). He sets out some of the consequences of
this prescription of a genuinely religious encounter: 'It must be free

from Particular Apologetics', for 'if the Christian or Buddhist approaches another religious person with the *a priori* idea of defending his own religion by all (obviously honest) means, we shall have a valuable defence of that religion and undoubtedly exciting discussion, but no religious dialogue, no encounter, much less a mutual enrichment and fecundation.' Apologetics has, he says, its proper place but 'we must eliminate any apologetics if we want to meet a person from another religious tradition'. As a corollary to this Panikkar goes on: 'It must be free from General Apologetics', when this would imply some kind of intention to enlist the other person into a religious league against 'un-religion' or irreligion. 'If to forget the first corollary would be to indicate a lack of confidence in our partner . . . to neglect the second point would betray a lack of confidence in the truth of religion itself, and present an indiscriminate accusation against "modern" Man.' This, he says, may be understandable but it is not in his terms 'a religious attitude', or in our terms ethically good practice.

Myth, Faith and Hermeneutics contains, as has been indicated, the theoretical hermeneutical basis for such encounter of free persons. He argues there that we must be freed from what he sees as the enslaving Western Myth, the myth of history, into a Myth of tolerance and communion, in which faith is understood as the constitutive human dimension.[14] In this we are taken beyond mere awareness of plurality into an acceptance of *pluralism*. This cannot belong within what he calls the 'order of the *logos*': 'pluralism cannot be accepted within an ideology. On the ideological level you cannot compromise with error. Just so, two contradictory conceptual statements cannot be both true at the same level, or according to a single perspective'.[15] Panikkar is here directing our attention to the realities of discourse in a world in which there is not a single system of logic and philosophy. Modes of analysis which appear to make sense in discussions taking place within the Western philosophical framework are rendered inoperable in encounters between cultures which have arisen from fundamentally different propositions. 'To assume *a priori* that a given conceptual form can serve as a framework for an encounter of cultures represents, from a philosophical point of view, an unacceptable, uncritical extrapolation. Sociologically speaking, it represents yet another vestige of a cultural colonialism that supposes that a single culture can formulate the rules of the game for an authentic encounter between cultures.'[16] So we have this formulation: 'Pluralism is grounded in the belief that no single group embraces the totality of human experience. It is based on trust in the other, even though I do not understand him and from my point of view I will have to say that he is quite wrong. Pluralism does not absolutize error because it does not absolutize truth either.'[17]

We have already looked at Wilfred Cantwell Smith's understanding of faith 'as a characteristic quality or potentiality of human life: that propensity of man that across the centuries and across the world has given rise to and has been nurtured by a prodigious variety of religious forms, and yet has remained elusive and personal, prior to and beyond the forms'.[18] Because faith is this primary constitutive human reality, we meet other persons as people of faith and not primarily as Hindus and Buddhists. Indeed, as we have seen,[19] it was Smith himself who taught us in *The Meaning and End of Religion* to set fundamental question marks against the unthinking use of the concept 'a religion' or 'a faith' and against the usage of the terms 'religions' and 'faiths' to indicate contraposed socio-theological communities.[20]

In his latest book, *Towards a World Theology*, he returns to these issues as they confront the academic community, and especially those professionally involved in humane sciences. In a chapter entitled 'Objectivity and the Humane Sciences', he writes: 'my contention is that objective knowledge in the humane realm is an inherently immoral concept. Many practitioners of this brand of knowledge are, of course, better than their theories; many are better men and women personally than individual scholars with more humane ideas. The goal of an objective scientific knowledge of man, however, is wrong. One element in this inadequacy, shall we say, is its moral wrongness'.[21] Writing primarily as a comparative religionist, his further remarks chime in with Panikkar's as he reflects on cultural superiority: 'Such learning requires, of course, a certain humility . . . and respect *vis-à-vis* men and women of other cultures, a humility that . . . neither Christians nor Western secularists regularly had. Sceptic and believer, at loggerheads at home, joined company to feel superior when they looked abroad: the one presuming that the religious faith of all humankind was superstitious error, the other that that of non-Christian was. At very least, both for a time lacked that humility that recognizes that one can learn about oneself and about one's own world from other civilizations'.[22]

He continues, a few sentences later, and now perhaps more overtly as a Christian theologian: 'Man cannot know man except in mutuality; in respect, trust and equality, if not ultimately love . . . One must be ready not only to receive the other but to give oneself. In humane knowledge, at stake is one's own humanity, as well as

another person's or another community's. At issue is humanity
itself.'[23]

In all this Smith is concerned about how we know another person,
and about our not being caught up in 'objective ideology'. As in
Panikkar, and both WCC and BCC *Guidelines*, the ethic is 'persona-
list' through and through. How strikingly this all reflects what we
learnt in a previous generation from a Jewish theologian who taught
us to distinguish between I-it and I-thou relationships. I refer, of
course, to Martin Buber, who also wrote on 'Dialogue' (*Zwiesprache*)
as 'speech from certainty to certainty . . . from one open-hearted
person to another open-hearted person. Only then will common life
appear, not of an identical content of faith which is alleged to be found
in all religions, but that of the situation, of anguish and
expectation'.[24]

3 Dialogue Depends upon Mutual Understanding and Mutual Trust

Put in ethically prescriptive terms engagement in dialogue is in order
to remove misunderstanding and to build up friendship. The BCC
Guidelines see this happening, in so far as Christians are concerned, by
the deliberate avoidance of misleading and hurtful terminology about
other people, in the refusal to dismiss other religions as human
attempts to reach God with nothing of his grace in them, by allowing
other people to define themselves in their own terms, and lastly by
accepting responsibility to help other people to clear away misconceptions about what Christians themselves believe and teach. About
such a programme, the WCC *Guidelines* say: 'Dialogue can be
recognized as a welcome way of obedience to the commandment of
the Decalogue: "You shall not bear false witness against your
neighbour". Dialogue helps us not to disfigure the image of our
neighbours of other faiths and ideologies' (para 17).

Such propositions clearly belong to the realm of axioms in
theological ethics, because both truth and love are involved here.
They are to be tested by applications in particular contexts, and we
content ourselves in this section by indicating some of the considerations that affect each context in which the search for mutual trust
and mutual understanding takes place.

First, from Panikkar's 'Rules of the Game', concerning the
avoidance of false witness: ' . . . the golden rule of any hermeneutic is
that the interpreted thing can recognize itself in the interpretation. In
other words, any interpretation from outside has to coincide, at least

phenomenologically, with an interpretation from within, i.e. with the believer's viewpoint. To label a *murtipujaka* an idol worshipper, using idol as it is commonly understood in the Judaeo-Christian-Muslim context rather than beginning with what the worshipper affirms of himself is to transgress this rule. An entire philosophical and religious context underpins the notion of *murti*; we cannot impose alien categories upon it'.

And sometimes it is even less forgivable because the misinterpretation, the false witness, happens within the Judaeo-Christian-Muslim tradition. Since in a moment I shall go on to speak of other people's failures let me record a characteristic Christian error, but one of my own. I had for several months been telling the story of the conversion of a well-known black entertainer to Judaism. He is reputed to have replied to the question, 'Why Judaism rather than Christianity?' by saying, 'Because Christians talk about love, but the Jews about justice'. This I had been doing in good faith, to illustrate the individualism and privatization of Christian ethics, compared with Jewish concern for how people live together, *Torah, Talmud, Halakhah* and so on. I mentioned this story to a Rabbi friend of mine. 'But', he said, 'we Jews also believe in love'. I could tell that he felt I had simply been reinforcing the stereotype of legalism that Christians lay upon the Jews. I apologized then, and I apologize now, for that is indeed what I had been doing, however unintentionally.

Secondly, there is the need to avoid language which is dismissive of other religious traditions. Stanley Samartha, the first Director of the WCC Sub Unit on Dialogue, has reported on the reactions of the guests of other faiths at the Nairobi WCC Assembly in 1975: 'they were', he writes, 'not sure why dialogue should be suspect to some Christians and attacked by others. They were disappointed that the question of seeking community in the contemporary world was not taken up with a greater sense of urgency. They felt uneasy to discover that they were part of the statistics that made up the 2.7 billion who were the objects of the proclamation of the gospel.' Dr Samartha reflects accurately on the unhappy paradox here: 'The missiologist who described all non-Christian religions as demonic missed the chance of personally meeting these "non-Christian" guests to discover and perhaps to do battle with "demonic" elements in them. At least one of these guests expressed disappointment that no one among those who talked loudest about proclamation actually came to him or others personally to proclaim the love of God in Jesus Christ.'[25]

The question raised in this last paragraph is not, I think, so much about theological ethics as the ethics of theologians, and you may like to be reminded of a story concerning one of the greatest of Protestant theologians with one of the greatest of Protestant evangelists of our century. D. T. Niles of Sri Lanka met Karl Barth for the first time in 1935. In the course of conversation Barth said, 'Other religions are just unbelief'. Niles asked, 'How many Hindus, Dr Barth, have you met?' Barth answered, 'None'. Niles said, 'How then do you know that Hinduism is unbelief?' Barth replied, '*A priori*'. Niles concluded, 'I simply shook my head and smiled'.[26]

Part of the problem for the Christian theologians, and especially for those who see their first task as the articulation and explication of the faith of the church, the formulation of 'Church Dogmatics',[27] is that they are driven by circumstances to use the third person plural as an exclusive: there is 'us' and there is 'them'! The 'we' form articulates subjective, firsthand knowledge, and the 'they' form necessarily suggests objective knowledge. Here is Wilfred Cantwell Smith again: '(Objective knowledge) . . . does not yield personal understanding, or the kind of knowledge on which to found friendship. One may remark that last century's missionaries, who were objective in another fashion (individually very friendly, but in their group's theoretical relation to the "other" religion, and in their writings, objectivist, alienist) were victims essentially of the same we-they fallacy . . . mutual understanding between groups is part of the truth, in this realm; it provides a criterion, a verification principle.'[28]

It would go far beyond the limits of this chapter, and way beyond my own competence, to discuss the philosophical and theological issues involved here, but I may be permitted to refer to John Macmurray's first volume of his Gifford Lectures, *The Self as Agent*, whose declared intention was to construct and illustrate in application the 'form of the personal', that 'personal existence is *constituted* by the relation of persons'. You may recall the words of his introductory preface 'The simplest expression I can find for the thesis I have tried to maintain is this: All meaningful knowledge is for the sake of action, and all meaningful action is for the sake of friendship'.[29]

4 *Dialogue Makes It Possible to Share in Service to the Community*

The guests from other faiths at the Nairobi Assembly of the WCC in 1975 were, we learnt from Dr Samartha, disappointed that the question of seeking community in the contemporary world was not taken up with a greater sense of urgency. A number of hypotheses might be advanced as to why this may have been so, and some of them need extended consideration and indeed condemnation from within the Christian ethical tradition. David Jenkins, now Bishop of Durham, writing out of his experience in the *Humanum* programme of the WCC, discusses some of the factors involved in the first chapter of *The Contradiction of Christianity* in which he refers to the tribalism of Christian traditions. He quotes Niebuhr's remark in *Man's Nature and his Communities*, 'The chief source of man's inhumanity to man seems to be the tribal limits of his sense of obligation to other men'.[30]

This is painfully true, and yet there may also be for some Christians deeply held theological beliefs which are not necessarily epiphenomenological to the preservation of cultural identity. For it may be, for example, that the church, 'the people of God in world-occurrence', is qualitatively different from all other communities. So Karl Barth, in the very act of arguing eloquently and persuasively that the church is 'the community for the world', seeing and finding its own cause in that of the world, and that of other men in its own, remarks, 'Now there can be no doubt that in the discharge of its mission to them the community has in a sense to keep its distance, and even to contradict and oppose them. Without saying No it cannot really say Yes to them'.[31] He speaks of this withdrawal as 'well-founded and solemn', this contradiction and opposition as 'well-meaning and justifiable' even at the same time as it proceeds from the 'profoundest commitment to the whole of humanity and each individual man'.[32]

Here is another instance. The Nairobi 1975 Assembly took place within the context of the whole 'humanization' debate begun in the late sixties, and still reflected in internal Christian discussion in various ways even now. Peter Beyerhaus, professor of missions and ecumenics at Tübingen, was one of the architects of the 1970 'Frankfurt Declaration on the Fundamental Crisis in Christian Mission'. About such propositions as 'we have lifted up humanization as the goal of mission' Beyerhaus says: 'Here, it seems to me we are encountering nothing less than the bankruptcy of responsible mission theology . . . In former ages people were religious and asked for the true God, and Christian missions directed them to Him. Today people do not care for gods any more, but for better human relations. Thus mission does not speak of God but directs them to the humanity in Christ as the goal of history.' 'True all this is done in the concern of missionary accommodation. By confining ourselves to the concept of humanization we hope to find a field of common concern with Hindus, Muslims, Marxists and Humanists. For according to the concept of the anonymous Christ *extra muros Ecclesiae* we are already sharing in Christ if we work together with them for the humanization of mankind. Perhaps by means of dialogue if the others ask us for the motives of our actions, they might even become disposed to accept Christ and integrate him into their present faith.'[33]

I have given these rather extended quotations for fear lest I caricature or misrepresent either Barth or Beyerhaus and those of Christian traditions who responsibly feel the force of these or similar arguments. There are also, of course, many other Christians who would not even be concerned to enter this discussion, for it is foreclosed by the very nature of the views of salvation which they hold.[34] But we have sufficiently established the point that the BCC's third Principle: 'dialogue makes it possible to share in service to the community' is affected by prior theological understandings.

We take notice, therefore, that Paragraph 18 of the WCC *Guidelines* is deliberately and consciously 'ethical' when it states: 'Dialogue is a fundamental part of service within community. In dialogue Christians actively respond to the command to "love God and your neighbour as yourself". As an expression of love, engagement in dialogue testifies to the love experienced in Christ. It is a joyful affirmation of life against chaos, and a participation with all who are allies of life in seeking the provisional goal of a better human community. Thus "dialogue in community" is not a secret weapon in the armoury of aggressive Christian militancy. Rather it is the means of living our faith in Christ in service of our neighbours.'

Yet, because of the issues we have raised by citing Barth and Beyerhaus, i.e., that for many within the Christian community theological presuppositions still govern the way in which they may behave towards people of other faiths, these statements are still likely to be seriously questioned: what is meant by 'provisional goal'? what is meant by 'a better human community'? what is this 'life' which is to be affirmed over against chaos? How does all this fit in with traditional understandings of e.g. 'the Church', 'the World' and 'the End'?[35]

If we have spent so much time on the Christian theological considerations anteceding the ethics of co-operating with people of other faiths, this is only because such considerations are the nearest home for most of us. With the necessary changes in terminology or patterns of thinking, similar issues affect other communities of faith. For example, many Muslims might have the gravest reservations about working with non-Muslims for 'the provisional goals of a better human community'. For non-Muslims traditionally belong to the *dar ul harb*, literally the 'house of war': a better human community could only come into being as the house of war becomes the *dar ul islam*, the house of peace wherein Muslim *mores* are normative. For such

Muslims their concept of *jihad*, striving for God, would be seriously jeopardized by co-operation with those who do not believe. The same could be said about many other religious groupings, bearing in mind that the force of Niebuhr's comment about 'tribal limits' applies across the board. Questions of cultural identity and absolute religious truth are inextricably intertwined for them as for Christians.

In this context the WCC *Guidelines* are right to locate their·ethical imperative not so much in romanticized (or even realistic) ideas of 'community' or 'humanization' as in the love of God and the love of neighbour, two axioms of theological ethics neither of which is peculiar to Christianity.

So it is no surprise that my own experience of expounding these 'four principles of dialogue' to inter-faith gatherings has often found the greatest response at this point. One could, if space permitted, first indicate the ways in which the several traditions echo the command to love thy neighbour; secondly the ways in which the old exclusiveness is being re-interpreted; and thirdly, some of the areas which are already being tackled in this kind of inter-religious co-operation.[36]

5 Dialogue Becomes the Medium of Authentic Witness

We have seen how insistent Raimundo Panikkar is in his 'Rules of the Game' that '*the Religious encounter must be a truly religious one*', or in his other words, it is more than 'just a congress of philosophy', more than 'merely an ecclesiastical endeavour'. In his discussion Panikkar touches on many of the themes covered in the first three of our 'Four Principles' and here we highlight those that belong specifically to the areas of 'authentic witness'. Panikkar is clear, as are the WCC and BCC *Guidelines*, that one must face the challenge of conversion: 'to enter the new field of religious encounter is a challenge and a risk. The religious person enters this arena without prejudices and preconceived solutions, knowing full well that he may have to lose his life – he may also be born again'.[37]

Here is one of the clearest statements of the openness and vulnerability that can be expected of participants in the deepest forms of 'dialogue'. This should not, however, be set out as the *sine qua non* or absolute condition for earlier stages in inter-religious encounter represented in some part by the first three Principles. It is certainly possible, for example, to work in a dialogical relationship with people of other religious commitments for a better human community without this form of openness and vulnerability.[38] It is equally

possible for people utterly committed to their own faith-understand-
ings to explain themselves to each other without expecting that they
should be, in Panikkar's expression, 'without prejudices and preconceived solutions'. If this were the necessary condition, almost every
possibility of discourse in this area would be foreclosed, and few
members, if any, of the world religious traditions could ever set out on
this path.[39]

And yet vital ethical issues here are at stake. The WCC *Guidelines*
wrestle with the problem of 'integrity' in commending the way of
inter-faith dialogue to Christians, recognizing that Christians (no
more or less than Hindus, Buddhists, Muslims and everyone else)
enter into such dialogue with prior commitment, in the Christian case
commitment to Jesus Christ. As an attempt to deal with this, the
WCC formulation runs like this:

> In dialogue Christians seek to 'speak the truth in a spirit of love',
> not naively 'to be tossed to and fro, and carried about by every wind
> of doctrine' (Eph. 4.14–15). In giving their witness they recognize
> that in most circumstances today the spirit of dialogue is necessary.
> For this reason we do not see dialogue and the giving of witness as
> standing in any contradiction to one another. Indeed, as Christians
> enter into dialogue with their commitment to Jesus Christ, time
> and again the relation of dialogue gives opportunity for authentic
> witness. Thus to member churches of the WCC we feel able with
> integrity to commend the way of dialogue as one in which Jesus
> Christ can be confessed in the world today; at the same time we feel
> able to assure our partners in dialogue that we come not as
> manipulators, but as genuine fellow-pilgrims, to speak with them of
> what we believe God to have done in Jesus Christ who has gone
> before us, but whom we seek to meet anew in dialogue (para. 19).

We may note, but refrain from commenting on at this moment,
the christological proposition embedded in the last fourteen words of
this passage. Let us concentrate on the phrase 'not as manipulators
but as genuine fellow-pilgrims', as pointing to the major ethical issue
here.

Stanley Samartha's invaluable collection of essays *Courage for
Dialogue* contains more than one reference to the reactions of people of
other faiths to new-found Christian enthusiasm for dialogue. Here is
one such:

> Do not think I am against dialogue . . . on the contrary, I am fully
> convinced that dialogue is an essential part of human life, and

therefore of religious life itself . . . Yet to be frank with you, there is something that makes me uneasy in the way in which you Christians are now trying so easily to enter into official and formal dialogue with us. Have you already forgotten that what you call 'inter-faith dialogue' is quite a new feature in your understanding and practice of Christianity? Until a few years ago, and often still today, your relations with us were confined, either merely to the social plane, or preaching in order to convert us to your *dharma* . . . For all matters concerning *dharma* you were deadly against us, violently or stealthily according to cases . . . [40]

This Hindu from North India was politely declining to take part in a dialogue instigated by Christians: the memory of past attacks and derogatory remarks was too fresh in his mind. What also perhaps he was too polite actually to express in words was the fear that others have made explicit, that in this context dialogue remains a disguised form of mission: 'you have failed to convert us by direct methods, now you will try to manipulate us by dialogue'.

Many on the Christian side hear this charge with too great an arousal of guilt feelings, for it often goes along with other indictments like 'cultural imperialism', 'Western feelings of superiority' and so on. At this point certain strategies are adopted, sometimes consciously but more often in an unreflecting and unaware manner. We must spend a little time on such moves, for they are quite simply *unethical* or, in Panikkar's terminology, *irreligious*.

One such move is to relativize the concept of truth itself, and to describe it in cultural terms. Christopher Lamb describes it thus: ' . . . one strong defensive tendency among British Christians is to adopt a "cultural-bound" interpretation of faiths, saying in effect "Jesus is the way for me because other religious traditions are culturally inaccessible to me. My western upbringing makes them opaque to me, and I presume that Christian tradition is equally opaque to their followers".'[41] Paradoxically there are many who are willing with this understanding to engage in a dialogue of a kind, though such a position would at first sight suggest that inter-religious understanding is impossible from the start. My own work takes me constantly to local groups in Britain who desire to have closer relationships with, say, the local mosque, and who are startled when I suggest that they should want to talk to Muslims as it were 'from faith to faith'. To meet, yes; to build up trust and friendship, yes; to work together on city and neighbourhood issues, yes . . . but to witness to Christ . . . ? That is a much more doubtful proposition.

And so it often comes about that 'truth-claims' are excluded from the agenda of inter-faith dialogue. Let another Hindu hold the mirror up for us here. Lesslie Newbigin tells us of the comments of Dr R. Sundarara Rajan of Madras. Dr Rajan suggests the emphasis on a self-critical attitude, the demand that each party should try to see things from within the mind of the other, and the disavowal of any attempt by either side to question the faith of others, can easily mean that dialogue is simply an exercise in the mutual confirmation of different beliefs with all the really critical questions excluded. 'If it is impossible to lose one's faith as a result of an encounter with another faith, then I feel that the dialogue has been made safe from all possible risks.'[42] Newbigin adds 'A dialogue which is safe from all possible risks is no true dialogue'.[43]

It is on grounds such as these that Panikkar and both WCC and BCC *Guidelines* reject explicitly or implicitly the 'congress of philosophy' or 'parliament of religions' approach to dialogue. It is vitally necessary in serious dialogue that the partners come with open commitments, not 'hidden agendas' or worse 'concealed ideologies'. So the WCC *Guidelines* believe that we must come as 'partners, genuine fellow-pilgrims, to speak of what we believe God to have done in Jesus Christ . . . '. The BCC *Guidelines* affirm, 'If we are concerned with religion we cannot avoid being concerned with truth – otherwise we are playing games, and dangerous games at that', and 'Christians will wish to be sensitive to their partners' religious integrity and also to witness to Christ as Lord of all'.[44] And Panikkar writes 'If the encounter is to be authentically religious, it must be totally loyal to truth and open to reality'. The last word comes from Dr Samartha: 'The freedom to be committed and to be open is the pre-requisite of genuine dialogue'.[45]

Once again we have approached the ethical and religious issues from a viewpoint within the Christian tradition. Strictures against less worthy forms of behaviour in dialogue have been charged to the account of Christians: positive precepts and prescriptions have been couched in Christian terms and Christian language. But it is re-assuring that the fundamental positions and commitments are susceptible to interpretation in the terms of the other religious traditions of humankind, and indeed that from time to time it is possible to hear people within those traditions expounding them for their communities. Just as we Christians have to hear, mark and inwardly digest comments like those of the two Hindu scholars quoted in this section, so there are comments made by Christians to, say, Muslims or Hindus that have to be heard on their side, for we, too, sometimes find ourselves 'manipulated', and not treated as 'fellow-pilgrims'.[46] Part of truth-seeking dialogue is to help one another in this process, so that all of us become as 'the disciples of Aaron, loving peace and pursuing peace', loving our fellows and drawing them nearer to God.[47]

⫞7⫞

Towards a New Spirituality

In the previous chapter I set down some of the firm results of the experience of inter-faith dialogue in terms of ethical principles. I was even able to assert that people of faith other than Christian would be able to assent to them. In what now follows everything has to be tentative and the form is that of an essay in the strictest sense. It can be no more than an attempt at understanding, a raid on the inarticulated feelings and experiences of those who already have entered into a new relationship. All prayer is by nature precarious, an act of faith, and the spirituality of the new relationships to which God calls us in our time is hardly yet worked out. What I write here must also be an act of faith. So then recognizing that it is not my duty to finish the work but that equally I am not at liberty to neglect it, I must here try to say something.

First, a comment on the term 'spirituality' itself is necessary. It is not a favourite word among many of us. This is partly because it is of such recent usage in the Christian church. Principal Gordon Wakefield writes 'it is a word that has come much into vogue to describe those attitudes, beliefs and practices which animate people's lives and help them to reach out towards super-sensible realities'. He points out in the same article that in the seventeenth century 'spirituality' bore a pejorative sense, describing a type of piety which was 'too refined, rarified, insufficiently related to earthly life'.[1] This phenomenon was well known in the earliest days of Christianity. In Corinth, for example, Paul had to deal with self-appointed 'spirituals' (*pneumatikoi*) whose notion of the Christian life was extractionist and other-worldly to the point of turning the mighty act of God in Jesus into a gnostic redeemer myth.[2] We have all of us had to do with those who have made the fallacious distinction between spirit and flesh, this world and the other world, to have become, in the words of the old gibe 'so heavenly minded to be of no earthly use'. For some of us the word 'spirituality' is still off-putting for it is still much in captivity to those whose concerns are refined, rarified and insufficiently related to earthly life.

But it is equally clear that Paul himself wished to address his awkward squad in Corinth as mature spiritual men and women, even though the circumstances forced him to speak to babies unweaned as yet to solid food (see I Cor. 3.1–2). His own teaching relates to the hard realities of discipleship which he describes in chapter 4, not to the spurious feelings of the Corinthians which he describes so sarcastically 'Already you are filled! Already you have become rich! Without us you have become kings' (I Cor. 4.8). Against this false spirituality he sets the teaching about spiritual gifts in I Cor. 12. This reaches unparalleled heights in the more excellent way of chapter 13 which concerns faith and hope and love and 'the greatest of these is love . . .' That the struggle against spirituality falsely conceived went on throughout the New Testament period needs no demonstration here.

If Paul is among the earliest writers on what is necessary for Christian attitudes and lifestyles, the Gospel and the Letters standing in John's name in the New Testament show clearly the same struggle. For there were many who held docetist or gnostic views of redemption. 'Beloved do not believe every spirit but test the spirits to see whether they are of God: for many false prophets have gone out into the world.' (I John 4.1). Some of these false teachers denied that Jesus was human, asserting that he was only a divine emanation (II John 8). For, as C. H. Dodd has made clear: 'any "Gnostic" was bound to find some way to avoid the scandalous idea that the Son of God, the Revealer, the Intermediary between the Divine and the human suffered the degradation of direct contact with matter, the embodiment of all evil; and above all he was bound to deny that the Divine could suffer.'[3] But other consequences appeared to follow from this false apprehension of Christian reality. There is no direct evidence, I think, that phrases such as 'we are born of God' (I John 4.7), 'we are in the light' (I John 2.9), 'we have no sin' (I John 1.8), 'we abide in God' (I John 2.6), 'we know God' (I John 4.7) were used in the gnostic literature but they are certainly analogous to gnostic phraseology.[4]

Nevertheless, it is clear that John the Elder is perfectly willing to take these terms on board as descriptive of Christian life and spirituality with his own striking insistences that each of them has ethical this-worldly content. The claim to mystical experience is transmuted into love of the brethren, service to the community, this-worldly directed behaviour: 'God is love and he who abides in love abides in God . . . if anyone says "I love God" and hates his brother, he is a liar, for he who does not love his brother, whom he has seen, cannot love God whom he has not seen' (I John 4.16, 20; cf. 2.29; 3.10; 3.16; 4.17).

But this kind of loving and serving in Johannine thought, just as much as Pauline teaching, has everything to do with 'abiding in Christ' (Paul's phrase is about the mind of Christ being in us (Phil. 2.5)). The followers of Jesus are invited to serve as well as to worship and pray. The incident of the washing of the disciples' feet (John 13) says it all. They can do this says the Fourth Gospel only as they abide in Christ and he abides in them (John 15.4). John the Elder affirms this: 'All who keep his commandments abide in him as he is in them. And by this we know that he abides in us, by the Spirit which he has given us' (I John 3.24).

It is with this tradition that we are concerned. We cut our way therefore through the syncretistic accretions in the long history of Christian teaching about spirituality to affirm, with Gordon Wakefield, that 'mutual indwelling with God in Christ is at once the means and the end: but this is a being caught up into the paschal mystery, not an absorption into the infinite, and it cannot deliver us from the sometimes unbearable tensions, dangers and sufferings of the "world of action"'.[5]

So this is the first concern in our statement now: we shall have to affirm the primacy of love in the shaping of the spirituality required of us in our new relationships. That love for us is known through and motivated by Jesus our Lord and Master. We must remain totally committed to him for he is the Way, the Life and the Truth. But we have already seen that this Way, this Life and this Truth lived out in Jesus of Nazareth is the very essence of how the Word by which all things were made fills the universe.[6] Committed to what we know of his life and his relationships with other people – whether they were members of the Occupation Forces, despised Samaritans, a semi-pagan Syro-Phoenician woman, or whether they were members of his own community who had made shipwreck of their inherited faith – we enter in our own time into fresh life-giving relationships with other men and women beyond the boundaries of the Christian church. So we shall speak first of all of a spirituality of commitment and openness.

How this is worked out we shall try to show by using three further categories. We shall speak of a spirituality which recognizes that there is 'a time for keeping silence'; then of a spirituality of crossing over and coming back; and finally of a spirituality of a once and future kingdom, using under this last heading such key and inter-related concepts as pilgrimage, provisionality, and spiritual poverty. We live still with the question of Thomas: like him, we go with Jesus in order that we may die with him, as well as live with him.

1 Commitment and Openness

Let us draw once more on the Wesleyan strand within the Christian tradition and examine that quite extraordinary openness to other traditions which marked the spirituality of the founder of Methodism. John Wesley's sermon on the 'The Catholic Spirit' (Sermon XXXIV) has begotten and nourished many followers in the same path, whose contribution both to the Christian ecumenical movement and our new inter-religious patterns of obedience is inestimable. So in itself it is worth a great deal of attention.

John Wesley's text for this Sermon comes from one of the most unlikely areas of the Old Testament for either his or our own purposes, namely the Second Book of Kings. The two partners in the conversation, however, were taking part in an inter-faith dialogue of a kind. Jehonadab we know of from a reference in Jeremiah 35 where he appears as a fanatical Yahwist and the founder of an extremist sect opposed to the sedentary culture of the Canaanites. Jehu goes on from his meeting with Jehonadab to slaughter the prophets and priests of Baal. Well, that too, is a kind of inter-faith encounter! But, its context apart, the sentiments and force of the text itself much impress themselves on John Wesley's succeeding generations: 'And as he was departed thence, he lighted on Jehonadab the son of Rachab coming to meet him, and he saluted him, and said to him, Is thine heart right, as my heart is right with thy heart? And Jehonadab answered: It is. If it be, give me thine hand.' The oddity of the encounter between Jehonadab and Jehu was not lost on John Wesley. He notes that it may be very possible that many good men may now 'also entertain peculiar opinions; and some of them may be as singular herein as even Jehonadab was'. But Wesley thinks it is the inevitable consequence of the present weakness and shortness of human understanding that different men will be of different minds in religion as well as in everyday life. 'So it has been from the beginning of the world and so it will be "till the restitution of all things".'[7] The wise man will therefore recognize his own fallibility as well as the fallibility of others and will bear with those who differ from him and will only ask him with whom he desires to unite in love that simple question, 'Is thine heart right with my heart?'.

And this, says Wesley, applies even unto the question of the

different ways of worshipping God in which he notes among
Christians that 'the particular modes of worshipping God are almost
as various as among the heathens'. So Wesley denies any relevance to
questions about forms of church government or modes of administer-
ing the sacraments, pointing rather to the central matters of faith:
'But what is properly implied in the question? I do not mean what did
Jehu imply therein? But what should a follower of Christ stand
thereby when he proposes it to any of his brethren.'

So he comes to part II of the Sermon which deals with the force of
the words: 'If it be, give me thy hand.' Wesley says this cannot mean
'be of my opinion. You need not, I do not expect or desire it . . . ' He
does not mean, "embrace my mode of worship" or "I will embrace
yours". This also is a thing which does not depend on either your
choice or mine. We must both act as each is fully persuaded in his own
mind. Hold you fast that which you believe is most acceptable to God
and I will do the same'. But positively he does mean: 'Love me, and
not only as thou lovest all mankind . . . love me as a companion in the
kingdom and patience of Jesus, and a joint heir to his glory'. Secondly,
'commend me to God in all thy prayers', thirdly 'provoke me to love
and good works' and, lastly, 'love me not in word only but in deed and
in truth so far as in conscience thou canst (retaining thine own
opinions, thine own manner of worshipping God) join with me in the
work of God and let us go on hand in hand, and thus far, it is certain
thou mayest go. Speak honourably wherever thou are, of the work of
God by whomsoever he works and kindly of his messengers'.

All this, he says, teaches us what a catholic spirit is and is not. For
one thing is certain, it is not 'speculative latitudinarianism'. It is not
an indifference to all opinions! That, he says, would be the 'spawn of
hell, not the offspring of heaven'. Nor is a catholic spirit indifference
as to the ways of public worship or to life within a given congregation.
But, and here we must quote him in full:

> While he is steadily fixed in his religious principles, on what he
> believes to be the truth as it is in Jesus; while he firmly adheres to
> that worship of God which he judges to be the most acceptable in
> His sight, and while he is united in the tenderest and closest ties to
> one particular congregation – his heart is enlarged towards all
> mankind, those he knows and those he does not; he embraces with
> strong and cordial affection neighbours and strangers, friends and
> enemies. This is catholic or universal love. And he that has this is of
> a catholic spirit. For love alone gives the title to this character:
> catholic love is a catholic spirit.

This, Wesley concludes, is the path set before us:

> And now run the race that is set before thee, in the royal way of
> universal love. Take heed, lest thou be either wavering in thy
> judgment, or straitened in thy bowels: but keep an even pace,
> rooted in the faith once delivered to the saints, and grounded in
> love, in true catholic love, till thou art swallowed up in love for ever
> and for ever!

So clear is this, despite its eighteenth-century turns of phrase (or
maybe because of them), that no further comment is needed. For my
part the openness and commitment spoken of here is the reason why I
return again and again to my Methodist roots as I enter into inter-
faith dialogue. Wesley's Sermon forms itself the answer to the
question once sharply put to me by a colleague: 'What is one of Mr
Wesley's preachers doing in the inter-faith movement?' I, for one,
have no doubt on the evidence that I presented in the first chapter
that Wesley himself would have recognized faith and love and hope in
the people that I have to deal with and would have walked the same
way with us. What he wrote of the universal catholic love applying to
all human beings is surely seminal, but like him, I also hold fast to
what I know of Jesus. I am open to God at work everywhere but
committed to Jesus through whom I know God.

2 'A Time to Keep Silent'

Openness and commitment are the twin themes of every section of
this chapter. Holding fast to the truth we know in Jesus, we are free to
move out in universal love to every human creature touched as they
all are by God.

It is therefore at this point that something must be said about the
spirituality adequate to those situations where we find ourselves with
those who are also praying but not through Jesus Christ. In other
words, we speak now of the vexed issue of inter-faith worship. In 1983
the Autumn Assembly of the British Council of Churches received
with cordial appreciation the first set of guidelines published
anywhere in the world addressing the issue of worship in a multi-faith
society. The document itself was called *Can we Pray Together?*.
Subsequently several friendly reviewers suggested that the question
mark was unnecessary. The booklet in their view should have been
called 'We Can Pray Together' or even 'Let Us Pray Together'. Let us
see why they reacted in this way.

The Methodist theologian, Roy Pape, whose meticulous and sensitive work played so great a part in the production of the book points out that when Christians make a serious attempt to get to know people of other faiths, it is very early on in this new relationship that the way the other people worship is encountered. 'For', he writes, 'people are usually more ready to show one another how they worship than they are to articulate for one another what they believe.'[8] I do not propose to go into the wealth of detailed comment that *Can We Pray Together?* provides, but point rather to one section of these guidelines which touches more intimately upon the issues of shared spirituality. I acknowledge here all that I have learnt from Sister Hannah of the Community of St Francis in London. She meditated for us on that lovely image in the book of Wisdom: 'For while gentle silence enveloped all things, and night in its swift course was now half gone, thy all powerful Word leapt from heaven from the royal throne' (Wisd. 18.14–15). Believing as we do that God continually is making himself known to individuals and communities the Christian church has always given space for him to speak in liturgical silence. This may be in a pause after a scripture reading or in intercessory prayers, or be the whole act of worship as with a Quaker meeting or within the monastery of a contemplative religious order. 'Wherever we are as Christians and in whatever way we worship we seem to leave some space at least for the Word to leap from heaven.'[9]

The search for a contemporary Christian spirituality has also led many to a rediscovery of silent prayer. As N. W. Goodacre perceptively comments: 'A common concern for silence draws eastern and western Christendom together. Aspirants are able to study the masters of spirituality in Christianity and other faiths. The art of contemplation can be learnt in all faiths. For Christians the writings of John of the Cross, Francis de Sales, Père Grou, Evelyn Underhill, Staretz Silouan, R. Somerset Ward and many others all emphasize silence in the inner life of the soul . . . in silence we begin to ask the right questions about God, about the world and about ourselves.'[10] All this is consonant with the work of modern psychologists and psychotherapists who have taught us so much about non-verbal communication. We meet not only with the aloneness of the soul before God but with each other at a level where words are inappropriate or simply inadequate. For silence, says Sister Hannah, is the prayer of friendship:

Few of us can withstand long periods of silence in conversations with strangers or acquaintances. It is only with those we know well and trust that silence can comfortably and naturally become part of our relationship. Shared silence, when it is mutually desired, is an intimate experience and therefore not one to be entered into lightly. If we are led to share such silence with those of other religions it is likely to be a leading of the heart rather than the mind. We are bound to enter such an experience with questions and perhaps doubts. We shall be wanting to share what is most precious to each of us in the hope that it will lead to further truth rather than hinder it; but theology will be a second step.[11]

There lies behind this succinct statement much experience and a notable amount of serious thinking. The common fund of experience, not altogether surprisingly, has been largely contributed to by members of religious orders both Roman Catholic and Anglican. Sister Hannah is herself a case in point, but I refer also to the considerable literature now available to us from people like Abhishiktananda (the chosen name of the French Benedictine Monk, Henri Le Saux), the English Benedictine Bede Griffiths, the American Cistercian Thomas Merton, the Irish Jesuit William Johnston, the Indian Carmelite Albert Nambiaparambil, or the Sri Lankan Jesuit Aloysius Pieris – names that spring instantaneously to mind from the midst of a great roll call.

Swami Abhishiktananda was the first to speak of the meeting between Hindus (particularly of the Advaitist tradition) and Christians in the 'Cave of the Heart'. He speaks in this way in his report of a meeting of a small group of Christians of different denominations who met in Nagpur at Christmas time in 1963 to read and ponder the Upanishads together:

> Faith can only be recognised by faith, in the same way that only a *jnāni* understands a *jnāni*. It is only in the depth of their spiritual experience that Christians and Hindus alike are able to understand each others' sacred books, and thereby to outgrow the limitations inherent in every particular tradition.

Abhishiktananda was given the task of writing the report of this meeting. He wrote that fellow Christians should look for:

> the treasures hidden in India's ancient scriptures and even more in that *guha* or secret place of the heart in which they were first heard. For this *guha*, from which the Upanishads welled up as from a spring of living water, is the inmost heart of every man: and it is to that inner centre that the Christian is invited to penetrate under the guidance of the Spirit, to discover in its fulness the mystery of the

atman, the Self which was glimpsed there by the rishis. There in fact is the place of the ultimate encounter; there man's spirit is henceforth one with the Spirit of God, the Spirit who proceeds from the Father and is communicated by the Son, the Spirit who is that essential non-duality *advaita*, which held the seers spellbound and who at the same time is perfect communion, flowing from the Father's heart and shared with us by his Incarnate Son. There the Spirit, drawing us into the mystery of his own indivisible unity, teaches us to say to God: 'Abba Father!'[12]

How Henri Le Saux trod the path that led him into his reconciliation of 'the mystery that has a face' (as the gospel presents itself in the person of Jesus Christ) and at the same time 'the mystery that has no face' as it is revealed in the heart of India's rishis need not be entered into here. Using his chosen name Abhishiktananda he has told us the story of his period in the ashram of the Hindu sage Gnanananda in his book *Guru and Disciple*.[13] The fruits of his reflection on the meeting of advaitist Hinduism and Catholic Christianity may be found in two books, *The Further Shore*,[14] and *Saccidananda: A Christian Approach to Advaitic Experience*.[15] One of his translators, Sister Sara Grant, may have a last word:

> Only in the cave of the heart can true dialogue between Christianity and Hinduism take place: contact at any other level can never be more than superficial and fleeting. Too often in the past Christians have given the impression that we are not even aware of the existence of this space within the secret place of the heart, (cp. Ch. Up., 8.1.1.6) where resides the Supreme Bliss (cp. Taitt Up. 2.9): and too often, perhaps the impression was true. Now, however, the time has come for Christians and Hindus to recognize in each other the gift of the Spirit, and for that both must go silently down to the depths of their own being, to the 'place where the Glory dwelleth'.[16]

Bede Griffiths knew both Henri Le Saux and his distinguished colleague, the Abbe Jules Monchanin, when they lived together at their ashram on the banks of the river Kavery in South India. He describes how they both lived there in the utmost simplicity wearing the dress of the Hindu holy man, going barefoot, sleeping on a mat on a floor and adapting themselves in all their habits of food and behaviour to Hindu customs. Those who visited them there, he writes, 'know how deep was the silence and the solitude, the atmosphere of peace and of the "desert" in this ashram'.[17] A similar atmosphere still pervades this place and countless others where the same vision of the dialogue of silence, 'in the cave of the heart' holds sway. 'Poor little talkative Christianity' is giving way to the Christian rediscovery of interiority and contemplation.

The theology for all this comes very much in second place, as the quotation from the BCC guidelines *Can We Pray Together?* made clear. But this is not to say that no attempt to speak of the issues raised here has been made. We turn now to the Jesuit scholar of mystical theology, William Johnston, born in Belfast in 1925 but domiciled in Japan since 1951, where he teaches in the Sophia University in Tokyo.[18] He writes in the Preface to his study *The Inner Eye of Love*: 'I am aware that for many professional theologians mysticism is a peripheral affair – an esoteric and embarrassing subject which has rightly been relegated to an obscure position in the curriculum of any self-respecting school of theology.'[19] But he argues that this cannot be allowed to remain so, and following the 'method' of Bernard Lonergan, he believes that mysticism is at the centre of religion and theology. This he is convinced is of utter importance for the future: 'One need be no great prophet to predict that Western theology of the next century will devote itself primarily to dialogue with the great religions of the East. And I myself believe that this dialogue will be a miserable affair if the western religions do not re-think their theology in the light of mystical experience.'[20]

Johnston's central argument, following Bernard Lonergan,[21] is that it is possible to distinguish in religious experience between a superstructure which he calls 'belief' and an infrastructure which he calls 'faith'. 'The superstructure is the outer word, the outer revelation, the word spoken in history and conditioned by culture. The infrastructure, on the other hand, is the interior word, the word spoken to the heart, the inner revelation.'[22] It is an inner gift which at first is, so to speak, formless. It is present in the heart prior to any outer cultural formulation.[23]

So Johnston can offer his own interpretation of what happens in the deep silence of shared spirituality, especially in cases where the theological expressions differ so vastly as in the case of Christianity and Buddhism. He describes that kind of silence which is almost palpable, uniting people more deeply than any words. What, he invites us to ask, is this silence which unites both Christians and Buddhists?

His answer is threefold. First, there is the existential level. 'When we sit together in silent meditation, just being, we are experiencing our true selves at the existential level, we are all doing the same thing, just being. And that gives birth to a powerful unity.'[24] Many experiences of inter-faith gatherings over the past years has given me much the same understanding. Just being together in this silence of friendship is itself a profound aspect of the spirituality for the new relationship between people of differing faith. But Johnston, still following Lonergan, goes one step further. Here, he says, is the practical form of that distinction between the superstructure of belief and the infrastructure of faith. 'Here we have the situation in which the eyes are turned away from words and concepts and images to remain in empty faith . . . This is the union of people who are in love without restriction or reservation and whose love has entered the cloud of unknowing. They are one at the centre of things: they are one in the great mystery which hovers over human life and towards which all religions point.'[25]

Yet neither Johnston himself nor his mentor Lonergan would want to stop there and suggest that the outer world of belief is unimportant. First, there is a mediation of meaning given in the tradition. What is it that is being experienced in the silence of empty faith? For Christians it is doubtless the presence of Christ but it is also the presence of Christ for those who have never heard of him. The distinction then may be made between the universal grace of God acting salvifically towards all human beings (I Tim. 2.4) and the fullness of the Christian meaning of that grace. In Lonergan's words: 'What distinguishes the Christian then is not God's grace, which he shares with others, but the mediation of God's grace through Jesus Christ our Lord.'[26]

The second point is that the inner gift of faith must always seek outward expression. In itself it is always imperfect and incomplete. The analogy Johnston chooses to illuminate this for us is the profoundly inter-personalist one of two people who love one another. Even if they both feel the same way about each other, and yet never confide their feelings to the other one, they cannot be said to be in love with each other. 'Their very silence means that their love has not reached the point of self-surrender and self-donation.'[27] We should not conclude therefore that all is silence and silence is all. Far from it. Rather the outer word is not merely incidental but has a constitutive role, both in the commitment to each other of wife with husband or friend with friend. It is in accordance with this sense that Gordon Wakefield rightly declares 'Let heart speak to heart, but there must be an engagement of the mind which demands its own asceticism'.[28] It is to this asceticism of the mind that we turn in the next section of this essay on the spirituality required for inter-faith relationships.

3 Passing Over and Coming Back

'Passing over' and 'coming back' are expressions borrowed from the writings of the American Roman Catholic professor of theology, John S. Dunne, whose writings are not so familiar on this side of the Atlantic as perhaps they ought to be.[29] But I do not intend to follow Dunne's thought in this section overmuch, save to use the fertile image he has created for us in these two expressions: 'Passing over is a shifting of standpoint, a going over to the standpoint of another culture, another way of life, another religion. It is followed by an equal and opposite process we might call "coming back" with new insight into one's own culture, one's own way of life, one's own religion.'[30] With these words Dunne helps us to focus on the twofold nature of the spirituality of empathy and imagination which I see as so desirable for us all as we enter into the new relationships between people of differing faith commitment. For here we come to speak of the inner changes wrought by exposure to other faith and culture on the point of view of Christian belief. We are not here concerned with the scholarly processes of understanding the nature of another religion or ideology or world view. Much work on this kind of endeavour has been done by twentieth-century scholars following the pioneers in the nineteenth century.[31] Through their explorations into the nature of the study of religion we have all been taught the processes whereby we 'distance' ourselves from our own set of attitudes in order to gain a sympathetic yet objective understanding of the religion of other people. They have taught us about 'bracketing' our own beliefs, in which we hold all our own convictions as it were in abeyance as we seek to enter the enormous complexity of the religious world of another person.[32] Many of us whose primary concern is with the living encounter and dialogue between people of different faith would wish to acknowledge profound indebtedness to those who pioneered in the universities the study of what used to be known as 'comparative religion' but is now more often referred to as 'religious studies' or 'the history and phenomenology of religion'.[33] But we should note that this study exists in its own right, and can in no way be seen as merely ancillary to the Christian theological task. But equally it has to be affirmed most emphatically that the Christian theological task is not to be defined or perhaps even approached, in terms of the study of religion.[34]

I am therefore in this section as much concerned with the 'coming back' as with the 'passing over'. This must be seen in terms of

Christian commitment as well as Christian openness. 'Passing over' and 'coming back' belong within the same dynamic pattern. Both are aspects of that enlargement of mental horizon, and of personal growth which, as Gordon Wakefield reminded us, demand their own asceticism. We address ourselves therefore to the rigours, the disciplines, the sheer hard work of being open and committed in a religiously plural world.

In my own reflections on this theme I am much helped by analogies with the learning of other languages and the entering into the experiences of others mediated through literature. Let me describe what I mean.

There is, I am told, a Czech proverb which says that as often as you learn a new language you become a new person! It is notable, but unsurprising, that there is no similar aphorism in the English language. The linguistic insularity of these islands goes back a long way. Nonetheless, there have always been those amongst the British people who have transcended our monoglot condition. These are the men and women who have discovered an expansion of mental and spiritual horizons, for they have learned to see the world through the eyes and perceptions of people of different cultures and different world views. They have understood from their experience that language determines how we think. But this insight is at least as old as that grandson of Jesus Ben Sirach, who committed himself to translating the works of his grandfather's writings somewhere about the middle of the second century before the Christian era. His translation is known as *Ecclesiasticus*. In asking for indulgence and care as we read his Greek translation, he wrote: 'For what was originally expressed in Hebrew does not have exactly the same sense when translated into another language.'[35] Because of detailed studies in the field of semiotics we can say much more about language today. Language is made up of more than words with their meanings. The words themselves are part of much larger patterns of meaning belonging to whole cultures. In learning another language we learn about another culture system. When we begin to speak another language we are enabled to stand within the framework of another cultural system. The pioneering sociologist Max Weber once spoke of the human being as 'a creature suspended in webs of significance that he has spun'. He meant that there is no 'human nature' as such, but only individual men and women who have been moulded as persons by their language.

I may therefore pass over into the experience and the world view of another human being only as I learn his or her language. I need to know how that other person uses words, not simply by knowing the meaning of those words as a lexicon might explain them to me, but by gaining some kind of insight into the way those words are used within the total framework of meaning. Learning a language means a long wrestling with grammatical structures and acquiring basic vocabulary. Most of us know the painful discipline of this. But it is only after we have gone through such a struggle that we can even begin to enter into that other framework. We begin to think then in that other language and no longer sound like P. G. Wodehouse's Englishman preparing to speak French. We have crossed a frontier and stand within a new circle of relationships and perceptions. In this there is at once both an enormous exhilaration ('I have become another person') but also an overwhelming sense that there is so much that one does not know that will forever remain opaque yet is clearly luminous and evident to the native speaker.

Many of the features of this process are comparable to entering into inter-faith relationships. Sometimes the experiences precisely overlap, as friends of mine throughout Britain are discovering for themselves, as they try to learn Gujarati or Bengali or any of the other languages now spoken in the great cities of the United Kingdom. They are automatically involved in inter-faith conversation, which in turn leads to an interior dialogue in their own hearts and minds. But most of us will never, in the nature of our short lives, be able to master Arabic or Urdu, yet we have to talk to Muslims from the Middle East or Pakistan; we will never master Sanskrit or Hindi, yet we must speak to Hindus; we will never master Pali or Singhalese, yet we must enter into dialogue with Buddhists.

The process and the commitment to such dialogue are analogous to learning another language. To enter another's religious world is not done easily. There is the unavoidable *ascesis* involved. There is a grammar and a vocabulary to be mastered. There is the moment to be reached when we begin to think, however fleetingly, like a Hindu or a Buddhist, even to the point of realizing that this view of life 'makes sense'! This will not be only at an intellectual level, though often we shall find ourselves 'almost persuaded' to become a Jew or a Muslim, or whatever else. These are intellectual systems which carry great majesty. But there may also be that intense immediacy of realizing in the depths of our spirit that there is a whole new world open to us, and for a moment we may respond with our whole being to this new world. But just as we find ourselves in the process of learning another language with that exhilaration of having become a new person and yet, at the same time, realizing that we shall never totally understand the world in the same way as a native speaker of that language, so in our inter-faith passing over we realize that this Muslim or Jewish or Hindu or Buddhist world will never be ours. At this point we come back. That which has made us is our native language, our mother tongue. This is the language we use for our deepest expressions, our ultimate perceptions. However much of the grandeur and profundity of another world view we may perceive through learning another language, our self-expression in moments of either ecstasy or crisis is in our own tongue. However much we pass over into the other linguistic frames of reference, ultimately we come back to that which grasped us and moulded us from the beginning of our lives.

That this analogy has commended itself to others may be demonstrated from Monica Furlong's beautiful biography of Thomas Merton. Merton died in an accident in Bangkok in 1968, but he has left us an account of his South East Asian journey, which has become one of the great contemporary spiritual classics, in his *Asian Journal*. Monica Furlong writes:

> Yet even as he set out on that last journey, with so much of his inner journey completed, he knew that something had still eluded him and hoped very much that he would find it in the Asian religious communities. Some Christian observers have seemed to take offence at this, as if Merton might only be permitted to drink truth from a Christian source and as if all other springs might be contaminated, like the spring behind the hermitage. But Merton never thought or wrote of ceasing to be a Christian. Christianity was, quite simply, his language, and could not more be renounced than any native tongue; but this did not mean that other languages might not be loved and yield striking new insights in the old familiar phrases and ideas. In a number of the Buddhist and Hindu teachers Merton met in Asia, he found holiness and a deep knowledge of the realities of prayer, and he was humble enough to listen and to learn.[36]

Another fruitful analogy, which helps us to see the process of passing over and coming back in terms of the spirituality required of us in a religiously plural world, may lead on from the domain of literature and of literary studies. William Walsh, formerly Professor of Education in the University of Leeds, once wrote: 'A literary education has not been fully effective if Literature still means to the student an array, however splendid, of distinct and independent works, however intimately known.' In his view a great literary talent offers to the rest of us an extension of the range of possibilities, 'a means of attaining, and a standard of judging, a discovery of self'.[37]

Walsh wrote these words at the beginning of a critical study of John Keats. Keats may be taken as one model of what he himself called 'Negative Capability', by which he meant the ability to be in 'uncertainties, mysteries, doubts, without any irritable reaching after fact and reason'.[38] It is this state of receptivity and openness to experience that marks a certain type of creative genius. Shakespeare, for example, possessed this ability supremely. Keats wrote elsewhere: 'let us not therefore go hurrying about and collecting honey, bee-like buzzing here and there impatiently for a knowledge of what is to be aimed at; but let us open our leaves like a flower and be passive and receptive'.[39] Keats's own ability in this area was most marked. He speaks of the way in which other people would impose their personalities to such an extent that he himself felt that he had to leave a room lest he be annihilated. Charmingly he tells us that 'if a sparrow come before my window I take part in its existence and pick about the gravel', and elsewhere he tells us that 'I lay awake last night listening to the rain with a sense of being drown'd and rotted like a grain of wheat'.[40] It is clear from many of the sayings of Jesus that our Lord had this same insight into the feelings of others, as well as kinship with natural things. W. H. Auden also speaks of this extraordinary openness and passivity which a poet experiences in a simple verse, which in itself has much to do with the theme of inter-faith relations:

> Whatever their personal faith
> All poets, as such,
> Are polytheists.[41]

Auden means that the poetic imagination is capable of taking in all kinds of other ideals and aspirations and hopes, things that are to be loved and worshipped. But Auden, a great Christian poet, and Keats, who could hardly be called that, are far from suggesting that the poet as such is a cipher. The negative capability is part of a total, strong integrity of mind and spirit. The great talent of Auden or Keats or any other poet is to unite the perceptions of their openness and receptivity within a single controlling vision.

It seems to me that many of those whom I count among my personal friends, who have entered joyfully the new world of inter-religious relationships, have demonstrated both this negative capability, this ability to be in uncertainties, mysteries, doubts, without an irritable reaching after fact and reason, alongside a single controlling vision of Jesus and their commitment to him. Just one illustration of this form of spirituality I draw now from Roger Hooker. He has given us three splendid accounts of his life in Varanasi, better

known to some of us as Benares. Writing perceptively in the Foreword
to the last of Roger Hooker's three books about Varanasi, Simon
Barrington-Ward describes Roger Hooker's distinctive method: 'If
you ask him – outstanding guide as he is – to show you what
Hinduism or popular Islam are, he responds by telling stories, by
introducing you to places and above all to people who have become
his friends.'[42] The reason why Roger Hooker responds with stories is
that he himself spent thirteen years patiently and receptively waiting
and listening to people of many different traditions. He speaks of the
need to 'submit ourselves to the patient and humble discipline of
listening to others, of being content to spend time with them because
God loves them infinitely more than we do. It is only in this context
that we can discover how strange and incomprehensible other people
find our language, our customs and our beliefs. And it is only when we
have made that humiliating, painful and very necessary discovery
that we learn that communication is not an automatic process that
happens by itself, but an art which has to be learnt, and it is precisely
our friends of other faiths who are our teachers in it.'[43] Roger Hooker
here speaks, as one who is well qualified so to do, words of rebuke to
all who are impatient, unimaginative, and 'bee-like, buzzing here and
there'.[44] Speaking in the context of much missionary work he says:
'Our evangelism is still far too often limited to traditional stereotyped
language. We do not stop to ask ourselves what effect our words really
have on those who hear them or why so many do not think what we
say is worth hearing anyway. A narrow and self-justifying concentra-
tion on "results" produces an impatience which betrays the very love
we seek to proclaim. A Hindu friend once remarked to me: "In the
past the missionaries did not want to spend time with someone like
me, they went where they thought their efforts would be more
fruitful".'[45] Roger Hooker's writings are supreme examples of the
process of passing over and coming back and, as such, models for
future spirituality.

4 The Once and Future Kingdom

But what we have said about spiritualities of keeping silence, of
passing over and coming back, of creative expectancy and self-
discovery must be set within a larger context, otherwise they lose the
sense of the kingdom of God, and, though in vastly different form,
become just as much escape routes from the harsh realities of this
world as the spiritual ecstasies of the Corinthian gnostics. I hasten to
add that none of the scholars and teachers I have referred to remotely

comes within such categorization. I refer simply to the possibility that such forms of spirituality become ends in themselves, and fail then to serve God's ultimate purposes in and for his world. So our last section must refer to a theology of creation and redemption. As Christians, we affirm that this is not a random universe to which we bring our own meanings, but that in Jesus Christ God has revealed both the heart of his relationship to us, and the way in which that relationship will work itself out in the unfolding of the future. In Jesus Christ God has revealed the heart of the relationship that each human being is to have to every other man or woman. Christian relations with those who cannot or do not believe as Christians do are part of those same relationships. These relationships God has with all his human children, and these relationships themselves are part of the kingdom of mended relationships, symbolized as we have seen, in the vision of the City of God in Revelation 21–22.[46]

We use, therefore, the symbol of the kingdom for both the relationship that God has to us ('Yours is the kingdom') and for that mended creation of the future ('let your kingdom come'). These petitions from the Lord's Prayer give us the two polarities lying at the heart of Christian faith. We believe that in the life, teaching, witness, suffering and death of Jesus, we have seen the mystery of redemption. It is through suffering that God reigns. Pilate, according to the records, at least made this clear, that Jesus reigns from the cross (John 19.19; cf. John 12.31–32). St Paul saw in this the establishment of a new creation, for in this death was God himself, reconciling the world unto himself (II Cor. 5.17). Here everything turns upon christology: neither *avatār* nor *sannyāsi*, neither a divine apparition nor just another of a series of persecuted prophets, this man is for us Lord and Christ. But if he is the Christ of God, we have serious problems, for the world apparently goes on its way without any significant difference. Not only has the desert not yet blossomed like the rose (Isa. 35) and the lion not lain down with the lamb (Isa. 12); nowhere are there any signs of lesser (or perhaps greater) miracles, as, for example, peace between Catholics and Protestants in Northern Ireland, or the feeding of the starving in the Horn of Africa. It is not apparent that God rules in his world.

Clearly many ways to deal with this problem have been developed in Christian history, and it would be far from my purpose to analyse them now. But the false step is always to imply that the kingdom of God has nothing to do with the trials and tribulations of this world. We are not permitted to preach Jesus instead of the kingdom that Jesus preached. For the central prayer of the church is inescapably the 'Our Father'. This is the Lord's Prayer, and there is no other prayer comparable to it. We have to emphasize this again and again, not least in our context of inter-religious relationships.[47] For in no way is the content of the prayer a private possession of an exclusive group, any more than that same content can allow the idea of an extractionist salvation in which individual souls enjoy eternal bliss in some realm far above the bright blue sky. For in these words of Jesus the Christian community still prays for a kingdom to come, and for God's will to be done on earth. As part of that coming of the new world, the church prays that it may be given strength for its pilgrimage ('our daily bread') and that it may already be the community of the future, a community of mutual forgiveness, ('forgive us our sins as we forgive one another'). All this is about what Bishop Krister Stendahl calls 'the mended creation'.[48]

A community which prays such a prayer is one marked by the future, not by the past. The consequences of this for our inter-faith spirituality are fourfold: first, we affirm that all Christian spirituality is that of people on the way, '*in via*', for which the best image is perhaps precisely that of pilgrimage. Flowing as a consequence from that, is the Christian's spiritual dependence on just enough bread sufficient for the journey, that daily provision upon which the ancient people of the exodus had to learn to trust (Ex. 16). The experience of total dependence upon God, as well as the sense that here in the present world we have no abiding city, leads us to affirm, thirdly, that condition of spiritual poverty of which the monk or nun, Eastern or Western, is the exemplar. Fourthly, to use Gordon Wakefield's words once more, Christian spirituality is not an absorption into the infinite, but rather 'a being caught up into the paschal mystery'. For Christians there is no by-pass around the tensions, dangers and sufferings of this world. Yet all these are made luminous by the cross and resurrection. We speak very briefly of these four marks of Christian spirituality in relation to our religiously plural situation.

5 Pilgrimage

One key image in the BCC Guidelines on Relations with People of Other Faiths is that of the Christian as a 'fellow-pilgrim' with others who are seeking a new future.[49] This image is derived from the WCC *Guidelines* which said: 'we feel able with integrity to assure our partners in dialogue that we come not as manipulators but as genuine fellow-pilgrims, to speak with them of what we believe God to have done in Jesus Christ . . . '[50] It is, I believe, a most happy metaphor, for

it reminds us that we ourselves are Abrahamic people, still looking for
'a city which has foundations, whose maker and builder is God' (Heb.
11.10). Such a self-conception belongs to the heart of Christian
understanding: we are not to be a settled community, living on the
traditions of the past, but rather are those who realize that 'here we
have no abiding city . . . '. The image of the quest or sacred journey
may well be universal, and that will in itself link us with all human
beings, but it is decisive for the community that has as one of its
profoundest symbols the image of the *Parousia* (the advent of Christ at
the end) and the continual prayer 'thy kingdom come'. Consequently,
the language of the Church of England document, *Towards a Theology
for Inter-Faith Dialogue* . . . is singularly well-chosen when in its 'Final
Reflections' it speaks of a 'journey through unfamiliar territory':
'Those who would journey with us into the unfamiliar territory must
learn to accept the stance of vulnerability which dialogue brings with
it. Our discipleship is revealed for what it is, as our understanding
and faith are put to the test. We discover that it is out of weakness and
not strength that we make our witness and our appeal.'[51]

It is not agreeable to our natural bents and inclinations to be thus
vulnerable. We would – left to ourselves – prefer to live in a well-
walled city, and even within that fortress, clothed in suits of armour.
But the pilgrim sets out from the place of security in quest of the holy
place – a city or a kingdom which lies somewhere over the rainbow,
beyond the furthest horizon. He or she sets out, too, knowing that
there will be perils, dangers, vicissitudes all along the way.

For through going on pilgrimage, and here is the second aspect of
the image, there comes self-knowledge. As the BCC *Guidelines* put it:
'Pilgrims learn truths about themselves and their fellow pilgrims
when they travel on the road together, sharing its rigours, its
difficulties and dangers. They come to understand their common
humanity.'[52] We discover, as we live alongside our partners in
dialogue that we at once share the same fears, the same griefs, the
same needs, and along with this goes the sharing of such resources as
we have: 'Pilgrims', we wrote, 'have gifts and strengths that they may
share with others, and that their fellows have gifts and strengths to
share with them.' We then went on to suggest in this context our
authentic witness to the dialogue partner would find its proper place,
using precisely 'pilgrimage' descriptions of Jesus and his gifts:
'Through dialogue in commitment to our own faith with others we are
able to point fellow-pilgrims to where we have found Bread and
Water, Rest and Healing (see John 6.51; John 7.37; Matthew 11.28;
Matthew 9.1ff).'

It is with the 'Bread' for the journey that we are concerned in the next mark of a proper Christian spirituality.

6 Provisionality

The fourth petition of the Lord's Prayer is endlessly fascinating to New Testament scholars. There are within the two versions that we have in the gospel records (Matt. 6.11 and Luke 11.3) two major questions of interpretation. One of these turns on the form of the verb, 'Give'. Is this to be translated, following Matthew, 'Give us once and for all', or should it be, following Luke, 'Keep on giving us'? In the one case the appropriate adverb of time will be 'this day' (as in Matt. *sēmeron*) and in the second case, 'each day' (as in Luke, *to kath' hēmeran*). The second crux lies in the interpretation of the adjective applied to 'bread', usually translated 'daily', *epiousios*. As Raymond Brown has written: 'In the third century the word puzzled Origen, who could find no example of it in other Greek writers. Seventeen centuries later we are not much better off.'[53] The only real help is in etymology, and Brown's detailed discussion leads him to the conclusion that we should not take this petition to be understood as a prayer expressing the daily needs of the Christian community, as in Luke, but much rather as pointing to the new future of God, i.e. as eschatological in its reference. This is the Bread of Tomorrow, (Heb. *lehem mahar*) the food of the Messianic Banquet. (Luke 14.15; Matt. 8.11; Luke 22.29–30; cf. Rev. 7.16). But on the way to that day of feasting, the church needs its provisions for the journey, in the understanding of which we have the powerful imagery provided by Exodus 16. 'The Lord said to Moses, "Behold, I will rain bread from heaven for you; and the people shall go out and gather a day's portion every day, that I may prove them whether they will walk in my law or not"' (Ex. 16.4). So we pray for *manna*, the daily provision, until we all sit down together in the kingdom of God.

But, as the Exodus story goes on to tell us, the people were not content with this provisionality. Instead of gathering a sufficiency for one single day, they wanted to ensure that they would have an adequate supply for the future . . . 'and it bred worms and became foul' (Ex. 16.20). As a pilgrim people we are entitled to ask from God some of tomorrow's bread today, sufficient to get us through, and no more.

All this is of course figurative. In rejecting the Lucan interpretation of the Fourth Petition, we are compelled to think not of the daily needs of bread for our stomachs, but rather of the sustenance of heart and mind (John 6.27; 6.47ff.). We may apply it to the kind of theology and spirituality we need to sustain us in the religiously plural world. David Brown, whose death was so severe a blow to us, reminded us always of the 'provisionality' of theological formulations as we have received them so far in our Christian history. It is therefore to him that the chief reference is made in a further paragraph in *Towards a Theology for Inter-Faith Dialogue* . . .: 'Those who have already begun the journey into such unfamiliar territory have reminded us that theology is always provisional. It is out of experience in dialogue with our tradition, under the power of the Holy Spirit, that our theology flows. We are given to the Spirit, who is with us and who goes before us.'[54] I take these words to be a kindly but firm warning that we may not have either a theology or a spirituality which is armour plated, an impregnable fortress. The pilgrim does not move towards the new age in the spiritual equivalent of a Chieftain tank, nor does he or she have the spiritual equivalent of a mobile Sainsbury's as logistical back-up. Jesus did not say, Blessed are those who are rich in spirit, any more than he said, Those who seek to save their souls will save them.

7 Poverty

On the contrary, he affirmed both the blessedness of the poor as such (Luke 6.20), and the blessedness of the poor in spirit (Matt. 5.3) which may or may not be the same thing.[55] Here we have no need to decide on which interpretation we would like to follow, for people of other faiths have already done that for us. Since I am going to use the thought of the Sri Lankan Jesuit, Aloysius Pieris in this section, let me set down an experience of my own in Fr Aloysius' house on the outskirts of Colombo. I discovered there a Buddhist monk, working at the invitation of Fr Aloysius on a wall sculpture of Jesus in the act of washing the disciples' feet. Now in Theravada Buddhist cultures it is quite a familiar event that a disciple should wash the feet of a monk. But hardly that a monk should wash the feet of a disciple. All the shock of that action has been brought out on the face of St Peter and of the disciples standing with him. Fr Aloysius told me of the many exchanges he had had with the monk while he was working on portraying this incident. One day he said to Fr Aloysius: 'If you Christians had looked like this (and he then pointed to the kneeling Jesus) we Buddhists would not have turned to Marxism . . . ' The panoply of wealth and power of Western Christendom, and its individual representatives, some of whom have the temerity to call themselves 'born-again' Christians, impress the monks and nuns of the east very little.

But there has always been the Christian protest against Christendom and we know this chiefly in the form of monasticism.[56]

Thus Thomas Merton's last recorded talk was on 'Marxism and Monastic Perspectives', filmed by an Italian television company in Bangkok. Monica Furlong describes this: 'What interested him, Merton said in his lecture, was the man who took up a critical attitude towards the world and its structures, whether Monk or Marxist . . . ' Such a one believes that 'the claims of the world are fraudulent'. Both monk and Marxist want a world open to change: 'the world refusal of the monk is in view of his desire for change'.[57]

It is therefore of extreme interest to me to find Fr Aloysius Pieris weaving the insight of Merton's spirituality into his own perception of the way in which Christians relate in the east to the existing monastic traditions of Hinduism and Buddhism.[58] He says that if the church really wishes to enter into dialogue with Asia, it will be necessary for it to learn from its own monks the language of interiority, which is equally that of Asian monastic tradition, as well as the language of *agapē*, love, which is the only language the poor of Asia can understand. The first of these speaks about a spiritual illumination which leads to an inward liberation from the instinct to acquire ever more things, and the second calls for an emancipation on the social level from all the structures of oppression, which are created by that same instinct to possess.

In Sri Lanka there are already examples of the coming together in 'basic communities' of Buddhist monks with Christians who have embraced monastic patterns of life. Father Aloysius describes the Satyodaya Group in Kandy which he calls a real miracle from the social point of view. This multi-racial, multi-linguistic, multi-religious community is offering an example of a classless society in a country torn asunder by racial tension. Similarly the Christian Workers Fellowship is another group which gathers together Buddhists, Hindus, Christians and Marxists. This Fellowship is at work in many regions of Sri Lanka in many 'basic communities'.[59] Aloysius Pieris concludes his article with a call for assistance from such representatives of the Western monastic tradition as Thomas Merton who have reactivated in themselves what Pieris calls the 'oriental' part of their being. Such people are able to defuse the tensions within the Christian churches set amid the grinding poverty of Asia when they proclaim the gospel 'to our people in our own languages'. For the gospel of Jesus Christ is the new covenant into which God and the poor have entered against Mammon, their common enemy. 'When that happens', says Father Aloysius, 'liberation and inculturation will no longer be two things, but one in Asia.'[60]

Fr Aloysius was dealing with the situation of the south east Asia countries, but what he wrote has its implications for the way we are in inter-faith dialogue in the West. For the same patterns of 'basic communities' are beginning to emerge amongst us. I think for example of the 'Inter-faith Conference' of Washington, DC, with its community centre set in downtown Washington, dealing with urban deprivation just fourteen blocks away from the White House itself; and in the British Isles of the network of new communities in the poorest part of our cities whose story has begun to be told in the survey conducted by Barbara Holden and Eric Rolls, *Christian Community and Cultural Diversity*.[61] I wrote in the Introduction to this little book: 'We know that monasticism was never a phenomenon limited only to the Christian tradition but has its counterparts in Buddhism, Hinduism and many other traditions. Men and women have always been drawn to find ways of living together in common testimony to other realities than the conventional wisdoms in their own societies. Now, with the coming of a consciously pluralistic religious world, it seems that the same Spirit is acting to bring these various traditional monastic forms into close association with one another, and monks and nuns, or their contemporary equivalents, are now meeting in new and remarkable ways.'[62] I went on to say that it seems likely that the BCC's fourth principle of dialogue (i.e. 'that dialogue becomes the medium of authentic witness') will find its most complete fruition in the realm denoted by 'spirituality'. When we move beyond intellectual discussion to mutual endorsement, mutual support, mutual testimony in shared life and shared prayer, new things are born in us. The calling of basic communities in this regard is clear, for here as in many other areas they are to be part of, in Alan Ecclestone's phrase, 'the dawn chorus of the new creation'.[63]

8 The Paschal Mystery

The attitude of the pilgrim, the vulnerability of those who have left aside the old securities, the trust that there will be provision adequate for one day at a time, the commitment to a new poverty of spirit for the sake of the oppressed, make sense only in the light of the pattern of death and resurrection which we call the paschal mystery. Jesus has become for us the man who reigns from the tree, and in his total obedience even unto death on the cross we have seen into the heart of

God. Because of this obedience God has highly exalted him (Phil. 2.11). He is the once and future king. With this insight into the way the kingdom once was, we go then towards that future kingdom. But Thomas's words form still the counterpoint. 'Let us', he said, 'go that we may die with him'. Again he said, 'Lord, we do not know where you are going, how may we know the way?' Jesus said, 'I am the Way, the Truth and the Life'. So be it. We will follow that Way, that Truth, that Life now, in the midst of our religious plural world. We will ourselves assuredly see the marks of the nails, for dialogue is an element of the cross we are called to bear.[64] Our spirituality cannot be an avoidance of the tensions, dangers of 'the world of action'. But the living out of the paschal mystery means that there is also the release of creativity, openness, joy in the power of the resurrection. So we go on, in Wesley's words: 'rooted in the faith once delivered to the saints and grounded in love, in true catholic love' until we are 'swallowed up in love for ever and ever!' Then there is an end of religion,[65] and God will be 'all in all to everyone' (I Cor. 15.28). In that day he will 'be King over all the earth', and we will join with all those who have come from 'the east and the west who will sit at table with Abraham, Isaac and Jacob in the Kingdom of Heaven' (Matt. 8.11).

Appendix A: A Bibliography on Jewish-Christian Relations

From the days of the first Christian missionaries to the present time church and synagogue have had to live side by side. So St Paul goes to Ephesus first to the synagogue, 'entering into dialogue and arguing persuasively about the Kingdom of God' (Acts 19.8). The great argument has continued through the centuries. From time to time the dialogue has broken off, deteriorating into mere abuse, as for example with St John Chrysostom or with Martin Luther. Often, tragically, abuse has turned into torture and death for the weaker partner. This past and its consequent literature cannot be ignored as we think of Jewish-Christian relations.

But we shall not start back in these bad times. For in our own period something unprecedented is taking place. For whatever reasons and motives – maybe the traumas of the Nazi time, maybe the establishment of the State of Israel, or perhaps the awareness of the shared uncertainty in the face of secularization, or the same distress at the prospect of a world apparently out of the control of its Creator – we Jews and Christians are engaged with a quite new seriousness and depth in dialogue together. Rabbi Irving Goldmann goes so far as to call our age 'a moment of Messianic promise'. The wonder and the excitement of this needs to pervade even a bibliography.

There are great gains for Christians in all this new exploration, and a bibliography on Jewish-Christian relationships should point to three positive ways in which our self-understanding is enlarged through this particular encounter.

1. First in the way we learn to read scripture afresh (and not only the Old Testament!). In a most important sense, Christianity and Judaism do not stand, as is so often said, in the relation of mother and daughter, but rather as the two offspring of the same stock. They form two differing ways of understanding the Law, the Prophets and the Writings. They are two different modes of exegesis of the single concept of Covenant. They represent two different religious ways of responding to the great cataclysms of the first century of the Common

Era, namely the fall of Jerusalem and the destruction of the Temple. When Christians and Jews read the same scriptures together, there is so much that is still held in common, and yet there are the riches of divergent interpretations to be explored. Of course much of this can be learnt through books, but when we actually work together on the same materials Jewish-Christian dialogue is at its most penetrating and most illuminating. A sense of this must come through this bibliography, to whet the appetite for fuller engagement.

2. Secondly, we may expect vast enrichment in our own Christian perceptions, particularly at the level of systematic theology and ecumenical understanding. I turn often to the words of Karl Barth in the *Church Dogmatics*, IV/3, pp. 876–8. He wrote there: ' . . . in relation to the Synagogue there can be no question of the community proclaiming the true faith in place of a false one, or opposing the true God to an idol. The God whose work and Word it has to attest to the world was the God of Israel.' For this reason mission is not what the church owes to the Jewish People. Rather we should be asking what we have still to learn from them. I think this suggestion works itself out in two ways. First, as we put to ourselves with increasing intensity (as a result of our re-discovery of the faith of living Judaism) the question 'what more do we have through our faith in Jesus Christ?', we shall find new depths in the symbols of the Death and the Resurrection. Secondly, we shall be brought to a realization that the first and gravest of all the schisms in the people of God is the cleavage between church and synagogue. Catholic, Protestant and Orthodox Christians will discover a new identity as one part of the equation in Romans 9–11, and through dialogue with Jewish teachers ways of breaking some of the contemporary theological log-jams. This is why Barth affirmed that ' . . . the modern ecumenical movement suffers more seriously from the absence of Israel than of Rome or Moscow' (he was writing before 1961). We shall see how the force of this is being brought home to us through many of the books listed below.

3. Thirdly, Christian-Jewish dialogue takes place within the greater context of dialogue with people of all the other living faiths and ideologies. Christians engage in this dialogue with a mixture of hope and trepidation, uncertain as to quite how they are to be faithful to Christ in an age of religious pluralism. As we all seek for an adequate theology of religions and inter-faith dialogue it seems to me that the engagement with those who are nearest to us is the one which will throw most light on how we must live with those who differ from us. Indeed, I register a further conviction that we will not get our

relationships to Muslims or Hindus or Buddhists right, if we fail to get ourselves right in relation to Israel. Hence the sense of urgency which I hope underlies the compilation of this bibliography, and the final criterion of the selection of the books which appear in it.

Please note that there are many important books on Jewish-Christian relations published in the USA (and therefore not easily obtainable here), or in German and Dutch (and therefore not easily accessible to most English readers). I have deliberately avoided referring to them, as well as to books that have long been out of print, except in the section on the 'precursors of today's dialogue'.

One Essential Tool

We are extremely well served in Britain by a comprehensive quarterly journal of record, *Christian-Jewish Relations: A Documentary Survey*, which is published by the Institute of Jewish Affairs, 11 Hertford Street, London, W1Y 7DX. This should be available in all theological libraries, and anyone who wants to take Christian-Jewish dialogue seriously will find it extremely worth-while to subscribe as an individual. Each issue contains documents and articles from both Jewish and Christian sources all round the world. It is referred to below as *CJR*.

The Precursors of Today's Dialogue

As Christians and Jews move towards each other in the new stages of our dialogue, we need to remind ourselves of those who in previous generations pioneered the new ways. Space forbids the full listing of their writings, and in some cases, their books are now obtainable only through libraries. I suggest here just one or two titles in each case. On the Jewish side important names are those of Martin Buber, Franz Rosenzweig and Hans-Joachim Schoeps. Martin Buber has had a quite special influence on Christian theology through his *I and Thou*, T. and T. Clark 1970 (there are several other translations in existence). But two other works bear more directly on our theme. *Between Man and Man*, Kegan Paul 1947 and Fontana 1961, is R. Gregor Smith's translation of a number of writings, the most important of which is Buber's *Zwiesprache*, literally 'Dialogue' (1929). These meditations are often deeply moving, and give practical expression to the often rather difficult thought in *I and Thou*. *Two Types of Faith*, Routledge & Kegan Paul 1951, is controversial and illuminating by turns, and still germane to our dialogue.

Martin Buber's great contemporary was Franz Rosenzweig, and happily his great work *The Star of Redemption*, second edition 1934, ET, Routledge & Kegan Paul 1971, makes his thought easily accessible. During the First World War Rosenzweig exchanged letters with the Eugen Rosenstock-Huessy, and these have been called 'the purest form of Judaeo-Christian dialogue ever attained'. They are conveniently summarized in *F. Rosenzweig: His Life and Thought* by Nahum N. Glatzer, New York, Shocken Books 1953. One other precursor to the present stage of Jewish-Christian dialogue was Hans-Joachim Schoeps who, among many other valuable writings concerning Christian origins, also contributed an exceedingly valuable introduction to our whole theme: *The Jewish-Christian Argument, A History of Theologies in Conflict*, Faber 1965.

On the Christian side it will suffice to recall three names who made outstanding contributions to bring us to the present time and place. The first is James Parkes, an Anglican priest who gave his whole life to the combatting of anti-semitism and Christian misunderstanding of Judaism. I find these two books invaluable: *Judaism and Christianity*, Gollancz 1948, and a collection of lectures and papers, *Prelude to Dialogue*, Vallentine Mitchell 1969. Another Anglican priest who toiled throughout his too short life for better relationships was Peter Schneider, whose 'Christian Presence' series book *Sweeter than Honey*, SCM Press 1966, is still one of the most helpful introductions for Christians to Judaism as a living faith. Lastly may I recommend a seminal work by a Canadian, Roland de Corneille *Christian and Jews: The Tragic Past and Hopeful Future*, New York, Harper and Row 1966. It contains not only a vivid historical survey but also a wealth of practical suggestions.

Introductions to Jewish Belief and Practice

Many Christians will want to begin with material which will give them a sense of Judaism as a living faith. The following are admirable and readable exercises in Jewish self-description: Moshe Davis, *I am a Jew*, Mowbrays 1978; Herman Wouk, *This is my God*, Fount 1976; Lionel Blue's two books, *To Heaven with Scribes and Pharisees*, Darton, Longman & Todd 1975, and *A Backdoor to Heaven*, Darton, Longman & Todd 1979; for more detailed historical and theological information there is Alan Unterman, *Jews: their Religious Beliefs and Practices*, Routledge & Kegan Paul 1981, Albert Polack and Joan Lawrence, *Cup of Life: A Short History of Post-Biblical Judaism*, SPCK 1976, and in the Argus Major World Religions Series, Samuel T. Lachs and Saul

P. Wachs, *Judaism*, obtainable from Fowler Wright Books, Leominster. Two items from the Reform Synagogues of Great Britain (33 Seymour Place, London W1) lead into an immediate apprehension of Jewish worship and devotional life: the *Forms of Prayer for Jewish Worship: 1. Sabbath and Daily Prayers* (1977) and Jonathan Magonet, *Returning: Exercises in Repentance* (1975). Two books by a non-Jew give fine insight into Jewish tradition: William W. Simpson, *Jewish Prayer and Worship*, SCM Press 1965, reprinted 1982, and *Light and Rejoicing: A Christian's Understanding of Jewish Worship*, Belfast Christian Journals, 1976.

The Church and the Jewish People

We enter into the contemporary dialogue with Jews and the entailments of Christian history and tradition. We need to understand, with deep penitence but not with total despair, something of that history. Hugh Montefiore's 1983 Stepney Lecture, *The Church and the Jews*, available from Church House, Harborne Road, Birmingham, B17, and reprinted in *CJR*, Vol. 16, No. 2, June 1983, pp. 3–19, is a brief, deeply felt survey by an Anglican Diocesan who is Jewish by race. A far more detailed account of where we have gone wrong is in Charlotte Klein, *Anti-Judaism in Christian Theology*, SPCK 1978. Here the whole issue of Christian origins is raised, and it is important to look at recent studies by New Testament scholars as, for example: Krister Stendahl, *Paul among Jews and Gentiles*, SCM Press 1977, along with such near-classical studies as Johannes Munck, *Paul and the Salvation of Mankind*, SCM Press 1959, W. D. Davies, *Paul and Rabbinic Judaism*, SPCK, second edition 1955, and E. P. Sanders, *Paul and Palestinian Judaism*, SCM Press 1977. In their various ways these scholars emphasize that Paul did not, as has been so often suggested, break from Judaism because it represented for him a legalist way of establishing human self-righteousness, but rather (and only) because of his christology. Obviously pivotal to Christian understanding of God's continuing purposes with the Jewish people is the interpretation of Romans 9–11. One very recent study of these chapters and related material is Marcus Barth, *The People of God*, published as *Supplement 5* to the *Journal for the Study of the New Testament* 1983, and obtainable from the Department of Biblical Studies at the University of Sheffield. Marcus Barth takes up here many of the themes with which his father was concerned, relating his exegetical work to the contemporary ecumenical log-jam and to the political conflicts surrounding the State of Israel.

The New Approaches

Here we mention three books which have particular significance. Alan Ecclestone, *The Night Sky of the Lord*, Darton, Longman & Todd 1980 is a most powerful reflection upon how the 'furnaces of Auschwitz . . . may be the fires in which the heart of mankind may be purged anew'. A group mainly composed of scholars from the Church of Scotland tries to discern in *The Witness of the Jews to God* (ed. David W. Torrance), Handsel Press 1982, what God is saying to Christians through the Jewish people now, after the Holocaust and with the establishment of the Jewish State. As a symposium it is uneven, and contains a number of rather startling perceptions, as for example, Thomas Torrance's view that the church has to 'take seriously the divine election and mission of Israel to the world' and then 'to incorporate the distinctive witness of the Christian Church within it'. But is there any evidence of our being so invited from the side of our Jewish partners? Awareness of what we have to explore together and to witness to in common does mark many contemporary Jewish statements, for example, those of the participants in the consultation referred to at the beginning of the next section, but perhaps the most substantial recent expression of such feelings from a Jew is in Dow Marmur, *Beyond Survival: Reflections on the Future of Judaism*, Darton, Longman & Todd 1982. He writes: 'this book is intended as a modest manifestation of the belief in a common understanding between exponents of Judaism and Christianity in the face of a world whose leading intellectual figures have sought to encourage us to live without hope.' He says elsewhere: 'The lack of a serious dialogue between Christians and Jews is not only jeopardizing the future of Judaism, but is harmful to Christianity.' Yes, we do have earnest and serious Jewish partners in dialogue.

Dialogue: Things We Have in Common

In 1980 the first Jewish-Anglican consultation took place in Andover, Wilts. Its theme was 'Law and Religion in Contemporary Society'. In the next year there was the first official international consultation of Lutherans and Jews in Copenhagen. Its theme was 'The Concept of the Human Being in the Lutheran and Jewish Traditions'. The papers given at these consultations have been published in *CJR*, Vol. 14, No. 1, March 1981, and Vol. 15, No. 2, June 1982 respectively. As well as being profoundly instructive in themselves, these documents represent precisely a discovery of common understanding and joint responsibility. Christians and Jews are drawn into dialogue by the force of their shared ethical convictions in the face of the general crisis of relativism: 'our shared concerns for God's concrete, earthly, creation could greatly benefit from a true dialogue' affirms one of the Jewish participants. The co-Chairman of the Andover consultation was the then Archbishop of York, and it is partly in tribute to his leadership in the field of Christian-Jewish dialogue that we use his recent book as a further example of where we may share common perceptions. Stuart Blanch, *The Trumpet in the Morning; Law and Freedom Today in the Light of the Hebraeo-Christian Tradition*, Hodder & Stoughton 1979, is an excellent example of how a Christian Old Testament scholar as well as one with high responsibility in Church and State, cannot stop at the reading of the Hebrew Bible as a historical document but must go on to relate positively to the perceptions of contemporary Judaism. Other Christian Hebraists are increasingly demonstrating the same need and the same ability to respond. For an insight into the way in which German Old Testament scholars are thinking, see two important articles reprinted in *CJR*: Hans-Joachim Kraus, 'The Jewish and the Christian Understanding of the Bible', *CJR*, Vol. 14, No. 2, June 1981, pp. 3–12, and Rolf Rendtorff, 'The Bible and its Anti-Jewish Interpretation', *CJR*, Vol. 16 No. 1, March 1983, pp. 4–20.

Dialogue about Jesus

That the Jewishness of Jesus is one area where Christians have much to learn from our Jewish partners, hardly needs to be stressed. Perhaps the latest in a goodly succession of Jewish scholars (C. Montefiore, I. Abrahams, J. Klausner, D. Flusser, Shalom Ben Chorin *et alia*) who have given close attention to the Gospel narratives is Geza Vermes, in *Jesus the Jew: A Historian's Reading of the Gospels*, Collins 1973 reissued SCM Press 1983, and *The Gospel of Jesus the Jew*, Newcastle-upon-Tyne, University of Newcastle Riddell Memorial Lecture 1982, reprinted in *Jesus and the World of Judaism*, SCM Press 1984. Vermes shows a Jesus who belongs within a context of ancient Palestinian charismatic Judaism. But this is not where the problem lies. The assertion that Jesus is Messiah is still the *skandalon* (I Cor. 1.23). The best historical introduction to what lies between us is undoubtedly Jakob Jocz, *The Jewish People and Jesus Christ: A Study in the Controversy between Church and Synagogue*, SPCK 1954. An intensely moving novel which brings home the human issues involved after the centuries of 'the teaching of contempt', of pogrom and Jew-baiting, of persecution and finally of the Holocaust is to be found in Chaim Potok, *My Name is Asher Lev*, Penguin Books 1973. To have read these two books is to be at least a little prepared for the sensitive task of speaking with Jews about the mystery of the crucified Messiah. It still turns, or so it seems, on the nature of the kingdom of God, concerning which Paul was in dialogue according to Acts 19.8. My own experience suggests that probably the three most helpful books here are Jürgen Moltmann, *The Crucified God*, SCM Press 1974 (arising very much out of the German post-Holocaust experience, it reflects itself constant dialogue with the thought of Jewish teachers like Emile Fackenheim, Shalom Ben-Chorin, Abraham Heschel, Franz Rosen-zweig and others); Kazoh Kitamori, *Theology of the Pain of God*, SCM Press 1965 (significantly the work of a Japanese theologian who lived through the events leading up to and after Hiroshima and Nagasaki); and C. S. Song, *Third-Eye Theology*, Lutterworth Press 1980. In this last book we have a Taiwanese theologian, writing against a background of Buddhism, who refers constantly to the *hesed* of God as the pain-love of God. Powerfully and imaginatively he can speak to Christian and Jew alike about the way in which all the pain and agony of history is taken into God himself to redeem and create anew.

Dialogue about the Land

For Christians the hardest issue to face in the dialogue is the Jewish attachment to the Land of Israel and to the city of Jerusalem. Even though Jews do in fact differ as to the secular and religious significance of the State of Israel, for all of them the Land is part of the divine promise, a central feature of Jewish hope, constituting therefore an essential component of faith, and intimately linked with the question of Jewish survival. It is important therefore to have some aids for reflection on these issues from Christian perspectives of various kinds. The following will be found to be of great value. First, we need to get our contemporary bearings right. The report of a British Council of Churches' delegation which visited the Middle East in 1981, *Towards Understanding the Arab-Israeli Conflict*, BCC 1982, begins with a most illuminating 'travel diary' and then goes on to deal with the major political issues. It warns against support by Christians for '*political* Zionism on *theological* grounds', i.e., the appeal to certain understandings of Christian scripture as offering justification for the establishment of modern Israel. Insight into the contemporary experience of Israelis, together with some pungent analysis of how the State of Israel became embroiled in the terrible present-day conflicts is to be found in Amos Elon, *The Israelis: Founders and Sons*, Penguin Books 1983. Another approach to the secular, political background is through Everett Mendelsohn, *The Compassionate Peace: A Future for the Middle East*, Penguin Books 1982. Written on behalf of the American Friends' Service Committee, it covers the whole of the Middle East region, and sets the present conflict in that wider context. Then Christians in Britain need to know much more than we usually do about the history of the Holy Land between the years 70 and 1948. The most helpful guide to this is James Parkes, *Whose Land? A History of the Peoples of Palestine*, Penguin Books 1970. After that we need to have our biblical exegesis clear in our minds, and here there is nothing finer than W. D. Davies, *The Gospel and the Land*, Berkeley and London, University of California Press 1975. In briefer compass two recent articles by Christians long experienced and uncommonly wise in these matters will help a better approach to Jewish partners when the question of the State of Israel arises: A. Roy Eckhardt, 'Towards a Secular Theology of the State of Israel', reprinted in *CJR*, No. 72, September 1980, pp. 8–20, and Allan R. Brockway, 'The Christian Facing Israel', in *CJR*, Vol. 14, No. 2 June 1981 p. 13–23.

The Churches' Official Statements

There is an ever-flowing stream of official statements, sets of guidelines, pastoral instructions and so on from the churches, and in general terms, these are all to be welcomed. While they are not normally the most readable or stimulating of documents they do provide important checks and parameters for Christians as they go on in dialogue, as well as material which is most important to set before our Jewish partners, both as restitution for ancient wrongs and as assurance that the Christian churches as corporate entities are committed to new relationships. The fullest collection of such statements, on the Protestant side and from Roman Catholic circles alike, is Helga Croner (ed.), *Stepping Stones to Further Jewish-Christian Relations*, London and New York, Stimulus Books 1977. It contains, for example, Vatican II on the Jews in *Nostra Aetate* as well as pastoral guidance from Bishops in the USA and Western European countries, and WCC Member Churches' statements from 1948 onwards. Since Helga Croner's compilation appeared we have had the English and Welsh Roman Catholic 'Pastoral Guidelines' conveniently available together with the *Nostra Aetate* documentation in *Catholic-Jewish Relations*, Catholic Truth Society 1981. *The Church and the Jews*, also published by the CTS in 1981 in the same format, is the most recent statement from the German Roman Catholic Bishops, and a valuable study outline. From the WCC we now have a full set of Guidelines, *Ecumenical Considerations on Jewish-Christian Dialogue*, Geneva, WCC 1983. Behind the production of these guidelines lies an enormous process of consultation between the churches themselves and between the WCC Consultation on the Church and the Jewish People with Jewish representative groups, and some of this work is recorded in *Jewish-Christian Dialogue: The Quest for World Community*, Geneva, WCC 1975. *Christian-Jewish Relations in Ecumenical Perspective*, Franz von Hammerstein (ed.), Geneva, WCC 1977 also contains much valuable material.

The Task in Britain Now

We end this bibliography by signalling the advent of a little book whose significance is out of all proportion to its size, and which takes us into a new dimension of our dialogue. *Christians and Jews in Britain: a Study Handbook for Christians*, United Reformed Church 1983, is the first example of a new *genre*. In it Christians and Jews are talking together about themselves, rather than Christians talking about Jews, or Jews talking about Christians. For several years a widely representative group of Rabbis and Jewish lay people met with Christians from many denominations in a series of residential conferences. As a result of the most detailed and painstaking discussions they have been able to produce this handbook for further work at all kinds of levels. All the important issues are touched upon, and it now forms the basic document in Britain for dialogue to continue. Please make use of this book as much as you can, for future developments are in your hands. Study and action go together.

Appendix B: Resources

A Note About Resources

Most of the resources already offered for guidance in the main text, in the notes and in Appendix A are literary. Adequate reference has been supplied in each case for those who want to take up specific issues through printed material. But as those of us already at work in inter-faith relationships never cease to reiterate: reading books about other religions is no substitute for the actual encounter with the human beings who live within those religious traditions. This, however, looks like a pious wish incapable of fulfilment to those who do not have immediate access to a neighbour of another commitment. Resources are necessary for such people who hardly know where to begin in this complex area.

Secondly, and this will have been apparent throughout my writing, we Christians stand just at the beginning of the journey into unfamiliar territory which in due course will revolutionize our understanding of the nature of the Christian mission, the teaching of the Christian church, and the foundations of Christian theology. We will have to do much thinking and praying together before we come to a common heart and mind about such matters in the church of the future. We will so much need the specialist groups set up at national and international levels as resources in this process of corporate thinking. I try to list some of these in the second part of this note.

Towards Engaging in Dialogue

Resources here are three-fold: First, the specifically inter-faith organizations which themselves feel increasingly part of a single 'inter-faith movement'; secondly there are international and national organizations within other world communities of faith dedicated to inter-religious understanding; thirdly there are groups within National Christian Councils and their member churches who can give wise counsel and advice about meeting people of other faith. It is impossible to give exhaustive lists, but a few pointers may be valuable.

Inter-faith Organizations

At a world level

The World Congress of Faiths (London); The International Association for Religious Freedom (Frankfurt); The Temple of Understanding (New York); The World Conference on Religion for Peace (Geneva) are examples of the international inter-faith movement. They are beginning to work co-operatively.

At a national level

Inter-faith groups and associations exist in most countries in the English-speaking world. Addresses of these are obtainable from the National Councils of Churches. In the United Kingdom inter-faith organizations and local groups are listed in *Interfaith News*, a bulletin which appears three times a year available from the World Congress of Faiths office and from the BCC, 35–41 Lower Marsh, London SE1 7RL.

Dialogue with Specific Traditions

Christian/Jewish Relations

The International Council of Christians and Jews has its Headquarters in West Germany and links Councils of Christians and Jews in various English speaking countries. There are Study Centres in Jerusalem and Birmingham, UK details of which are available from the BCC and similar National Councils of Churches.

Christian/Muslim Relations

The Study Centre for Islam and Christian/Muslim Relations in Selly Oak, Birmingham, is the first point of contact. Other Study Centres exist in the USA, Canada, Pakistan, the Philippines, South India, Nairobi and elsewhere. Addresses available from National Councils of Churches.

Christian/Buddhist Relations

An international point of reference is the Study Centre at the University of Hawaii. Other important study centres are in Colombo, Sri Lanka and Hong Kong. Addresses available from the BCC and similar National Councils of Churches.

Christian/Hindu Relations

This is more difficult to deal with as the term Hinduism covers a wide range of different social and religious understanding. The church in India itself has many ways of relating in dialogue with Hindu traditions but in the UK and North America there are as yet few serious centres functioning as a resource for Christian/Hindu dialogue. Specific advice may be obtained through the BCC Committee for Relations with People of Other Faiths and its equivalent Committee in other National Councils of Churches.

Christian/Sikh Relations

In the UK there is an important initiative in the United Reformed Church. Contact the Secretary of the Mission and Other Faiths Committee, URC, 86 Tavistock Place, London WC1H 9RT. A Study Centre in Batala, Punjab, Northern India is a major resource.

Other world religious traditions, e.g. Zoroastrianism, Jainism, Baha'ism have fewer followers but are not less important for that. However, there are no major resources for Christian relations with these smaller groups.

Christian Resources for the Theological Task

The Sub Unit for Dialogue with People of Living Faiths of the World Council of Churches, 150 route de Ferney, 1211 Geneva 20, Switzerland is the international point of reference for the Protestant and Orthodox Churches.

For Roman Catholics it is the Secretariatus Pro Non Christianis, Citta Del Vaticano, Roma, Italy.

Most National Councils of Churches in the English-speaking world have now an inter-faith or dialogue desk in some form. In addition Christian denominational structures are increasingly taking religious pluralism seriously, and individual Christians should approach the headquarters of their own churches for help and guidance. In the UK the BCC will supply on request a list of the relevant church agencies and their Secretaries or Co-ordinators.

NOTES

Introduction

1. Three recent studies offer reliable and scholarly overviews of the whole field: Alan Race, *Christians and Religious Pluralism: Patterns in the Christian Theology of Religions*, SCM Press 1983; Paul F. Knitter, *No Other Name? A Critical Survey of Attitudes Toward the World Religions*, SCM Press 1985, and Willard G. Oxtoby, *The Meaning of Other Faiths*, SPCK 1984. The last of these is no less discerning than the other two but is more directed towards a non-specialist readership. Each is invaluable in helping to map out the areas that theologians are now engaged in exploring. A fourth book, edited by John Hick and Brian Hebblethwaite, *Christianity and Other Religions: Selected Readings*, Collins, Fount 1980, is a convenient source book for many of the writers discussed by Race, Knitter and Oxtoby. Detailed guidance to the other recent contributions will be found in the notes to the following chapters, and, specifically with regard to Christian/Jewish understanding, in Appendix A. But some readers may wish to start further back, with as it were 'pre-theological considerations'. Here the outstanding work of Christopher Lamb, *Belief in a Mixed Society*, Lion 1985, is essential reading for its accurate and sensitive appraisal of the practical issues in living in a multi-faith society.

1 About the Old Relationships

1. Cf. the famous report of the 'Christian Missionary Activities Committee' appointed by the State of Madhya Pradesh in 1954; 'missions are in some places used to serve extra religious ends' and 'evangelization in India appears to be part of the uniform world policy to revive Christendom for re-establishing western supremacy, and is not prompted by spiritual motives'. Continuing difficulties in obtaining visas for missionary work in India, Burma and many other countries indicate that these perceptions are still very real to many non-Christians.

2. The formula *'extra ecclesiam nulla salus'* is in fact derived from Cyprian: in *De Catholicae Ecclesiae Unitate* 6 he writes with true rigor, *'Habere non potest Deum patrem qui ecclesiam non habet matrem'* and the phrase *'salus extra ecclesiam non est'* itself appears in Epistulae LXXIII 21.

3. Denziger/Schonmetzer, *Enchiridion Symbolorum*, Friburg-in-Bresgau, Herder, Editio 29, No. 1354.

4. Cf. Pope Boniface VIII, who affirmed and professed 'without qualification' that 'outside the one and only Catholic Church there is neither salvation, nor the remission of sins'. The reason for this is stated thus – 'it is a matter of absolute necessity for salvation for every human creature, to submit to the Roman pontiff'. Of course Boniface was more interested in the political rather than the theological battle, but the thought form is clear. *Enchiridion Symbolorum*, No. 469.

5. In *All Have the Same God*, St Paul Publications 1979, p. 21.

6. Augustine's early works like *De moribus ecclesiae Catholicae et Manichoeorum, De vera religione, De libero arbitrio* and *De utilitate credendi* show that Augustine like Athanasius was capable of speaking of divine immanence, and incarnation necessarily consequent upon that as a revelation of divine nature, the love of God as the ground or

determination of his will, of humankind having power to read the divine character because of an inward light in the reason – and reason itself as the evidence of an indwelling God. Cf. also the later *Retractiones* 'that which we now call the Christian religion was present in antiquity . . . ' 1, 13, iii. Augustine was also quoted favourably at the Tambaram Conference by the Norwegian scholar Karl Ludvig Reichelt who in a paper entitled 'The Johannine Approach' attributed these words to Augustine without naming the actual source (possibly it is rather a free translation of the passage in the *Retractiones*: 'In all religions some truths are to be found. And these truths in all religions are really Christian truths although the name Christianity had not yet appeared'). Tambaram Report Vol. I, *The Authority of the Faith*, Oxford University Press 1939, p. 94.

7. This passage and the two that follow are to be found in Henry Beveridge's translation of the *Institutes of the Christian Religion* published by James Clarke of Edinburgh, II, 2, 18, p. 238. Calvin's doctrine of general revelation may be studied in the *Institutes* I, 6, 1ff. The 'effulgence which is presented to every eye . . . leaves the ingratitude of many without excuse, since God, in order to bring the whole human race under condemnation, holds forth to all, without exception a mirror of his Deity in his works'. However, 'it is impossible for any man to obtain even the minutest portion of right and sound doctrine without being a disciple of Scripture' (I, 6, 2, Beveridge translation, p. 66).

8. Karl Barth's actual words are: 'Religion ist Unglaube: Religion ist eine Angelegenheit, man muss geradezu sagen, die Angelegenheit des gottlosen Mensch-en', *Die Kirchliche Dogmatik*, 1/2, 17.2. 'Religion is unbelief. It is a concern, indeed we must say that is the one great concern, of godless man'. *Church Dogmatics*, 1/2, 17.2, pp. 299–300. The whole of section 17 has to be studied, however, before we may allow ourselves to say that Barth is a Calvinist! Note the following repudiation of Calvin from *Church Dogmatics* 4/2: 'Calvin's doctrine of the *participatio Christi* has one weakness which we can never too greatly deplore and which we can never forget in all his thoughtful and instructive presentation of justification and sanctification. This consists in the fact that he found no place – and in view of his distinctive doctrine of predestination he could not do so – for a recognition of the universal relevance of the existence of the man Jesus, of the sanctification of all men as it has been achieved in him. The eternal election which according to Eph. 1.4 has been made in Jesus Christ was referred by Calvin only to those who in God's eternal counsel are foreordained to salvation and therefore to reconciliation, justification and sanctification in Jesus Christ, while His existence has no positive significance for those who are excluded from this foreordination, from the reprobate.' In the four trenchant comments that Barth goes on to make in this extended note we point to only the one which is most relevant to our theme: that while the *participatio Christi* of the Elect does serve the glory of God, it is an end in itself and has no positive function in relation to the rest of God's creation. It therefore serves only to attest the holiness of a God whose mercy is limited to them and whose love is restricted by a limit which he himself has arbitrarily and inscrutably set. 'But', says Karl Barth, 'since this is not a total love it cannot be accorded a total confidence' (p. 520).

9. Weimar, *Collected Works*, 51, p. 150ff. (my translation).

10. Ibid., 40, 2, p. 111 (my translation).

11. Ibid., 40, 1, p. 609 (my translation).

12. Quoted from H. de Vos, *Het Christendom en de Andere Godsdiensten*, Nijkerk, Callenbach 1962, p. 32. Professor de Vos does not indicate the precise source in Luther's writings.

13. *Larger Catechism*, II. iii. Compare with this his commentary on Jonah at verse 1.5. 'Darumb ists gar eyn gros unterscheyd, wissen, das eyn Gott ist, und wissen, was odder wer Gott ist. Das erste weys die natur and ist ynn allen herztzen geschrieben. Das andere leret alleyne der heylige geist' – 'therefore there is a great distinction

between knowing that there is one God, and knowing what or who God is. The first is shown by nature and is written in every heart. The other is taught only by the Holy Spirit' – my translation.

14. Cf. Karl Barth again 'He (sc. the human creature) does not believe. If he did, he would listen; but in religion he talks. If he did, he would accept a gift; but in religion he takes something for himself. If he did he would let God Himself intercede for God; but in religion he ventures to grasp at God. Because it is a grasping, religion is the contradiction of revelation, the concentrated expression of human unbelief, i.e. an attitude and an activity which is directly opposed to faith. It is a feeble but defiant, an arrogant but hopeless, attempt to create something which man could do but now cannot do, or can do only because and if God Himself creates it for him: the knowledge of the truth, the knowledge of God' *Church Dogmatics*, 1/2, 17.2, pp. 302–303. Barth surveys Luther's own writings on pages 309ff. of the same volume.

15. In his *The Young Wesley: Missionary and Theologian of Missions*, Epworth Press 1958, ch. 3. Wesley's letter to John Burton is on pp. 44–8.

16. Ibid., p. 26.

17. The outline of the narrative *The Life of Hayy ibn Yakzām* may be found in R. A. Nicholson, *The Literary History of the Arabs*, Cambridge University Press 1966, p. 433. Wesley's surmise that the story was written 'a century or two ago' is mistaken, but he is correct in thinking that it is fictitious. The Arabic text together with a Latin translation was published in 1691 under the title *Philosophus Autodidactus*, and an English translation had appeared in 1708 and had been reprinted several times during Wesley's lifetime. For a recent study of the literary genre to which *The Life of Hayy ibn Yakzām* belonged see M. Mayerhof and J. Schacht (eds), *The Theologus Autodidactus of Ibn Al-Nāfis*, Oxford University Press 1968, esp. the section on 'Ibn Al-Nāfis' Theological Novel', pp. 28–36.

18. See below pp. 56ff.

19. See for this J. A. de Jong, *As the Waters Cover the Sea. Millennial expectations in the rise of Anglo-American Missions 1640–1810*, published in the Netherlands by J. H. Kok 1970. Note, too, Max Warren's comment that the late eighteenth- and early nineteenth-century missionary believed that 'the greatest purposes of God were about to be accomplished in the conversion of the nations to the faith of Christ'. Largely absent among missionaries of this period, 'in comparison with this note of hopefulness, is that emphasis on the heathen perishing in their blindness, which was to be so powerful a motive in the second half of the nineteenth century'. *The Missionary Movement from Britain in Modern History*, SCM Press 1965, p. 48.

20. 'To Jonathan Edwards the Great Awakening appeared to be the beginning of the latter days', J. A. de Jong, op. cit., p. 157. Out of his experiences Edwards wrote in 1746 his *An Humble Attempt to Promote Explicit Agreement and Visible Unity Among God's People in Extraordinary Prayer for the Revival of Religion and the Advancement of Christ's Kingdom on Earth, Pursuant to Scripture Promises and Prophecies Concerning the Last Time*. This *Humble Attempt* was instrumental in bringing the Baptist Missionary Society into being.

21. John Erskine worked for fifty years to awaken missionary interest in Scotland. He urged his Synod in 1750 to emulate Paul who was constrained by Jesus' love 'to fly like a flaming Seraph from pole to pole to proclaim the ineffable glories of his lovely Jesus'. See de Jong, op. cit., p. 166. He is remembered for his challenge at the General Assembly in 1796: 'Moderator, rax me that Bible.'

22. John Newton, the hymn writer, became Vicar of St Mary Woolnoth in 1779. In 1786 he preached a series of fifty sermons on the texts used by G. F. Handel in *The Messiah*, the oratorio composed in 1741. These sermons form part of the background of the founders of the Church Missionary Society (1799).

23. John Gill was a Particular (Calvinist) Baptist minister. The title of his book, published in 1753, speaks for itself: *The Glory of the Church in the Latter Day*. William Carey was a Particular Baptist.

24. Its proper title was 'The Particular Baptist Society for the Propagation of the Gospel among the Heathen'.

25. The story of how Carey and his colleague, William Marshman, issued for scholars a collated text and a translation of a large part of *The Ramayana* is not as well known as it should be. Carey and Marshman were not blind to its human interest and literary power, whatever doubts they may have had about its theology. But their home based colleague Andrew Fuller pleaded with them to desist. For Fuller, the *Ramayana* was 'a piece of lumber'. See the invaluable study *William Carey*, by S. P. Carey, published by the Carey Press in 1942, pp. 61ff. T. E. Slater (1840–1912) deserves a full study in his own right. So far we have only incidental comments in works devoted to other pioneers of a new relationship. In his excellent survey of the work of J. N. Farquhar, *Not to Destroy but to Fulfil*, Uppsala, Gleerup 1965, Eric Sharpe says of Slater that he 'was a layer of foundations and it is commonly the fate of foundations to remain hidden'. But until we have that fuller study, we may honour Slater for being among the first to perceive a new guiding principle in the presentation of Christian faith in India: 'Not to present Christianity as an antagonistic Religion among other Religions of the world, not as a voice sounding the knell of doom to non-Christian nations, but, in the firm persuasion that all are *by nature* Christians, to hold it up as that in which Hindus would find realized and satisfied the noblest and earliest ideas of their sages, and truest sentiments and yearnings of their hearts', *God Revealed* (1876), p. iii, quoted by Sharpe, op. cit., pp. 97–8. His most extensive book is called *The Higher Hinduism in Relation to Christianity* which first appeared in 1899.

26. This is the title he gives to Vols. IV, V and VI of his monumental *History of the Expansion of Christianity*, Eyre and Spottiswoode 1941–44.

27. I refer to the English, because I am English, but members of the other nations in the British Isles, and those who live in continental Europe as well as across the Atlantic Ocean can make their own substitutions. We have all confused culture and religion.

28. *Tom Jones* was published in 1749: in Henry Fielding's portrayal of Thwakum is of course intentionally appalling.

29. I deal here rather too summarily with the complexities of the forming of the 1944 Education Act. For an illuminating and detailed study see Dennis Starking's chapter 'World Religions and the Spirit of 1944' in *Approaching World Religions*, ed. Robert Jackson, John Murray 1982.

30. Because I hold the man in great reverence, and will be using what I think are some noble insights from his spiritual classic, *The Way The Truth The Life*, let me instance some words of F. J. A. Hort, quoted by Gordon Rupp in his lecture *Hort and the Cambridge Tradition*, Cambridge University Press 1970. Dr Rupp calls them 'terrible lines about the Negroes which may betray the disastrous influence of Kingsley's racism: "I hate slavery . . . much more for its influence on the whites than on the niggers themselves . . . they have surely shown themselves only as an immeasurably inferior race, just human and no more, their religion frothy and sensuous, their highest virtues those of a good Newfoundland dog"'. If so great a man can write so foolishly, we may perhaps not be too surprised at the wicked stupidities of lesser mortals.

31. Anthony Trollope wrote in 1872: 'We are called upon to rule them (the colonies) – as far as we do rule them, not for our glory, but for their happiness. If we keep them, we should keep them – not because they add prestige to the name of Great Britain, not because they are gems in our diadem, not in order that we may boast that the sun never sets upon our dependencies, but because by keeping them we may assist them in developing their own resources. And when we part with them, as part with them we shall, let us do so with neither smothered jealousy nor open hostility, but with a proud feeling that we are sending a son out into the world able to take his place among men.' Quoted from J. W. Davidson, 'The Idea of Empire', in *Ideas and Beliefs of the Victorians*, Sylvan Press 1949, p. 326.

2 Dialogue in the New Testament

1. Note the succinct statement of Ernst Käsemann: 'Luke was not simply a person who recorded facts. Where he appears as narrator or historian, he is really a theologian. Personally I should say that, considering the effect he had had, he is the greatest New Testament Theologian', in *Jesus Means Freedom*, SCM Press 1969, p. 121.

2. E. Haenchen, *The Acts of the Apostles: A Commentary*, Basil Blackwell 1971, pp. 526–7. Haenchen's reading of the matter is accepted by Wayne A. Meeks in *The First Urban Christians*, Yale University Press 1983, p. 62.

3. One of the most recent, and in many respects, certainly the most instructive accounts of Paul's relationships with his churches is Wayne Meeks' book just referred to. Meeks points out that the only mention of Athens in the letters of Paul is I Thess. 3.1 which merely confirms that he spent some time there waiting for Timothy to return from the north.

4. Haenchen, op. cit., p. 558. Haenchen adds that Luke wishes to portray Paul in Ephesus at the high point of his work. But Haenchen thinks this has more to do with the downfall of 'paganism as a cult religion'. The entire production of devotional artifacts in honour of Artemis faces ruin.

5. One scholar who does pay this incident some attention is Elisabeth Schüssler Fiorenza in her introductory chapter in a collection of papers she edited called *Aspects of Religious Propaganda in Judaism and Early Christianity*, University of Notre Dame Press 1976, p. 9: 'However, after some slanderous attacks and opposition from the side of the Jews, Paul separated the Christians from the Synagogue and established an independent Christian congregation. The new place for the Christian assembly was no longer the synagogue but the hall of Tyrannus. The new locale served to foster the image of the Christian community as a philosophical school and to depict Paul as a teacher in dialogue with not only the Jews but also the Greeks.' But I am quite sure that this is not all that Luke intends to tell us about!

6. Meeks thinks that this 'may be a sort of guildhall of a trade association', op. cit., p. 26 and cf. note 44 on p. 223.

7. For the concept of the *logos* in Stoicism any major commentary on St John's Gospel may be consulted. For the contemporary usage of the term *plērōma*, C. F. D. Moule's commentary on *Colossians and Philemon*, Cambridge University Press 1958, will be found particularly useful, see pp. 164–9.

8. Some New Testament scholars (Conzelmann, John Knox) have suggested that there was a quite definite 'school of Paul' in the sense that his ideas were worked on by a group of early Christian thinkers. Conzelmann suggested that this would have been centred in Ephesus, and cited the presence of Apollos, Aquila and Prisca, and the 'dialogues' in the *scholē* of Tyrannus. (I am indebted for this information to Meeks, op. cit., p. 82.) We do know that Ephesus became 'the city of dialogue' by the end of the century. Because it has some bearing on our later discussions it is worth quoting here the judgment of Raymond Brown about the provenance of the Fourth Gospel: 'Ephesus still remains the primary contender for identification as the place where John was composed. Besides the almost unanimous voice of the ancient witnesses who speak of the subject, we have an argument from the parallels between John and Revelation, for the latter work clearly belongs to the area of Ephesus. The anti-synagogue motif in the Gospel . . . makes sense in the Ephesus region, for Rev. ii 9 and iii 9 attest bitter anti-synagogue polemics in this part of Asia Minor. If there is in the gospel a polemic against the disciples of John the Baptist, the NT mentions disciples baptized with John's baptism at only one place outside Palestine – Ephesus (Acts xix 1–7). If there are parallels between John and the Qumran scrolls, is it an accident that Qumran parallels are most visible in Colossians and Ephesians, epistles addressed to the Ephesus region? Any incipient and anti-docetic and anti-Gnostic polemic would also have been at home

on the Ephesus scene.' *The Gospel According to John*, Anchor Bible Commentary, Chapman 1966, vol. 1, pp. ciii-iv.

9. Note the definition of the term '*Asiarch*': 'Each of the cities of proconsular Asia, at the autumnal equinox, assembled its most honourable and opulent citizens, in order to select one to preside over the games to be exhibited that year, at his expense, in honour of the gods and the Roman Emperor. Thereupon each city reported the name of the person selected to a general assembly held in some leading city, as Ephesus, Smyrna, Sardis'. Grimm-Thayer, *Greek English Lexicon of the New Testament*, ad loc., p. 80. Note Elisabeth Schüssler Fiorenza's comment: 'The second part of the story (19.29–34) demonstrates the support of the Asiarchs, the cultic officials of the Roman civil religion in Asia Minor, for the Christian missionary, Paul. Luke's point is quite clear: a sect, whose leader had such friends, cannot be at all dangerous to the Roman Empire', op. cit., p. 17.

10. The reference is to the great Dutch missiologist, Johannes Verkuyl, in his *Inleiding in de Nieuwere Zendingswetenschap*, J. H. Kok 1975, p. 234. Verkuyl goes on to remark that Paul points here to the fact of experience, that whoever shares the gospel with someone else, receives it again, freshly and with deeper meaning.

11. Ramsay wrote: 'It would appear that Paul was disappointed and perhaps disillusioned by his experience in Athens. He felt that he had gone at least as far as was right in the way of presenting his doctrine in a form suited to the current philosophy, and the result had been little more than naught. When he went on from Athens to Corinth, he no longer spoke in the philosophical style. In replying to the unfavourable comparison between his preaching and the more philosophical style of Apollos, he told the Corinthians that, when he came among them, he "determined not to know anything save Jesus Christ, and Him crucified" (I Cor. 2.2); and nowhere throughout his writings is he so hard on the wise, the philosophers and the dialecticians, as when he defends the way he had presented Christianity at Corinth.' *St Paul the Traveller and Roman Citizen*, Hodder and Stoughton, sixth edition 1902, p. 252. For an excellent recent missiological study of Acts 17.16–34, see Myrtle Langley, 'Paul in Athens: Pseudophilosophy or Proclamation' in the *Bulletin of the Evangelical Fellowship for Missionary Studies*, 1980.

12. A. Deissmann, as quoted by C. J. Bleeker, *Christ in Modern Athens*, Mowbray 1966, p. 7. Bleeker is quoting in German from *Licht vom Osten* (1923) but the English reference is to *Light from the East*, Hodder and Stoughton 1924, p. 391.

13. The fact, attested in the commentaries, that we have no further information about either person, actually testifies to the importance of these people within the non-Pauline Athenian church.

14. The Greek is *deisidaimonesterous*, the comparative form of adjective from *deisidaimonia*, 'fear of the gods'. It is used in both senses in Greek literature, and also in a neutral way. In Acts 25.19 Festus uses the word of the Jewish faith. Although the RSV translates *deisidaimonia* here as 'superstition' it is hardly likely that Luke thinks that Festus would have called Judaism a 'superstition' in adressing Herod and Bernice, both of whom needed the goodwill of their people, even if they were scarcely committed to the ancestral faith themselves.

15. Aratus, *c*. 270 BC, wrote: 'Let us begin with Zeus, streets and markets, oceans and harbours are full of him; we all need him, and we are of his family' (from the *Phaenomena* 1.5). His near contemporary Cleanthes, has these words in a hymn to Zeus: 'we are born of thee', *Ad Jovem*, line 4. From Epimenides, as it appears, we have these words: (they are put into the mouth of Minos, son of Zeus) The Cretans carve a tomb for thee, O holy and high, liars, evil beasts and slow bellies! For thou art not dead for ever, thou art alive and risen; for in thee we live and are moved and have our being.' For a discussion of these texts see Martin Dibelius, *Studies in the Acts of the Apostles*, SCM Press 1956, pp. 47–52.

16. Martin Dibelius wrote that the Areopagus speech is 'as alien to the New Testament (apart from Acts 14.15–17), as it is familiar to hellenistic, particularly Stoic, philosophy' (op. cit., p. 63), and distinguished between 'the Paul of the Acts of the Apostles from the real Paul' (p. 62). He also wrote that Acts 17.31 is 'the *only Christian* sentence in

the Areopagus speech' (p. 56, the italics are his). That I don't agree with either his interpretation of Paul, or with the theological presuppositions that he brings to this interpretation will be apparent from this and the following sections. Ferdinand Hahn writes, I think, more cautiously and more constructively about both Acts 14.15–17 and Acts 17. 22–31: 'The preaching to the Gentiles presupposes, not the covenant with and the promises to the fathers, but the care of the Creator', *Mission in the New Testament*, SCM Press 1965, p. 135.

17. I use here the term 'paganism' with its first connotation, i.e. the religion of country dwellers. Note Hahn's comment: 'Acts 14.15–17 is only a preparatory sketch of the sermon that is not developed in detail until the Areopagus speech of 17.22–31', op. cit., p. 135.

18. In his Bible Study 'It took a miracle to launch the mission to the Gentiles: the Cornelius story', in *Faith in the midst of Faiths*, ed. S. J. Samartha, WCC 1977, pp. 124–5.

19. The Greek expressions are *eusebēs kai phoboumenos ton theon, poiōn eleēmonsunas pollas tō laō kai deomenos tou thesu dia pantos* (10.2) *anēr dikaios kai phoboumenos ton theon* (10.22); his prayers and alms *anabēsan eis mnēmosunon emprosthen tou theou* (10.4). In 10.35 he is described as *ergazomenos dikaiosunen* and *dektos* to God. See for further comment *Towards a Theology for Inter-Faith Dialogue*, CIO Publishing 1984, p. 25. Geoffrey Lampe says 'Biblical language is thought by Luke to be appropriate for so "devout" a Gentile', *Peake's Commentary on the Bible*, Nelson 1962, p. 900.

20. I echo here Geoffrey Lampe's words: 'Those who live like Jews are accepted by God even though they live outside the boundaries of Israel'. This is a different doctrine from the Pauline teaching of justification though it has points of contact with the thought of Rom. 2.14–15, op. cit., p. 900. Why this is so may be shown from Paul's inherited traditions to which we turn in the rest of this chapter, and in chapter 3.

21. Lesslie Newbigin, *The Open Secret*, SPCK 1978, pp. 78–9. Chapters 4 and 7 are both excellent re-statements of what is meant by the biblical doctrine of election.

22. In *Christian Faith in a Religiously Plural World*, eds. D. G. Dawe and J. B. Carman, Orbis Books 1978, pp. 18–19.

23. See the whole passage Genesis 9.17–18, and my further comments on p. 45.

24. *The Anchor Bible: Genesis*, Doubleday, third edition 1981, pp. 99–109.

25. In Donald Senior and Carroll Stuhlmueller, *The Biblical Foundations for Mission*, SCM Press 1983, pp. 17–18. Senior wrote the New Testament section, Stuhlmueller the Old Testament.

26. H. H. Rowley, *The Rediscovery of the Old Testament*, James Clarke 1945, p. 79.

27. F. L. Moriarty, in the *Jerome Bible Commentary*, Chapman 1969, p. 95.

28. J. H. Hertz, *The Pentateuch and Haftorahs*, Soncino Press 1938, p. 670.

29. See p. 44.

30. *Ancient Near Eastern Texts*, ed. J. B. Pritchard, Princeton second edition 1955, p. 150.

31. Max Warren, 'Presence and Proclamation' in *Eye of the Storm*, ed. Donald McGavran, Word Books, Waco, Texas 1972, pp. 194–6. Among recent treatments of Idolatry, I commend one by Roger Hooker shortly to be published by the BCC, and the brief Bible Study in *Can We Pray Together*, BCC 1983, pp. 10–12.

32. Ernst Käsemann, *New Testament Questions for Today*, SCM Press 1969, p. 241. Cf. the striking exegetical statement in Käsemann's *Commentary on Romans*, SCM Press 1980, pp. 309–10: 'For Paul there can be no church of Gentile-Christians alone. Such a church would be a world alongside a world and an extract from the world, not the goal of God's plan of salvation for the world. It would be abstracted from pre-Easter history. God's claim to the whole world, established with and from creation, would be renounced, and the church would be reduced to a religious society. History would be sacrificed for the sake of spirit and a counter-world set up. The concept of the people of God growing out of the root of Israel has, therefore, an indispensable function in

Paul's ecclesiology, even though it is only one of its aspects and not even the center. For the apostle there is no salvation apart from the history of Israel.'

33. A powerful statement of this repudiation has come recently in Kenneth Leech (ed.), *Theology and Racism 1*, CIO Publishing 1985, with contributions on anti-semitism in Christian theology from John Austin Baker, Rosemary Reuther and John Pawlikowski.

3   God and the Nations

1. This and the following quotation come from p. 13 of *Guidelines on Dialogue*, Geneva, WCC 1979.

2. In *Dialogue in Community. Essays in Honour of S. J. Samartha*, ed. Constantine D. Jathanna, Mangalore, Karnataka Theological Research Institute 1982, pp. 1–15.

3. For some glaring examples of misleading translations of *ethnē* see the RSV at Matt. 28.19 (why should it not be 'gentiles' here?); Romans 11.25 (why should it not be 'the nations' here?); I Cor. 5.1 (is it necessary to use the term 'pagans' here? Would not 'gentiles' or 'nations' be less emotive?) and I Cor. 12.2 where the word 'heathen' is used almost gratuitously. It is instructive to examine the usage of all modern versions at these four points.

4. There is a very instructive article on these themes by Nils A. Dahl, called 'Nations in the New Testament' in *New Testament Christianity for Africa and the World*, ed. Mark Glasswell and Edward W. Fashole-Luke, SPCK 1974, pp. 54–68.

5. See his essay 'The impact of the Ancient Near East on Israelite Tradition', in *Tradition and Theology in the Old Testament*, ed. Douglas A. Knight, SPCK 1977, pp. 32–46.

6. Two classic statements of this point are: G. Ernest Wright, *The Old Testament against its Environment*, SCM Press 1950, and Norman H. Snaith, *The Distinctive Ideas of the Old Testament*, Epworth Press 1944.

7. For this see Ringgren, op. cit., pp. 45–6.

8. In his Commentary on *Genesis*, SCM Press, second edition 1963, p. 46. He is specifically referring to Gen. 1–24a but these words would apply to his whole approach to succeeding chapters.

9. For detailed discussion of the etymology of the name *Noah* see the commentaries.

10. Karl Barth has some important things to say about Gen. 9 as a covenant of 'redemption'. See *Church Dogmatics*, Vol. 4/1, T. and T. Clark 1956, pp. 26ff.

11. The reference is to the work of G. E. Mendenhall, *Law and Covenant in Israel and the Ancient Near East*, published by the Biblical Colloquium, Pittsburg, PA 1955. There is a convenient summary of his views in his articles 'Covenant' and 'Election' in the *Interpreter's Dictionary of the Bible*, Abingdon Press 1962.

12. C. S. Song, *Third Eye Theology*, Lutterworth Press 1979, writes of the Noachic covenant: 'God binds himself with a covenant as a sign of his repentance as well as his promise. The covenant is thus the reality of God's pain-love for his creation', p. 70.

13. Claus Westermann, *Handbook to the Old Testament*, SPCK 1969, p. 27.

14. See above pp. 34f. See on this Karl Barth, *Church Dogmatics*, Vol. 3/1, T. and T. Clark 1959, p. 46. The whole section on the covenant as the internal basis of creation, and on the creation as the external basis of the covenant are immensely important for our theme.

15. From the article on 'Nations' by S. Amsler in *Vocabulary of the Bible*, ed. J. J. von Allmen, Lutterworth Press 1958, p. 300.

16. See Johannes Blauw, *The Missionary Nature of the Church*, Lutterworth Press 1962, p. 40.

17. G. E. Wright, *Isaiah*, SCM Press 1964, p. 60.

18. A. Feuillet in *Recherches de Science religieuse*, Mélanges J. Lebreton 1951. I owe this reference to E. Jacob, *Theology of the Old Testament*, Hodder & Stoughton 1958, p. 222.

19. For a profound modern Jewish interpretation of the Book of Jonah see the

magnificent work of Jonathan Magonet, *Form and Meaning*. Sheffield, Almond Press 1983. He writes in conclusion: 'If . . . we may extract a theme which seems to have become clarified by our analysis, it is precisely the freedom of God to be beyond any definition by which man would limit Him. God is not contained in Jonah's categories. He is free to deal with Nineveh as He wants, not as Jonah wants. It may be that as regards Nineveh, Jonah wants "justice" – the destruction of the wicked, but God is ready to accept their repentance. Jonah wants his own relationship to God (a controlling one!) to be maintained (whether this is Jonah's egoism or Israel's particularism) – but God is free both to maintain this privileged relationship (though on *His* terms) yet extend His concern at the same time to all mankind, and all creation' (p. 112).

20. E. Jacob, op. cit., p. 222 (italics mine).

21. For a survey see R. Martin-Achard, *A Light to the Nations*, Oliver & Boyd 1962, pp. 42–46.

22. Ibid., p. 44.

23. H. H. Rowley, *The Missionary Message of the Old Testament*, Carey Kingsgate Press 1944, p. 73.

24. We are passing over much else that is of great importance, of course. See also the material in the Acts (e.g., 14.16ff. and 17.26ff.), and the letters of St Paul. On this see J. Munck, *Paul and the Salvation of Mankind*, SCM Press 1959; K. Stendahl, *Paul among Jews and Gentiles*, SCM Press 1976; and E. Käsemann, *Commentary on Romans*, SCM Press 1980, pp. 309ff.

25. Mathias Rissi, *The Future of the World*, SCM Press 1972, from the preface.

26. See on this M. Rissi, op. cit., p. 77, and his note on p. 110. We have given reasons for dissenting from the position of J. Jeremias in *Jesus's Promise to the Nations*, SCM Press, revised edition 1967, that 'the restoration of the Temple and the pilgrimage of the Gentiles are inseparably linked together', p. 66.

27. N. Turner, *Peake's Commentary, p. 1059.*

28. See above p. 49.

29. Stanley Samartha himself once told me of a Hindu visitor to his study who picked up a copy of a book called God's People in India (in itself an admirable essay about the church in India) and asked: 'Are not all the rest of us God's people also?' A similar question mark needs to be put against the Ecumenical Cycle of Prayer of the World Council of Churches: this is called *For All God's People*.

4   A Pluralist and Inclusivist Theology in the Making

1. See above, pp. 17f.

2. I use here the estimates of Prof. G. C. Oosthuizen in his *Die Godsdienste van die Wêreld*, Pretoria, NG Boekhandel 1977, p. 356. He wrote then that the Christian population could be estimated at thirty-eight per cent, but I am writing eight years later.

3. I offer some examples from some recent widely used theological handbooks from very different traditions: John Macquarrie in *The Principles of Christian Theology*, SCM Press, second edition 1977, ch. VII; Hans Küng, *On Being a Christian*, Collins 1977, Section A III; Jürgen Moltmann, *The Church in the Power of the Spirit*, SCM Press 1977, ch. 4, section 3; A. T. Hanson and R. P. C. Hanson, *Reasonable Belief*, Oxford University Press 1980, ch. 4; Stephen Neill in *The Lion Handbook of Christian Belief*, 1982; 'God in Other Religions', pp. 191–203; Geoffrey Wainwright, *Doxology*, Epworth Press 1980, ch. 7.

4. Cf. Matt. 8.11. This saying is found in the Gospel narrative immediately after the astonishing (to Jesus) declaration of faith by the non-Jewish centurion, as Donald Baillie comments: 'it is plain that Jesus came to single out this faith-attitude as a very vital one and to attach unlimited importance to it', in *Faith in God*, Faber, second edition

1964, p. 78. While it is true that this unnamed Roman soldier becomes in the story a model of faith in Jesus for the Christian audience, it is also clear that Matthew does not see him as a disciple, *mathētēs*, and there is no evidence of his recruitment into the membership of the Christian church.

5. John Hick, *God and the Universe of Faiths*, Macmillan 1973, Revised Edition, Collins Fount 1977.

6. John Hick (ed.), *Truth and Dialogue*, Sheldon Press, 1974.

7. See his article: 'The Outcome: Dialogue into Truth', ibid., p. 152.

8. John Hick, *God has Many Names*, Macmillan 1980, p. 58. Also in John Hick and Brian Hebblethwaite (eds) *Christianity and Other Religions*, Collins, Fount 1980.

9. The two seminal works of scholarship are The *Meaning and End of Religion* first published in the USA in 1963 (Macmillan 1963, Mentor Books 1964, Harper Books 1978), and with an English edition, SPCK 1978; and *Faith and Belief*, Princeton University Press 1979. More accessible for the non-specialist reader are *The Faith of Other Men*, first published in 1962, and Harper Torch Books 1972; *Questions of Religious Truth*, Gollancz 1967; and *Towards a World Theology*, Macmillan 1981. An admirable selection of Smith's writings has been made by Willard Oxtoby, in *Religious Diversity*, New York, Crossroad 1982.

10. W. Cantwell Smith, *The Meaning and End of Religion*, English edition, p. 51ff.

11. Ibid., p. 43.

12. See p. 36.

13. W. Cantwell Smith, *Questions of Religious Truth*, Gollancz 1963, p. 71.

14. Smith finds the first usage of the term 'Boudhism' in 1801, 'Hindooism' in 1829, 'Taouism' in 1839, 'Zoroasterianism' in 1854, 'Confucianism' in 1862 and so on. *The Meaning and End of Religion*, p. 61.

15. *Towards a World Theology*, p. 115.

16. Ibid., pp. 113–14.

17. *Faith and Belief*, p. 142.

18. *The Meaning and End of Religion*, p. 189.

19. *Towards a World Theology*, p. 127.

20. See above p. 15.

21. I am thinking here of the English Methodist layman, Dr John Taylor, formerly director of the WCC Dialogue Unit and now General Secretary of the World Conference on Religion and Peace; of Dr Wesley Ariarajah, the present director of the Dialogue Unit in the WCC, of the first two General Secretaries of the Council of Christians and Jews in Britain, William Simpson and Peter Jennings; of scholars in previous generations like James Hope Moulton, J. W. Sweetman, and in our own times, of the scholar-saint Lynn da Silva of Sri Lanka who died in 1982. Happily still at work is Professor Geoffrey Parrinder. It would be invidious to name Methodist scholars of the present generation, but I can think of at least a couple of dozen of my own friends all around the world, who as Methodists are making major contributions.

22. See below p. 131.

23. *Towards a World Theology*, p. 171.

24. In an essay first published in the *Occasional Bulletin* of the Missionary Research Library, New York, in April 1969. It is reprinted in W. Oxtoby, *Religious Diversity*, pp. 117–37, and G. H. Anderson and Thomas F. Stransky, *Mission Trends No. 2: Evangelisation*, Eerdmans 1975, pp. 219–29.

25. *Religious Diversity*, pp. 131–2; *Mission Trends No. 2*, pp. 222–3.

26. *Religious Diversity*, p. 137; *Mission Trends No. 2*, p. 229.

27. In *The Documents of Vatican II*, ed. Walter M. Abbott, Geoffrey Chapman, 1966, pp. 14–96, 584–630, 660–8.

28. *Partners in Dialogue*, Orbis Books 1983.

29. Ibid., pp. 81–2.

30. Ibid., pp. 83–4.

31. See above, p. 4, and note 4, p. 166.

32. My translation of the closing words of the original Dutch edition, *Christendom en godsdiensten der Wereld*, Baarn, Oecumene 1976, p. 94.

33. Published in the Netherlands by J. H. Kok in 1978. The contributions are in both English and Dutch, and Camps writes his article in English.

34. Also published by J. H. Kok of Kampen 1975. There is a translation of this work as *Contemporary Missiology* 1978, published by Eerdmans in the USA, but this is not accessible to me.

35. In *Zending op Weg naar de Toekomst*, p. 131.

36. Ibid., p. 135.

37. Kenneth Cragg, *The Christian and Other Religion*, Mowbray 1977, pp. 72–3.

38. David Brown, *A New Threshold*, BCC 1976.

39. Ibid., p. 21.

40. Ibid., p. 23.

41. Just before his untimely death, David Brown produced *All Their Splendour*, Fount Paperback 1982. This lucid book spells out how David Brown experienced both the joy and glory of which he speaks and how he saw a way of reconciliation between the world faith communities.

42. Donald G. Dawe and John B. Carman (eds) *Christian Faith in a Religiously Plural World*, Orbis Books 1978. Donald Dawe's paper is also called 'Christian Faith in a Religiously Plural World', see pp. 13–33.

43. Ibid., p. 22.

44. Ibid., p. 26.

45. Ibid., p. 28.

46. Ibid., p. 31.

47. See below pp. 107f.

48. By S. A. Nigosian of Toronto writing in *The Ecumenist*, June 1978, in a paper on 'The Challenge of Religious Pluralism'.

49. Anderson, *World Religions*, Tynedale Press 1968, p. 192.

50. Anderson, *Christianity and Comparative Religion*. Inter-varsity Press 1970, p. 104.

51. Ibid., p. 98.

52. Ibid., p. 110.

53. Anderson, *God's Law and God's Love*, Collins 1980.

54. Ibid., pp. 32–3.

55. Ibid., p. 33.

56. Ibid., p. 128.

57. Ibid., p. 128.

58. In *Living Faiths and the Ecumenical Movement*, ed. S. J. Samartha, WCC 1971, pp. 131–42, and in a slightly different translation, G. H. Anderson and Thomas F. Stransky (eds), *Mission Trends No. 5: Faith Meets Faith*, Eerdmans 1981, pp. 37–49.

59. *Living Faiths*, p. 138, cf. *Mission Trends No. 5*, p. 45.

60. *Living Faiths*, p. 162.

61. Ibid., p. 163.

62. *Relations with Peoples of Other Faiths*, BCC 1981, revised edition 1983.

63. *Towards a Theology for Inter-Faith Dialogue . . .* , CIO Publishing 1984.

64. Ibid., p. 27.

65. Ibid., p. 27.

66. Ibid., p. 18.

67. Ibid., p. 18.

68. Ibid., p. 19.

69. Ibid., p. 35. See chapter 7 below for an exposition of this 'provisionality' as a necessary aspect of the spirituality needed in inter-faith relationships.

70. Ibid., p. 31.

71. Ibid., p. 31.

5   A Christology for Religious Pluralism

1. In an essay 'The salvation of other men' in *Man and his Salvation*, ed. E. J. Sharpe and J. R. Hinnells, Manchester University Press 1973, p. 196.

2. See above p. 44.

3. Luther, *Auslegung des Evangeliums Johannes*, my translation.

4. David Tracy, *The Analogical Imagination*, SCM Press 1981, p. 163.

5. As a theologian working for the time being in a temperature of 70°F, I can never lose from my mind the excoriating challenge of Klaus Klostermeier in *Hindu and Christian in Vrindaban*, SCM Press 1969, pp. 40–1. 'Theology at 120°F in the shade seems, after all, different from theology at 70°F . . . The theologian at 70°F in a good position presumes God to be happy and contented, well-fed and rested, without needs of any kind. The theologian at 120°F tries to imagine a God who is hungry and thirsty, who suffers and is sad, who sheds perspiration and knows despair . . . The theologian at 70°F with a well-fed god compiles very nicely what other theologians at 70°F with well-fed gods have written before him. Everything is well documented; the footnotes take up almost half the page. French, English, Latin and Greek authors are quoted. They know exactly that God's grace, like American development aid, is intended for all heathen, for the pro-US ones as well as for others. The former get a little more. If only everybody follows nicely the road prescribed by their ministers and prelates, there will be enough for everyone. This is very convenient for the 70°F theologians; in that case they do not have to get themselves to where it is 120°F.' In the light of the implicit plea of Kostermeier anything I write in these pages seems timid and conventional.

6. Thomas is an interesting figure in non-Western church history. The *Acts of St Thomas* (second century) states that Jesus sent him specifically to India. This story is devoutly believed by all the *Mar Thoma* Christians of India and is accepted by many Roman Catholic and Protestant authorities, see Kenneth Scott Latourette, *A History of the Expansion of Christianity*, Eyre and Spottiswood, Vol. 1 1938, pp. 107–8. A recent visit to St Thomas' Mount, in Madras, made me aware of the credibility of this story. There is much evidence of lively trade between the Roman Empire and India and Sri Lanka in the first century and we are quite sure of the existence of the Christian church in South India by the fourth century at the very latest. Roy C. Amore, an American Methodist scholar has recently examined the links in the centuries immediately before and after the birth of Jesus in relation to the interaction of Christian and Buddhist teaching in his *Two Masters, One Message*, Abingdon 1978, and demonstrates the commercial and cultural contacts between the Mediterranean area and the Indian sub-continent. If Thomas was martyred in India, then it is not inconceivable that the writer of the Fourth Gospel knew that Thomas was not only apostle but also martyr, witness.

7. The references are to C. K. Barrett, *The Gospel according to St John: An Introduction with Commentary and Notes on the Greek Text*, SPCK 1955, p. 382; F. C. Grant, *Nelson's Bible Commentary*, Vol. 6, Nelson 1962, p. 386; William Temple, *Readings in St John's Gospel* (First and Second Series), Macmillan 1961, p. 222; Lesslie Newbigin, *The Light has Come*, Eerdmans 1982, p. 271.

8. In *The Interpreter's Bible*, Abingdon Press 1952, Vol. 8, pp. 700–1.

9. As with most commentators I take it that Ch. 21 is a later addition, for a discussion of its origin and purpose see R. E. Brown *Commentary*, Vol. 2, pp. 1077ff., and C. K. Barrett, *Commentary*, pp. 479ff.

10. The words are those of C. K. Barrett, *Commentary*, p. 476.

11. Docetism is 'the distinctive thesis which gave it its name (dokein = to seem) was that Christ's manhood, and hence his sufferings, were unreal, phantasmal'. J. N. D. Kelly, *Early Christian Doctrines*, Black, fourth edition 1968, p. 141.

12. The suggestion that someone else was substituted on the cross to die in Jesus's place was a very early suggestion (Basilides), as indeed are suggestions that Jesus was

given some powerful drug which induced the appearance of death, see e.g. the apocryphal *Gospel of Peter*, 4, 11.

13. In *The Real Resurrection*, Collins 1972, p. 82.

14. See on this aspect of 'explaining away' the Resurrection, Michael Perry, *The Easter Enigma*, Faber 1959, esp. ch. 9.

15. E. C. Hoskyns in *The Fourth Gospel*, ed. F. N. Davey, Faber, second edition 1947, p. 455.

16. F. J. A. Hort, *The Way the Truth the Life*, Macmillan 1893, p. 20.

17. Ibid., pp. 20–21.

18. I refer to the period of 'dialectical' theology associated particularly with the names of Karl Barth and Emil Brunner. See W. N. Pittenger, *The Word Incarnate*, Nisbet 1959, for the kind of criticism with which I would associate myself. Brunner, for example, wrote that Christ is *the* Revelation, 'absolutely different from all other events in history, from all other forms of religious and moral human development' (as cited in Pittenger, op. cit., p. 138). Pittenger concludes: 'While it is true that the "neo-orthodox" theology was valuable in emphasizing once again the great fact of God's transcendent majesty and glory, it has obtained its victory at the expense of destroying the significance of the world which God loved enough to "enter" and redeem. It is a hard saying, but I believe this theology is much further from the Christian gospel than the liberal school which it so despises.' Ibid., p. 144.

19. *The Oecumenical Documents of the Faith*, ed. T. H. Brindley, Methuen, second edition 1906, pp. 219ff.

20. *God was in Christ* was first published in 1948 by Faber with a second edition in 1955; *The Word Incarnate*, Nisbet 1959; *Christology Reconsidered*, SCM Press 1970; *Grace and Truth*, SPCK 1975 and *The Image of the Invisible God*, SCM Press 1982. A shorter statement of A. T. Hanson's position is in A. T. Hanson and R. P. C. Hanson, *Reasonable Belief*, Oxford University Press 1980.

21. *Methodist Hymn Book*, No. 283.

22. *God was in Christ*, p. 114.

23. Ibid., p. 117.

24. *The Word Incarnate*, p. 197.

25. For Pittenger see *The Lord Incarnate*, pp. 183–88, and *Christology Reconsidered*, pp. 12–13, and the whole of ch. 6. For Hanson see *The Image of the Invisible God*, p. 146 and *Reasonable Belief*, pp. 98–106.

26. For the importance of Trinitarian understanding in this context see *Grace and Truth*, pp. 83–95; *The Word Incarnate*, pp. 215–235.

27. See above p. 59.

28. *Partners in Dialogue*, p. 84.

29. Good and honourable scholars like W. E. Hocking have asked whether Christianity can 'so present the valid essences of religion as to give them unimpeded force, able to meet the issues created everywhere by the abstract universals of secularized arts and sciences'. He wants Christianity to 'meet the coming civilization' as a 'clarified messenger of the universal' (!), *The Coming World Civilization*, Allen & Unwin 1958, pp. 84–5. The desire for a universal 'essence of religion' faith is strong, and it would not be difficult to list a mass of titles and religious movements dedicated to such a search. But this could mean, as W. A. Visser t' Hooft once wrote, 'that we may find ourselves before long exceedingly rich in religion and exceedingly poor in real Christianity' *No Other Name*, SCM Press 1963, p. 9.

30. This is 'syncretism' properly so called. Note the definition of syncretism employed by the WCC. 'Conscious or unconscious human attempts to create a new religion composed of elements taken from different religions', *WCC Guidelines on Dialogue*, WCC 1979, p. 14.

31. For an excellent survey of the origins and development of the academic study known as 'comparative religion' see Eric J. Sharpe, *Comparative Religion: A History*,

Duckworth 1975.

32. Lionel Blue, *To Heaven with Scribes and Pharisees*, Darton, Longman & Todd 1975. Note also Lionel Blue's other attractive book *A Backdoor to Heaven*, Darton, Longman & Todd 1979.

33. The *Guide for the Perplexed* (Heb. *Moreh Nevukhim*) marks the high point of the 'golden age of Jewish learning' in the twelfth century of the Christian era. Maimonides was born in 1135, and wrestled with Aristotelian philosophy in order to give a rational basis for revelation and faith.

34. A. J. Arberry, *The Koran Interpreted*, Allen & Unwin 1955, Oxford Paperback 1983.

35. For further reflection on the Islamic theology from Christian standpoints see *Christians and Muslims Talking Together*, BCC 1984, and Kenneth Cragg, *Muhammad and the Christian*, Darton, Longman & Todd 1984; and *Jesus and the Muslim*, Allen & Unwin 1985.

36. I say strangely familiar because few people who use a version of these words know their ultimate origin in the Upanishads. Interestingly they are to be found in the Methodist Baptismal Service, see pp. A4 and A5 of the *Methodist Service Book*, Methodist Publishing House 1975. T. S. Garrett explains why these words found themselves in the Baptismal Liturgy of the Church of South India, from which they are directly borrowed by the *Methodist Service Book*: 'They are a baptizing of the ancient prayer of the Upanishads . . . The implication is that this agelong desire in the soul of India finds its fulfilment in Christian Baptism', *Worship in the Church of South India*, Lutterworth 1958, p. 41. For the CSI Baptismal Service see *The Book of Common Worship*, Oxford University Press 1963, pp. 120, 127. The only difference in the text is that the Methodist Service Book uses 'eternal' in the place of 'everlasting'.

37. For a brief discussion for the non-specialist Christian reader see Paul D. Clasper, *Eastern Paths and the Christian Way*, Orbis Books 1980, pp. 17–32.

38. My authority for this statement is M. A. Amaladoss in his essay 'An Indian Reads St John's Gospel' in *India's Search for Reality and the Relevance of the Gospel of John*, ed. C. Duraisingh and C. Hargreaves, Delhi, ISPCK 1975, p. 12.

39. The translation is that of Geoffrey Parrinder in *The Bhagavad Gita: A Verse Translation*, Sheldon Press 1974.

40. Ninian Smart, *Beyond Ideology*, Collins 1981, p. 107.

41. Jotiya Dhirasekera in 'God at the Head of Religion: A Search through Buddhism' in *God – the Contemporary Discussion*, ed. F. Sontag and M. D. Bryant, New York, Rose of Sharon Press 1982, pp. 74–5.

42. Westcott, *The Gospel according to St John*, reissued, James Clarke 1958, p. 202.

43. C. S. Song, *Third-Eye Theology: Theology in Formation in Asian Settings*, Lutterworth Press 1980, p. 17.

44. Professor S. G. Wilson has recently written a most important essay on 'Paul and Religion' in a *Festschrift* for C. K. Barrett entitled *Paul and Paulinism*, ed. M. D. Hooker and S. G. Wilson, SPCK 1982. He, as a New Testament exegete, is among the first known to me to imply that Romans 1–3 is not the last word to be said about the Christian judgment on other religion. He writes: 'Obviously, too, the admitted existence of unnamed pious Gentiles (Wilson is referring of course to Rom. 2.14–15) is an embarrassment to Paul's intended conclusion. It might thus be conceded that there is a need to cool his passion, tone down his polemics and straighten his logic, and in the process it would be legitimate to observe that Rom. 1–3 is a prophetic judgment and not a dispassionate report and that we should not expect the detail and accuracy from the one as we do from the other – though it would also be necessary to consider at what point the notion of a prophetic judgment ceases to be an excuse for misrepresentation' (p. 348).

45. *The Interpretation of the Fourth Gospel*, Cambridge University Press 1968, p. 19.

46. Brown, *Commentary*, p. 629. See further Raymond Brown's further reflections on the Johannine milieu in his *Community of the Beloved Disciple*, New York, Paulist Press

1979. This gives a vivid picture of the Johannine Community in dialogue or contention with a wide spectrum of religious faith and ideology in the first century. See also the chapter 'The Johannine Theology of Mission' in D. Senior and C. Stuhlmueller, *Biblical Foundations for Mission*, SCM Press 1983, pp. 280–96.

47. The phrase 'whatever path men choose is mine' comes from what Professor John Hick calls 'one of the great revelatory scriptures of the World', the *Bhagavad Gita*, iv, 11. But the verse remains for the Christian profoundly problematic in view of the paths that some people have chosen; neither John Hick nor I would want to agree that every form of religion is wholesome or salvific. Some forms of religion have plainly led away from a loving and saving God.

48. Isa. 55.8.

49. *Timaeus*, 28c. Justin Martyr quotes this sentence in his *Second Apology*, ch. 10.

50. Hans-Joachim Schoeps, *The Jewish Christian Argument*, Faber 1955, pp. 141–42.

51. Ibid., p. 142.

52. *Alternative Service Book*, Hodder & Stoughton 1981, p. 588. This prayer is simply an updating in language of the equivalent collect in the *Book of Common Prayer* which prays for 'Jews, Turks, Infidels and Hereticks'.

53. Barth, *Church Dogmatics*, Vol. 4/3, T. and T. Clark 1962, p. 877.

54. For some illuminating comments on the earliest understandings of God in the Old Testament, set against the background of 'the inter-faith dialogue' (my expression) of the Israelites, see Rudolf Ficker 'Uniqueness and Interdependence: Israelite Religion in its Religious Environment' in *Bangalore Theological Forum*, Vol. XV, No. 2 May-August 1983, pp. 87–127. The whole of this article is worth consulting, as reflecting the opinions of an Old Testament scholar who teaches in a multi-faith context, and therefore sees 'interdependence' as well as 'uniqueness' in the earliest biblical traditions.

55. Otherwise known as the *Shemoneh 'Esreh*, the Eighteen Benedictions.

56. *Returning: Exercises in Repentance*, published by the Reform Synagogues of Great Britain 1975.

57. See Appendix A, esp. p. 160.

58. Though sometimes this has been disputed, and Christian influence has been credited with such insights especially in Sikhism and the *Bhakti* tradition.

59. Hendrik Kraemer, *The Christian Message in a Non-Christian World*, third edition, James Clarke 1956, p. 102.

60. It might be said, for example, of the second example given below that Teja Singh's translation of the 'Sikh prayer' is influenced by his having attended a Christian school, and that therefore this evidence has to be discounted as being in fact more Christian than Sikh. But to say this would be to deny another person the right to define himself and his tradition. Teja Singh would in fact affirm that his translation brings out the heart of the Sikh teaching.

61. In George Appleton, *The Oxford Book of Prayer*, Oxford University Press 1985, p. 288. While this is the only prayer addressed to the 'Father' I cite directly from this magnificent anthology, a cursory reading through the section, 'Prayers from Other Traditions of Faith', pp. 269–357, reveals many other examples: Jewish at nos. 837, 840 and 846; Indian, nos. 859, 866, 874, 893, 909 ('Mother'); Muslim, no. 1050; African, nos. 1056, 1064, 1065, 1067; Canadian Indian, no. 1068 ('Grandfather'); Japanese Shinto, nos. 1081–3 ('God our Parent'). But such a selection takes no account of the tone and feeling of many other of the prayers in this section in which there is a profound sense of the fatherly relation of God to his human children.

62. In Teja Singh, *Sikhism: its Ideals and Institutions*, Amritsar, Khalsa Brothers, p. 125.

63. W. Owen Cole (ed.), *Comparative Religions*, Blandford Press 1982. In fairness to Dr Cole it should be stated that the title was determined by the publisher not by the editor.

64. I.e. the Sikh holy scriptures. A convenient English Anthology is G. S. Talib, *Selections from the Holy Granth*, Delhi, Vikas 1975.

65. W. Owen Cole, *The Guru in Sikhism*, Darton, Longman & Todd 1982, p. 16.

66. Quoted by W. O. Cole, ibid., pp. 15–16.

67. N. S. Dhillon, *Practical Sikhism* was published by the author in 1980 and is obtainable from 37 Rosebery Avenue, Manor Park, London E12 6PZ. His Sikh 'creed' is on p. 21.

68. Privately published.

69. Rudolf Otto, *Christianity and the Indian Religion of Grace*, Madras, CLS 1929 (in German as *Die Genadenreligion Indiens*, Gotha 1930). Otto defined this as 'faith in salvation through an eternal God and through a saving fellowship with Him', p. 29. For an account of the *bhakti* tradition by an Indian bishop who was very close to it, see A. J. Appasamy, *The Gospel and India's Religious Heritage*, SPCK 1942. Robin Boyd, *An Introduction to Indian Christian Theology*, Madras, CLS, revised edition 1975, has an excellent chapter on Appasamy entitled 'Christianity as Bhakti Marga', pp. 110–43. Incidentally British Methodists have been familiar with just one expression of this Christianized *bhakti marga* through the one hymn from anywhere outside Europe or North America in the 1933 *Methodist Hymn Book*, No. 159, 'One who is all unfit to count/As scholar in thy school'. The last verse matches the paradox of grace of Harriet Auber's hymn:

> If there is aught of worth in me
> It comes from Thee alone
> Then keep me safe, for so, O Lord
> Thou keepest but Thine own.

Its writer was Narayan Vaman Tilak (1862–1919), a first generation convert to Christianity whose Marathi devotional lyrics are part of the 'permanent treasury of devotion and theology for the Indian Church, comparable to the Latin hymns of the early Church, or Luther's chorales, or the great German hymnodists Gerhardt Tersteegen and Neander, or the hymns of Wesley and Watts in England', Robin Boyd, op. cit., p.117.

70. *Eastern Paths and the Christian Way*, p.24.

71. *Bhagavad-Gita*, 11.43; in op. cit., p. 67.

72. 18.62; in op. cit., p. 100.

73. 18.65–6; in op. cit., p. 101. Parrinder comments on this: 'The favourite final verse held to be the climax and summary of the Gita'.

74. For the sense of being found, see the story quoted from Klaus Klostermaier in *Relations with People of Other Faiths: Guidelines on Dialogue in Britain*, p. 5: '"it is not we who choose our God", replied Gopalji, "it is God who chooses us"'.

75. A. J. Appasamy (ed.), *Temple Bells: Readings from Hindu Religious Literature*, Calcutta, Association Press 1930.

76. Ibid., p. 47.

77. Cited in W. S. Deming, *Selections from Tukaram*, Madras, CLS 1932, p. 23. Deming comments: 'yet here again, as a *bhakta*, Tukaram approximates to the Christian position, when he thinks of salvation as release from the power of sin, rather than as release from the bondage of *karma*'.

78. *Temple Bells*, p. 55. 'Save as Thy servant I am nought', is of the same spirit, is it not, as Harriet Auber? See above p. 77.

79. *Temple Bells*, p. 62. I am grateful to the Methodist scholar of Indian Christian thought, Roy Pape, for calling my attention to this verse. He points out the affinities here with e.g., Psalm 51.

80. The *Gitanjali*, a collection of prose translations made by the author from the original Bengali were published in the UK by Macmillan in 1913 with an introduction by W. B. Yeats. I am told that many of these songs form the regular hymnology of the

Bengali Christian church, though Tagore never became a Christian himself– or, at least, 'a Christian like us'.

81. The great Methodist missionary, anthropologist and pioneering Africanist, Edwin W. Smith reported a conversation, now notorious, with the German intellectual, Emil Ludwig. In the course of the conversation Ludwig looked at Smith with perplexity: 'How can the untutored African conceive God? . . . How can this be? . . . Deity is a philosophical concept which savages are incapable of framing', *African Ideas of God*, Edinburgh House Press 1950, p. 1. The hurt that has been done to Africa because of the cultural assumptions of the nineteenth-century Europeans is inestimable. See further Kwame Bediako, 'Biblical Christologies in the context of African Traditional Religions', in V. Samuel and C. Sugden (eds), *Sharing Jesus in the Two Thirds World*, Bangalore, Partnership in Mission-Asia 1983, pp. 117–35.

82. Just a selection of recent work on African religious traditions by Africans themselves may be mentioned here: K. A. Dickson and P. Ellingworth (eds), *Biblical Revelation and African Beliefs*, Lutterworth 1969; E. B. Idowu, *African Traditional Religion*, SCM Press 1973; J. S. Mbiti, *Concepts of God in Africa*, SPCK 1970; G. I. Metuh, *God and Man in African Religion*, Chapman 1981. For a fuller bibliography see David Bosch's extended revue article 'Missionary Theology in Africa' in the South African Journal of Theology, No. 49, pp. 14–37. For a fascinating example of what happens if the Christian missionary takes African knowledge of God seriously see Vincent Donovan, *Christianity Rediscovered*, SCM Press 1982.

83. John S. Mbiti, *The Prayers of African Religion*, SPCK 1975, cf. his *Concepts of God in Africa*, SPCK 1970, pp. 64–70, and his *African Religions and Philosophy*, Heinemann 1969, esp. pp. 61–8. But note also Mbiti's telling comment from the last-named book: 'As for the love of God, there are practically no sayings that God loves. This is something reflected in the daily lives of African peoples, in which it is rare to hear people talking about love. A person shows his love for another more through action than through words. So, in the same way, people experience the love of God in concrete acts and blessings; and they assume that He loves them, otherwise He would not have created them' (p. 38).

84. *Prayers*, p. 143 (Nuer, Sudan).

85. Ibid., p. 151 (Kikuyu, Kenya).

86. Ibid., p. 139 (Ewe, West Africa).

87. Ibid., pp. 137–8 (Dinka, Sudan).

88. Ibid., p. 129.

89. Brown, *Commentary*, pp. 23–4.

90. See C. F. D. Moule, *The Birth of the New Testament*, Black 1962, p. 167: 'The Epistles to the Colossians (i.15ff) and to the Hebrews (i.1ff,) both contain a *"logos-doctrine"* in all but the actual term.' Cf. A. T. Hanson in *The Image of the Invisible God*, SCM Press 1982, p. 88: 'Colossians is particularly interesting because it has what is virtually a Logos doctrine without using the word Logos.'

91. Note, however, C. K. Barrett's argument that *phōtizein* may mean here 'to bring to light', rather than 'to illuminate', i.e. the true light 'shines upon every man' whether he sees it or not for judgment to reveal what he is. But it seems more likely, even on Barrett's terms to take it with the Rabbinic connotations he spells out in his previous comment and to translate it with e.g. Lev. R 31.6 which says 'Thou enlightenest those who are on high and those who are beneath and all who come into the world', *Commentary*, p. 134.

92. A. C. Bouquet, *Christian Faith and Non-Christian Religions*, Nisbet 1959, p. 160. I am grateful to Alan Bouquet for other sharp perceptions of the New Testament writers' basic stance e.g. in Acts 28.8 '. . . *autoi kai akousontai*'. The Gentiles will listen to the message of salvation. 'Why', asks Alan Bouquet, 'should the *goyim* do this?' Ibid., p. 159.

93. Ibid., p. 148. Bouquet goes on to make his point more vividly: 'It would have been tantamount to some British writer introducing a scientific term like "relativity" into a theological work, but intending it to mean something quite different from what it would have signified when used by Einstein. To make such a supposition in the case of the

Johannine author seems fantastic. Whoever he may have been, when he wrote "Logos" he meant "Logos", and he meant it to be taken in the sense in which a contemporary Stoic writer would have taken it', p. 157.

94. C. H. Dodd, *The Interpretation of the Fourth Gospel*, p. 9. Dodd is certainly not so emphatic as Bouquet that the Logos reference is merely intended for the Stoics: his work reveals a much wider range of reference to the many strands of religious thinking that would be present in 'the varied and cosmopolitan society of a great Hellenistic city such as Ephesus under the Roman Empire'.

95. A recent experience of the first joint Conference of the National Missionary Council (Roman Catholic missionary leaders) with the conference for World Mission (a division of the British Council of Churches) in September 1983 confirms this. Dr Hans-Ruedi Weber of the WCC, leading an extended session on Bible Study on the Johannine Prologue, posed the question: 'Where does the hymn and its annotation begin to speak about the *incarnate* Logos, the work of Jesus of Nazareth on earth (from verses 9ff. or only verses 14ff. onwards)?' Missiologists from many Catholic and Protestant traditions were virtually unanimous in deciding for the second alternative.

96. *First Apology*, ch. 46. Justin adds as examples: among the Greeks, Socrates and Heraclitus, and among the 'foreigners' Abraham, Elijah and the people we know as Shadrach, Meshach and Abednego (Dan. 1.7).

97. *Second Apology*, ch. 10.

98. *Second Apology*, ch. 13. Justin goes on to claim their insight for the Christian church: 'The truths which men in all lands have rightly spoken belong to us Christians.'

99. *First Apology*, ch. 5.

100. *Stromateis*, 6.8.

101. Ibid., 6.2.

102. Ibid., 1.9.

103. Ibid., 1.13.

104. A. T. Hanson, *The Image of the Invisible God*, p. 143.

105. Pittenger, op. cit., p. 286. See also pp. 236–44. Pittenger writes beautifully: 'We have argued in this book that . . . the only way to understand the Incarnation of God in Christ is in the context of an incarnational presence and operation of the Word of God in nature, in history and human life. What is "diffused" elsewhere, "at sundry times and in divers portions" is "focused" in our Lord Jesus Christ. There is always union between God and man, of some sort and in some way: in Jesus Christ there is *the* union towards which all others point and from which they are seen in all their rich potentiality yet in all their tragic failure' (p. 241).

106. Ibid., p. 286. Cf. his sharp criticism of 'neo-orthodox' christologies as based upon 'an irrational philosophy, a sceptical epistemology, and a dialectic theology'. He continues 'It is a hard saying, but I believe that this theology is much farther from the Christian gospel than the liberal school which it so despises. For even if man is in sin, he is still God's; of that fundamental fact Christian faith can never lose sight, and the "liberals" were at least near the truth in this. They did not cast away as rubbish the world which God created; nor did they despair utterly of the potential goodness of the men and women whom Christ came to save, the simple people whom he was not ashamed to call his brethren' (pp. 144–5).

107. Ibid., pp. 248–51, where he deals with the question, frequently posed by students, 'How can the Christian gospel, concerned with the salvation of man in this world, have universal significance when we know there may well be intelligent life on other planets?'

108. Ibid., p. 249.

109. Ibid., p. 219.

110. Temple, *Readings in St John's Gospel*, St Martin's Library edition, Macmillan 1961, p. 9.

111. Temple, *Christus Veritas*, Macmillan 1924, p. 140.

112. In 'Jesus and the World Religions' in John Hick (ed.), *The Myth of God Incarnate*, SCM Press 1977, p. 181, and reprinted in John Hick, *God Has Many Names*, Macmillan 1980, p. 75. It is from the latter that the citation is taken.

113. Cf. Irenaeus' phrase: 'the measure of the unmeasured godhead' and re-call the subtitle of Kenneth Cragg's book *The Christian and Other Religions: the Measure of Christ*, Mowbray 1977.

114. Barrett, *Commentary*, p. 382.

115. There is of course an exegetical problem here. In common with the majority of British commentators, I take *katelaben* in the sense of 'overcame', not least for the reason that the same word appears in John 12.35: 'walk while you have the light, lest the darkness overtake you' (RSV). Here the same three Greek words appear together: *phōs*, *skotia* and the verb *katalambanō*. To adduce connotations of incomprehensibility as, for example, Hendrik Kraemer did, seems to be a recipe for not getting the 'theology of religion' right. See further A. C. Bouquet, *Christian Faith and Non-Christian Religions*, pp. 155–59.

116. I have indicated that I owe much to A. T. Hanson's *The Image of the Invisible God* which is full of powerful insight into the relation of the ascended Christ to God and to believers. What I do not find is an attempt to relate the ascended Christ to those outside the Christian community. I note, however, the following comments in criticism of the traditional doctrine of the glorified humanity. Hanson says that this 'seems to suggest that some of the greatest figures of the Old Testament revelation, such as Hosea, Jeremiah, or the Servant of the Lord portrayed in Deutero-Isaiah, not to mention the anonymous authors of so many psalms of intimate communion with God, could not really have come close to God because they could not partake in the glorified humanity of the Word. But this is contrary to the evidence; what they lacked was scope of the knowledge of God, not intimacy of communion. We might add that many people in other religious traditions appear to have got very close to God, and I certainly would not want to deny the validity of their religious experience' (p. 57).

117. Geoffrey Lampe, *God as Spirit*, Oxford University Press 1977, reissued SCM Press 1983. Lampe continues 'Through the life and death, the words and deeds of Jesus, and his personal character, the power of the Kingdom of God, which is the creating and saving power of God as Spirit, was released into the world with new strength. Decisive as the act of God in Jesus was, it was not discontinuous with the creating and saving work through the entire historical process' (p. 31).

118. In *Christian Faith in a Religiously Plural World*, ed. Donald G. Dawe and John B. Carman, Orbis Books 1978, p. 29.

6   The New Relationship: The Way We Behave in Inter-religious Dialogue

1. The excellent series *Mission Trends* edited by Gerald H. Anderson and Thomas F. Stransky, published jointly by the Paulist Press and Eerdmans, contains selections from Christian missionary thinkers who are for and against 'dialogue', see especially No. 2, *Evangelization* and No. 5, *Faith Meets Faith*. We do not have similar collections of statements from representatives of other world religious traditions, but some of their thinking may be found in the WCC collections: *Dialogue between Men of Living Faiths* (papers from the Ajaltoun Consultation) WCC 1971, and *Towards World Community* (papers presented to the Multi-Lateral Dialogue, Colombo) WCC 1974. Two volumes of essays, published in India, have statements by non-Christians: *Meeting of Religions: New Orientations and New Perspectives*, ed. T. A. Aykara, Bangalore, Dhamaram Publications 1978, and *Dialogue in Community*, ed. C. D. Jathanna, Karnataka Theological Research Institute, Balmatta, Mangalore 1982.

2. Examples of this are Myrtle Langley's brief, perceptive essay, *Ethical Dialogue with Other Religions*, Bramcote, Grove Books 1979; John Ferguson's *War and Peace in the World's Religions*, Sheldon Press 1977, and a third type, S. C. Thakur's *Christian and*

Hindu Ethics, Allen & Unwin 1969.

3. Again we choose a few titles as examples of what is meant: there are Roger Hooker's three books about inter-faith relationships in Varanasi, all published by CMS: *Uncharted Journey, 1973; Journey into Varanasi, 1978; Voices of Varanasi, 1979.* On the Roman Catholic side there is Klaus Klostermaier's *Hindu and Christian in Vrindaban,* SCM Press 1969, and the various writings of Bede Griffiths and Abhishiktananda, e.g. *Christian Ashram,* Darton, Longman & Todd 1966; *Guru and Disciple,* SPCK 1974. These all have been from the Indian context: for the encounter with Buddhism see Donald Swearer, *Dialogue – the Key to Understanding Other Religions,* Westminster Press, Philadelphia, 1977, and William Johnston The *Inner Eye of Love,* Collins 1978. But this list could be much extended.

4. We cannot offer a full list of such guidelines. Sometimes they refer to relations between two faiths at national level, sometimes on an international level: sometimes they represent ecumenical effort, sometimes they are the effort of a single denomination. All the examples listed come from Christian traditions, but it should be noted that other communities are contemplating the production of 'Guidelines' for use within their own circles. The earliest effort in Britain at the ecumenical level was: *A New Threshold: Guidelines for the Churches in their Relations with Muslim Communities,* BCC 1976. (This has been translated with additional material into Danish and Swedish.) A Dutch counterpart to this is: *Anders geloven, samen leven* (To believe differently, to live together). A handbook for the Christian/Muslim encounter in the Netherlands, 1982. The German Protestant Church has published a number of booklets about Christian/ Muslim relationships, and the most important of these is *Christen and Muslime in Gespräch,* Frankfurt 1982. This has been translated into French, Dutch and English, *Christians and Muslims Talking Together,* BCC 1984. The Secretariat for Non-Christians of the Vatican has produced: *Guidelines for Dialogue with Muslims,* and *The Attitude of the Church Towards the Followers of Other Religions,* 1984. Relations with the Jewish people are especially problematic and this had led to a number of statements, the latest from the WCC is: *Ecumenical Considerations on Jewish/Christian Dialogue,* WCC 1983. British denominations have produced their own Guidelines to inter-religious relationships on a general level: United Reformed Church has: *With People of Other Faiths in Britain,* 1980, and the Methodist Church has: *Shall We Greet Only Our Own Family?: On Being a Christian in Today's Multi-Faith Society,* 1981. There is also Christopher Lamb's leaflet: *I don't think we've met before . . . Do's and Don'ts in approaching those of other faiths in Britain,* 1982.

5. 'The Church has to provide guidelines for its members as they confront the problems of how to act, and sometimes these guidelines may be simply prohibitions to keep them from wandering too far.' John Macquarrie, *Principles of Christian Theology,* SCM Press 1966 edition, p. 461.

6. I would be most grateful for any information there may be about this being done.

7. Five that are: *The Unknown Christ of Hinduism,* 1964, Darton, Longman & Todd, second edition 1981; *The Trinity and the Religious Experience of Man,* Darton, Longman & Todd 1973; *Worship and Secular Man,* Darton, Longman & Todd 1972. *The Intrareligious Dialogue,* New York, Paulist Press 1978 and *Myth, Faith and Hermeneutic,* New York, Paulist Press 1979.

8. There is a good deal of highly condensed but extremely suggestive material on the theological significance of people of other faiths and ideologies and on the concept of ideology especially in relation to 'syncretism', pp. 11–15.

9. 'As the member churches of the WCC consider, test and evaluate these guidelines they will need to work out for themselves and with their specific partners in dialogue statements and guidelines for their own use in specific situations.' WCC *Guidelines,* p. 21.

10. The General Synod of the Church of England, for example, adopted the BCC *Guidelines* by some 300 votes to 2 against.

11. 'A man will not really be intelligible to you if, instead of listening to him and sympathizing with him, you determine to classify him.' F. D. Maurice, *The Religions of the World*, Macmillan, sixth edition 1886, p. 96.

12. Cf. the Qur'anic statement: '(the Jews) . . . slew him not nor crucified, but it appeared so unto them: and lo! those who disagree concerning it are in doubt thereof; they have no knowledge thereof save pursuit of a conjecture, they slew him not for certain. But Allah took him up unto himself . . . ' (Surah 4.157–158).

13. 'The Rules of the Game' are reprinted conveniently in *Mission Trends No. 5: Faith Meets Faith*, pp. 111–12.

14. Op. cit., pp. 99 and 24–25. Cf. p. 69, 'Faith is not *a* religion but stands at the basis of *all* religions'.

15. Ibid., p. 101.

16. Ibid. p. 102.

17. Ibid.

18. *Faith and Belief*, Princeton University Press 1979, p. 4. I have a vivid recollection of my first meeting with Dr Smith on the back seat of a bus showing members of a conference around Richmond, Virginia. I gave him my card on which was printed the name of the Committee I serve: The Committee for Relations with People of Other Faiths. Dr Smith put his finger on the 's' and raised his eyebrows. If up to this time I have not managed to get the 's' removed it is not because I do not assent wholeheartedly to Dr Smith's proposition. I do. But in a fallen world there is a certain convenience in using words as other people use them, and we have to call the 'cumulative religious traditions of humankind' by some shorter term.

19. See above pp. 55f.

20. W. Cantwell Smith, *Questions of Religious Truth*, Gollancz 1967, p. 71.

21. W. Cantwell Smith, *Towards a World Theology*, Macmillan 1981, p. 74.

22. Ibid., p. 77.

23. Ibid.

24. Martin Buber, *Between Man and Man*, trans. R. Gregor Smith 1947, and reissued Collins, Fontana 1961, p. 24.

25. *Courage for Dialogue*, WCC 1981, p. 57.

26. D. T. Niles, 'Karl Barth – a Personal Memory', *The S E Asia Journal of Theology*, No. 11, Autumn 1969, pp. 10–11. I re-tell the story as it is in the notes to Gerald H. Anderson's 'Religion and Christian Mission' in *Christian Faith in a Religiously Plural World*, ed. D. G. Dawe and J. B. Carman, Orbis Books 1978, p. 114. Actually Karl Barth has more to contribute to our theme than the stereotype (based solely on the *Church Dogmatics*, Vol. 2/1, 17) of this thinking might suggest. It is his disciples who have spoken of 'biblical realism' and 'radical discontinuity'. There is an intriguing paper by Arvind Nirmal, the Indian theologian, 'Some Theological Issues connected with Inter Faith Dialogue and the Implication for Theological Education in India' in the *Bangalore Theological Forum*, Vol. XII, No. 2, 1980, which takes up Barthian themes in inter-religious relationships.

27. It is not, I think, a problem at all if Brian Hebblethwaite's position is adopted: 'The prime task of theology is that of understanding. What makes a man or a woman a theologian is first and foremost a desire to know the truth about his or her religion or that of other people. To that end the theologian has to set aside both pietistic and apologetic motives. He is not primarily concerned, *qua* theologian, to deepen faith or to defend a gospel.' *The Problems of Theology*, Cambridge University Press 1980, pp. 20–21.

28. *Towards a World Theology*, p. 74. Compare this with the fascinating formulation which occurs on p. 101 of the same book: 'Several years ago I had occasion to characterise the study of comparative religion as moving from the talk of an "it" to talk of a "they"; which became a "we" talking of a "they" and presently a "we" talking of "you"; and finally – the goal – a "we all" talking together about "us".'

Smith is referring to a paper "Comparative Religion: Whither and Why?" in *The History of Religions: Essays in Methodology*, ed. Mircea Eliade and Joseph M. Kitagawa, Chicago 1959, pp. 31–58.

29. John Macmurray, *The Self as Agent*, Faber 1957, reissued 1969, pp. 14–15.

30. David Jenkins, *The Contradiction of Christianity*, SCM Press 1976, p. 15.

31. Barth, *Church Dogmatics*, Vol. 4/3, p. 773. Note the comment of a contemporary German missiologist: 'On the other hand the kerugmatic antithesis set over against everything religious in this period still functions as a detectable handicap for the missionary encounter with the other religions.' My translation of Horst Bürkle, *Missionstheologie*, Kohlhammer, Stuttgart 1979, p. 19.

32. Ibid., p. 773.

33. Art., 'Mission and Humanization', in the *International Review of Mission*, Vol. LX, No. 237, January 1971, p. 21.

34. As, e.g., discussed by David F. Wells, *The Search for Salvation*, Inter-Varsity Press 1978, pp. 34ff.

35. The sensitivity to issues like this in WCC circles is indicated by the title of a book by the Librarian of the Ecumenical Centre in Geneva: A. J. van der Bent, *The Utopia of a World Community*, SCM Press 1973.

36. 'Our purpose in dialogue should not be to eliminate differences, but to appreciate each other's faith, and cooperate with one another in overcoming violence, war, injustice and irreligion in the world . . . There are many devils to be cast out. World religions should come together to vanquish them, *before* they destroy human community completely.' K. L. Sheshagiri Rao speaking at a conference in the USA in 1976, see *Christian Faith in a Religiously Plural World*, p. 58.

37. Cf. Klaus Klostermaier: 'By dialogue I do not mean . . . the exchange of views between theologians of different religions. Interesting and necessary as it is, it is not "dialogue" but "comparative religion". The real dialogue is an ultimate personal depth – it need not even be a talking about religious or theological topics. Real dialogues . . . challenge both partners, making them aware of the presence of God, calling them to a metanoia from an unknown depth.' Art. 'Dialogue – the words of God', in *Inter-Religious Dialogue*, ed. Herbert Jai Singh, Bangalore, CLS 1967. Quoted in D. K. Swearer, *Dialogue – the Key to Understanding Other Religions*, p. 35.

38. See the comments of the BCC *Guidelines*, p. 6.

39. Cf. Hendrik Kraemer on the aims of inter-religious relationships: 'There may be two aims: a pragmatic or a fundamental one. The pragmatic has to aim first and foremost at removing mutual misunderstandings and serving common human responsibilities. This may lead on to a deeper exchange of witness and experience, but if so it is a by-product. The fundamental aim directly involves this open exchange of witness, experience, cross-questioning and listening. The seriousness of true religion demands that one shall really be one's true religious self . . . ' *World Cultures and World Religions*, Lutterworth 1956, p. 356. Panikkar and Kraemer would agree that one 'preconceived solution' would be that all religions say fundamentally the same thing.

40. *Courage for Dialogue*, p. 9.

41. In *Jesus Through Other Eyes: Christology in Multi-Faith Context*, Latimer House, Oxford 1981, p. 30.

42. In 'Negations: an article on dialogue among religions' in *Religion and Society*, Bangalore XX (4), p. 74.

43. Newbigin, *The Open Secret*, SPCK 1978, p. 211. Note, however, Newbigin's further comment 'The Christian will go into dialogue believing that the sovereign power of the Spirit can use the occasion for the radical conversion of his partner as well as of himself.'

44. Op. cit., p. 12 and 7.

45. *Courage for Dialogue*, p. 43.

46. We may for example not be treated as fellow-pilgrims because of 'colonialism'. It is often easier for Christians of the so-called Third World to express themselves clearly

about that. I remember a conversation about this with Dr Lamin Sanneh, now of Harvard, in which he gave thanks that he was not handicapped by guilt for Western imperialism in his dialogue with Muslims.

47. The *Pirke Aboth* (Ethics of the Fathers) 1.12, slightly modified. The original reads 'and drawing them nearer the Torah'.

7   Towards a New Spirituality

1. Art. 'Spirituality' in *A New Dictionary of Christian Theology*, ed. Alan Richardson and John Bowden, SCM Press 1983, p. 549.

2. Hans Conzelmann describes the situation in Corinth brilliantly: 'Paul attests the community's wealth of knowledge (1.5). But Christianity is on the way to being transformed into a mystery religion of the ancient style. Faith is oriented not to the death of Christ but to his heavenly glory. In the sway of the Spirit the believer experiences his own participation in this glory and hovers above the world.' *History of Primitive Christianity*, Darton, Longman & Todd 1973, p. 103. See also 'A Cloud of Witnesses' and 'Two Roots or a Tangled Mass', two articles by Frances Young in *The Myth of God Incarnate*, ed. John Hick, SCM Press 1977, for an excellent survey of the possibilities open to the early church in understanding who Jesus was. Theology has everything to do with spirituality.

3. C. H. Dodd, *The Johannine Epistles*, Hodder & Stoughton 1946, p. xix.

4. See further on this C. H. Dodd, *The Interpretation of the Fourth Gospel*, Cambridge University Press 1968, pp. 97–114.

5. Art. 'Spirituality' in *A Dictionary of Christian Spirituality*, ed. Gordon Wakefield, SCM Press 1983, p. 363.

6. For another way of putting this, compare these words of one of the great contemporary writings on the work of the Holy Spirit: 'For the patterns of the Gospel experience are the patterns of the very fabric of life. The free obedience of Jesus, his dying for us all and his rising again, are both history and universal reality. They happened and they are the way things always happen. And man is saved not by relating only to that historical life, death and resurrection in which the pattern was made plain once for all, but by relating to that true pattern wherever it emerges in the tissue of contemporary experience.' John V. Taylor, *The Go-Between God*, SCM Press 1972, 1980, p. 180.

7. Wesley accurately notes: 'although every man necessarily believes that every particular opinion which he holds is true; (for to believe that any opinion is not true, is the same thing as not to hold it), yet no man can be assured that all his own opinions, taken together, are true'. I find I have to get this across endlessly in discussing the processes of inter-faith dialogue. We are not, and cannot be indifferent about the opinions and beliefs that we hold – otherwise we should not hold them. Dialogue is not about being open-minded.

8. Roy Pape, *Can We Pray Together? Guidelines on Worship in a Multi-Faith Society*, BCC 1983, p. iv.

9. Ibid., p. 17.

10. Art. 'Silence' in *A Dictionary of Christian Spirituality*, p. 355. For a detailed study see William Johnston *Silent Music*, Collins 1974. Johnston's title comes from the words of St John of the Cross: 'My Beloved is in the mountains, the solitary wooded valley, strange islands . . . silent music'.

11. Pape, op. cit., p. 17.

12. *Hindu-Christian Meeting Point*, revised edition, Delhi, ISPCK 1976, p. xiii.

13. Gnanananda, *Guru and Disciple*, SPCK 1974.

14. *The Further Shore*, ISPCK, Delhi 1975.

15. *Saccidananda: A Christian Approach to Advaitic Experience*, ISPCK, Delhi 1974.

16. *Hindu-Christian Meeting Point*, p. viii.

17. Bede Griffiths, *Christian Ashram: Essays Towards a Hindu-Christian Dialogue*, Darton, Longman & Todd 1966, p. 63.

18. We have already noted his study *Silent Music*, note 10 above. Johnston is well-known for his studies of the Middle English mystical work, *The Cloud of Unknowing* and he becomes particularly important for our theme because he is so deeply versed in traditional Christian spirituality. His studies of Zen: *The Still Point*, Fordham University Press 1975, and *Christian Zen*, Dublin, Gill and Macmillan 1979, are written against this background. The *Inner Eye of Love* was published by Collins in 1978.

19. William Johnston, *The Inner Eye of Love*, p. 10.

20. Ibid., pp. 9–10.

21. Lonergan's two most important books for Johnston's purposes are: *Method in Theology*, Darton, Longman & Todd 1972 and *A Second Collection*, Darton, Longman & Todd 1974.

22. *The Inner Eye of Love*, p. 68.

23. Ibid., p. 69.

24. Ibid., p. 76.

25. Ibid., pp. 76–77.

26. Lonergan, *A Second Collection*, p. 156.

27. Lonergan, *Method in Theology*, p. 112, quoted by Johnston, ibid., p. 70.

28. Art. 'Spirituality' in *A Dictionary of Christian Spirituality*, p. 363.

29. For our theme Dunne's most important books are *The Way of All the Earth: An Encounter with Eastern Religions*, Sheldon Press 1973, and *The Reasons of the Heart*, SCM Press 1978. The latter contains a closing essay, 'A Note on Method' in which he says 'my method is my journey' (p. 151). 'It became a kind of odyssey, passing over into the great religions and coming home again to Christianity and my own life!' (p. 152).

30. *The Way of All the Earth*, p. vii.

31. For a thorough and reliable study of the history of all this, see Eric J. Sharpe, *Comparative Religion: A History*, Duckworth 1975. Eric Sharpe elsewhere writes pointedly of the distinction between the Comparative Study of Religion (CSR) and the theological task I am concerned with throughout this book: 'Let me make it quite clear I have no quarrel whatsoever with the attempt from the side of the Christian Church to work out a theology of confrontation with other religions; in view of the actual situation of the Church in many parts of the world, this is an imperative necessity and methodologically perfectly legitimate, providing always it is made quite explicit on what criteria the Christian is passing judgment. But in this, theological college and secular university part company; it is a confessional concern, and I hold no brief for Christian apologetics masquerading as CSR'. Art. 'The Comparative Study of Religion in Historical Perspective', in Whitfield Foy (ed.), *Man's Religious Quest*, Croom Helm 1978, p. 20.

32. For 'bracketing' or, more technically, *epoche*, see Sharpe, op. cit., p. 224.

33. The name of the subject itself remains a most controversial issue, not least among its practitioners. Even as I write, a ballot is taking place among members of the British Association for the History of Religion to see whether the name should be changed to 'The British Association for the Study of Religion'.

34. Note the strong words of Max Warren on this matter: 'But some would argue that for dialogue on religious matters to be genuine, each party has to suspend its own deepest convictions during the dialogue. There is a technical term for this suspension, *epoché*. I would suggest that this is, properly speaking, undesirable and, if we are both men of integrity, it is impossible. For, if he and I are to be honest with one another, we must bring to our talking the whole of ourselves. In doing so we shall become very vulnerable. Only so will there be a meeting at depth. *Epoché* is an illusion; more, it is an evasion not open to the man of any Faith.' *I Believe in the Great Commission*, Hodder and Stoughton 1976, p. 163. I keenly appreciate the reason for Max Warren's

speaking so forcefully, but suggest in what follows that we might still learn something from the method itself.

35. The Prologue to *Ecclesiasticus (Ben Sirach)*, line 30 in my edition of the RSV.

36. Monica Furlong, *Merton: A Biography*, Collins 1980, p. 339.

37. William Walsh, *The Use of Imagination: Educational Thought and the Literary Mind*, Chatto & Windus 1959, p. 86.

38. *The Letters of John Keats*, selected by Frederick Page, Oxford University Press 1954, p. 53.

39. Ibid., p. 80.

40. See Walsh, op. cit., p. 89.

41. Auden in *Thank You, Fog*, Faber 1974, p. 29.

42. *Voices of Varanasi*, CMS 1979, p. 5. The other two books are *Uncharted Journey*, CMS 1973, and *Journey into Varanasi*, CMS 1978.

43. *Voices of Varanasi*, p. 12.

44. I learnt, when I was in Nairobi, that this is precisely how the white missionary was perceived by the Swahili-speaking Africans. They call Europeans *mzungu*, the name given to a certain kind of buzzing insect!

45. *Voices*, pp. 10–11.

46. See above p. 51.

47. As does Krister Stendahl, for example, in *Christ's Lordship and Religious Pluralism*, ed. Gerald H. Anderson and Thomas F. Stransky, Orbis Books 1981, p. 10.

48. Ibid., p. 8.

49. BCC *Guidelines*, p. 7. 'Pilgrimage' is fruitfully used by Martin Forward as a key to interpret Luke's portrayal of both Jesus and the earliest disciples in 'Pilgrimage: Luke/Acts and the World of Religions', *King's College Theological Review*, Vol. VIII, No. 1 Spring 1985, pp. 9–11. Martin Forward contends that the writer of Luke/Acts makes use of 'the theme of faith as pilgrimage in order to impart the Christian message'. He adds 'In Luke's view the journey of faith requires metanoia, repentance, a change of orientation, a seeking to hear and do God's will, rather than taking a relationship with him for granted as a static event and an assured status'. For a study of pilgrimage in the wider religious context see the superb book of Diana L. Eck, *Banaras: City of Light*, Routledge & Kegan Paul 1983. Dr Eck is Moderator of the Sub Unit on Dialogue of the WCC.

50. Ibid., p. 11.

51. Ibid., p. 35.

52. BCC, *Guidelines*, p. 7.

53. In 'The Pater Noster as an Eschatological Prayer', *New Testament Essays*, Chapman 1967, p. 239.

54. *Towards a Theology for Inter-faith Dialogue* . . . , p. 35.

55. In recent times much attention has been given within the WCC and circles concerned with the theology of mission to the concept of the 'Gospel for the Poor', under the influence of Liberation Theology. The best critique I know of this is by J. D. Gort in an article 'Gospel for the Poor', in *Zending op weg naar de Toekomst*, Kampen, J. H. Kok 1978, pp. 80–109. Jerry Gort, who is a missiologist teaching at the Free University in Amsterdam is very far from attacking the whole idea. On the contrary, like all who have the privilege of travelling the world, Gort is very aware of 'the unspeakably wretched condition and deeply bitter suffering of huge masses of oppressed and pauperized people in the world'. Nor does he ask us to ignore the anger and the anguish of the prophetic voices whom God is using to challenge our sinful complacencies. But he does offer a deeply serious challenge to the materializing of the understanding of both the gospel and of poverty. Gort himself pays much attention to the exegetical issues concerning the interpretation of the terms 'poor' and 'rich' in the biblical witness. For my part I do not see the addition of the words 'in spirit' to the Lucan phrase 'Blessed are the poor' as a 'spiritualizing' of the Beatitudes. Rather Matt. 5.3 must be read as part

of a single poetic structure, describing the nature of discipleship. In Paul Minear's words: 'We should probably assume that all eight (Beatitudes) describe the same group of people and that the eight rewards portray a single condition of blessedness. When read in this way each beatitude clarifies and reinforces the others. For example, those who enter the kingdom of heaven . . . are the same as the "sons of God" who receive the vision of God and enjoy God's forgiveness and comfort, the satisfaction of their hunger and thirst, and the inheritance of the earth. Similarly, poverty of spirit is to be understood as roughly synonymous with mourning, meekness, mercifulness, peace-making, and suffering persecution for righteousness' sake.' *Matthew: The Teacher's Gospel*, Darton, Longman & Todd 1984, pp. 46–7.

56. I follow here the judgment, among others, of Stephen Neill: 'The increasing identification of the Church with the world resulted in an almost inevitable reaction. Those who despaired both of the Church and the world fled from both to seek salvation in the wilderness.' *The Christian Society*, Collins, Fontana edition 1964, p. 58. But he goes on immediately to suggest that the roots of monasticism are rather more complex, and a more balanced account may be found in Benedicta Ward's brief article on 'Monasticism' in *A Dictionary of Christian Spirituality*, pp. 267–9. She writes: 'Monastic renunciation which is the basis of its spirituality is not, however, meant to be a rejection of the created order.' She calls it an 'alternative interpretation involving the loss of self in order to grow into the reality of relationships in the love of Christ' (p. 268).

57. *Merton: A Biography*, p. 329.

58. Aloysius Pieris, in an article about the 'inculturation' of the Gospel in *Lumière et Vie*, No. 168, 1984, entitled 'L'Asie non sémitique face aux modèles occidentaux d'inculturation'. The Western models of inculturation which Pieris rejects are: the Latin model, or incarnation in a non-Christian *culture*; the Greek model, or assimilation to a non-Christian *philosophy*; the North European model, or adaptation to a non-Christian *religion*. He points, however, to a fourth model: the monastic model, or participation in a non-Christian spirituality. See pp. 51ff.

59. For the term 'basic community' see David Clark, *Basic Communities*, SPCK 1977. It is a literal translation of the French term *communauté de base*, or the Spanish *communidad de base*.

60. Aloysius Pieris, op. cit., p. 58.

61. Eric Rolls, *Christian Community and Cultural Diversity*, New Christian Initiatives Series, No. 2, 1982, published by the National Centre for Christian Communities and Networks, Selly Oak Colleges, Birmingham.

62. Ibid., p. 5.

63. Ibid., p. 7.

64. Father Thomas Michel SJ, of the Vatican Secretariat for Non-Christians, in a private conversation.

65. Cf. the words of Wilfred Cantwell Smith: 'the end of religion, in the classical sense of its purpose and goal, that to which it points and may lead, is God. Contrariwise, God is the end of religion in the sense that once He appears vividly before us, in His depth and love and unrelenting truth, all else dissolves; or at the least religious paraphernalia drop back into their due and mundane place, and the concept "religion" is brought to an end.' *The Meaning and End of Religion*, SPCK 1978, p. 201.

INDEX OF NAMES

INDEX OF BIBLICAL REFERENCES